EDITH STEIN AND COMPANIONS
ON THE WAY TO AUSCHWITZ

EDITH STEIN AND COMPANIONS

On the Way to Auschwitz

BY FATHER PAUL HAMANS

Translated by Sister M. Regina van den Berg, F.S.G.M.

Foreword by Ralph McInerny

IGNATIUS PRESS   SAN FRANCISCO

This book is based on the book by P. Hamans
entitled *Getuigen voor Christus:*
Rooms-katholieke bloedgetuigen uit Nederland in de twintigste eeuw
published in 's-Hertogenbosch, The Netherlands, 2008

Cover photographs, left to right:

Rosa Marie Agnes Adelheid Stein
Elvira Maria Josepha Sanders-Platz
Dr. Ruth Renate Frederike Kantorowicz
  (Photo: *Als een brandende toorts*, 281)
Helene Luise (Leni) Bock
Alice Maria Reis
  (Photo *Als een brandende toorts*, 281)
Sister Mirjam Michaelis, C.S.J.
  (Photo: *Schwester Mirjam Michaelis*, 28)

Cover design by Riz Boncan Marsella

ISBN 978-1-58617-336-4
Library of Congress Control Number 2009930113
Printed in the United States of America ∞

CONTENTS

FOREWORD

Once, in monasteries, religious houses, and seminaries, the Roman Martyrology was read in the refectory before meals. Each day some of those who had given their lives in witness to the faith were commemorated by name, and often the tortures they underwent were described. Each day's entry ended with a sentence beginning "et alibi aliorum plurimorum sanctorum. . . ." And elsewhere many other saints. . . . This tradition continues in some monasteries.

We may feel sad for all the anonymous martyrs gathered into that commodious final sentence, but that would be a mistake. They are all entered in the Book of Life, and the names of each are known to God. For all that, it is important for us, not for them, that the names and sufferings of some be explicitly known by us. The saints are put before us as models of the Christian life, and martyrs are the ultimate models. We need to know more about some of them.

In this remarkable book, Dr. Paul Hamans, Father Hamans, has undertaken the onerous task of compiling biographies, often accompanied by photographs, of many of the religious and laity who were rounded up from their various convents and monasteries and homes on the same day as Saint Edith Stein, August 2, 1942; most of them were taken to the Amersfoort concentration camp and from there put on trains to Auschwitz, where the majority, soon after their arrival at the camp, were gassed and buried in a common grave between August 9 and September 30, 1942. They were all Catholic Jews, and their arrest was in retaliation for the letter of the Catholic bishops of the Netherlands that was read from the pulpits of all churches on July 26, 1942.

Over the past few years, in striking contrast to contemporary acknowledgments and the magnificent book of Jewish theologian and historian Pinchas Lapide, many authors have accused the Church of silence during the Nazi persecution of the Jews. None of the counter-evidence to this shameful thesis has had any effect on the critics. The experience of Jews in the Netherlands, particularly Catholic Jews, is eloquent witness of what could result from public condemnation of the Nazis. The victims whose stories are included in this book were told that they were rounded up in direct retaliation of the condemnation of the Nazi "final solution" by the Dutch bishops. Elsewhere, as was once acknowledged and celebrated, the Church in many ways, and in many countries, provided the principal help to European Jews. Indeed, the Catholic Church, under the leadership of Pope Pius XII, is credited by Lapide with saving the lives of some 860,000 Jews. These efforts were effective largely because they were not accompanied by noisy public declarations. With the appearance of the mendacious play of Rolf Hochhuth, *The Deputy*, in 1963, the tide turned, and a series of progressively more intemperate accusations against the Church and Pius XII began to appear. Some Jews reacted to mention of the non-Jewish victims of the Nazi persecution as if it were in some way an effort to diminish the tragedy that had befallen the Jewish people under the reign of

Hitler. There were even objections from some Catholics when Edith Stein was canonized and characterized as a martyr. Their argument was that she was put to death as a Jew, not as a Catholic. And some sad souls objected to acknowledgment of what had happened to Catholic Jews like Edith Stein and her companions. This book is an indirect reply to such criticisms and will speak to all who have ears with which to hear.

That the ultimate sacrifice of the Catholic Jews arrested in the wake of the Dutch bishops' protest should become a cause of controversy is a sad indictment of these last days. But it cannot touch the nobility and holy resignation with which they met their end. Pondering the people commemorated in this book should be an occasion, not for argument, but for edification. Father Hamans has put us in his debt for having taken on the enormous task of making them flesh-and-blood persons for his readers. During the ordeal, one nun wrote to her superior that they had all become numbers to their captors. Lists had been drawn up with diabolical bureaucratic efficiency by the Nazis, which is why the arrests were made so promptly. Thanks to this book, they are no longer mere numbers. Like those mentioned in the Martyrology, their names have been restored. But, again, the importance of that is largely for us. They would have been content, like perhaps millions of others, with the collective mention of the army of martyrs in the *Te Deum Laudamus:*

Te martyrum candidatus laudat exercitus.

Ralph McInerny
University of Notre Dame
September 2010

INTRODUCTION

In 1994, in preparation for the new millennium, Pope John Paul II asked the local churches to do "everything possible to ensure that the memory of those who have suffered martyrdom should be safeguarded".[1] The bishops of the Netherlands fulfilled the Holy Father's request, drawing up a list of the local martyrs of the twentieth century.[2] This cataloging of the martyrs' names led to the publication of a book, the last portion of which concerned murdered Catholic Jews. It is this last section of the Dutch book about the blood witnesses of the twentieth century that is made available to the American public in the present publication.

The Nazis wanted to exterminate all Jews. This group of Jews who had become Catholic forms a separate whole. They became companions because they were arrested and murdered for the same reason. On July 26, 1942, the Dutch bishops, together with the Protestant denominations, publicly protested against the deportation of Jews. In retribution, the Nazis had more than four hundred Catholic Jews rounded up. Many were soon released, but 113 were murdered. The most well-known of them is

---

[1] Pope John Paul II, Apostolic Letter *Tertio Millenio Adveniente* (1994), no. 37.

[2] See Dr. P. W. F. M. Hamans, ed., *Getuigen voor Christus: Rooms-Katholieke bloedgetuigen ùit Nederland in de twintigste eeuw.* Published by the Liturgical Commission of the Dutch Bishops Conference, commissioned by the Bishops of the Province of Utrecht, 2008 ('s-Hertogenbosch, 2008).

surely the Carmelite nun and philosopher Edith Stein, who was canonized by Pope John Paul II on October 11, 1998. It is also widely known that her sister Rosa suffered the same fate.

For the first time in the English language, a still incomplete list of Edith Stein's eighty-two travel companions to Auschwitz is published in the present work. The lives of twenty-eight of these murdered Catholic Jews are depicted by means of individual biographies. In the interest of historical authenticity, the biographies were based, whenever possible, on accounts of those who saw and heard the events firsthand. However, this manner of presentation makes repetition inevitable. Situations are also described differently by various persons. For the most part, the Catholic Jews portrayed here are people who embraced the Catholic faith when they were older. They chose very consciously to be faithful to Jesus Christ and his Church. Theirs was a fidelity that was sustained by a great spirit of sacrifice unto death. They saw their death as an act of expiation as well as a means of obtaining the conversion of the Jews, the good of the Church, and the restoration of peace.

This fidelity to the faith, up to their sacrificial death, shows the extent to which these believers knew that the fulfillment of their lives was to be, not in this world, but in the house of the heavenly Father. They considered eternal life more important than earthly existence and everything that this earth had to offer. They knew that the resurrection of the body was the goal and future of their lives.

Their stories illustrate how worthwhile it is for a believer to suffer and to die in the service of God, of Jesus Christ and his Church, in service to one's neighbor, and for the Catholic vision of the human person. The *Catechism of the Catholic Church* describes martyrdom as "the supreme witness given to the truth of the faith: it means bearing witness even unto death. The martyr bears witness to Christ who died and rose, to whom he is united by charity. He bears witness to the truth of the faith and of Christian doctrine. He endures death through an act of fortitude" (CCC 2473).

Martyrdom is the "fullest proof of love", because the disciple becomes like the Master "by willingly accept-[ing] death for the salvation of the world".[3]

In the Post-synodal Apostolic Exhortation *Ecclesia in Europa*, Pope John Paul II calls martyrdom "the supreme incarnation of the Gospel of hope". He explains that martyrs "bear witness to it with their lives to the point of shedding their blood, because they are certain that they cannot live without Christ and are ready to die for him in the conviction that Jesus is the Lord and the Savior of humanity and that, therefore, only in him does mankind find true fullness of life. According to the exhortation of the Apostle Peter, their example shows them ready to give reason for the hope that is in them (cf. *1 Pt* 3:15)."[4]

Martyrs are not only earthly heroes in the Church. They are also examples and intercessors for the pilgrim and suffering Church as she makes her way through the desert of life to fulfillment in the promised land, eternal life.

From the perspective of persons with different backgrounds, the biographies of the murdered Catholic Jews

---

[3] Vatican II, *Lumen Gentium* (1964), no. 42.
[4] Pope John Paul II, *Ecclesia in Europa* (2003), no. 13.

also shed light on the situation of the Church in the first half of the twentieth century. The Church existed in the midst of the political, social, and economic crises that led to the Second World War. Under these circumstances, a notable number of Jews found their way to the Church because they recognized in Jesus Christ the Redeemer.

The life stories of the individuals recounted in this volume reveal how much their baptism cost them: problems with their families, loss of social status, impoverishment, misunderstanding, and the sacrifice of their lives.

ACKNOWLEDGMENT

I would like to thank the superiors of the Sisters of Saint Francis of the Martyr Saint George, who made it possible for three sisters to assist in preparing this text for publication in the United States. I thank Sister M. Regina van den Berg, F.S.G.M., for cooperating in preparing this work for publication. She provided the translation from the Dutch and made the necessary contacts in the United States that led to the publication of this book. I also thank Sister M. Maximilia Um, F.S.G.M. and Sister M. Anne Maskey, F.S.G.M. for proofreading the text and preparing it for printing.

Chapter 1

THE MURDER OF CATHOLIC JEWS IN RESPONSE TO THE DUTCH BISHOPS

On August 2, 1942, the Nazis arrested a large number of Catholic Jews in the occupied Netherlands and sent them to their deaths at Auschwitz. The provocation for this action was a pastoral letter that had been read in Catholic churches on the previous July 26. This letter included the text of a telegram that had been sent by the leaders of ten Christian denominations to the German occupying forces on July 11. Both the pastoral letter and the telegram protested the persecution of Jews in the Netherlands.

From various sides, the question has been raised whether these murdered Catholic Jews can be considered martyrs for the Catholic faith. Some respond that they cannot because, as they rightly point out, the Nazis had already determined to exterminate all Jews, and Catholic Jews were not exempt. The Catholic Jews were not murdered because they were Catholic, this position maintains, but because they were Jewish. This argument does not, however, do full justice to the reality. While Catholic Jews would have been murdered even without the telegram and pastoral letter, there are significant arguments for considering them a separate group, distinct from the other Jews who were killed during the Holocaust. That they

are blood witnesses for Catholic faith and morality is precisely what sets them apart.

The Catholic Jews who were arrested on August 2 form
a distinct group because their deaths can be directly linked
to actions taken by the Catholic bishops in the Netherlands. The occupying forces made the decision to arrest
Catholic Jews on July 27 because the bishops had stood
up for human dignity and human rights in accordance
with their Catholic vision of man. General Commissioner Fritz Schmidt made this motive publicly known
on the day of the arrests. They were taken prisoner, he
explained, because the bishops had protested the treatment of Jews in general, instead of restricting themselves
to concern for Catholic Jews. Edith Stein's canonization
demonstrates that the highest authority of the Church
considers hers to have been the death of a martyr—
willingly suffered for the Catholic faith. Her companions on the way to Auschwitz died as Catholic Jews just
as she did because the Church in the Netherlands, through
her bishops, dared to defend the Jewish people in the
name of Christ.

The lives of the murdered Catholic Jews reveal a certain internal unity to the group. These men and women
did not allot a mere token place of honor to God and
the faith, while leaving room for conflicting convictions
and pursuits. On the contrary, the martyrdom of this group
began with an uncompromising acceptance of God's will
and the faith of the Church, in which they persevered
unto death.

Edith Stein and her companions had already suffered
losses for the sake of Christ before they offered their lives
in the Nazi gas chambers. By becoming Catholic, many

had been rejected by family members and friends. Such was the case with Edith and Rosa Stein, Elisabeth Michaelis, Luise Löwenfels, and Sister Judith Mendes da Costa, who had become a stranger in her parents' house. Some of these Catholic Jews were prevented from gainful employment or from fulfilling their vocation. In some cases, they were unable to use their talents because others tried to protect them—as Jews—from the Nazi occupiers and from Dutch anti-Semitism. Others were hindered because they were at the end of their strength, having already suffered so much for their Catholic faith. Alice Reis, for example, had a mental breakdown, requiring her to enter a psychiatric institution and give up her life as a nun.[1] Ruth Kantorowicz could not be accepted into the Carmel of Maastricht on account of her weakened constitution.

Total fidelity to their faith was not the only characteristic shared by many of the Catholic Jews who were arrested in August 1942. It is also remarkable that the paths of some of them had already crossed earlier in time. Edith Stein had been in contact with Ruth Kantorowicz, Alice Reis, and Annemarie and Elfriede Goldschmidt. They met one another again on their way to death.

Occupation

On May 10, 1940, the Germans invaded the Netherlands, though the Dutch, as they had done during World

---

[1] All cities mentioned, unless otherwise noted, are cities in the Netherlands. In every chapter, the first mention of a given city outside the Netherlands is followed by a parenthetical reference to the country in which it is located.—TRANS.

War I, had declared themselves neutral. On May 15, the Dutch army capitulated, and the German occupation began; it would last until May 5, 1945. After the Dutch surrender, the Germans created a civilian government under the sovereign authority of Government Commissioner Arthur Seyss-Inquart (1892–1946). Under him were four general commissioners, among whom Friedrich Wimmer was in charge of Internal Affairs and Justice, and Hans Albin Rauter was Commissioner of Public Safety and the HSSPF (Höherer SS und Polizeiführer: Higher SS and Chief of Police). These men played key roles in the extermination of the Dutch Jews.

Nazi Plan for the Jews

Although it is not clear when Hitler decided to exterminate the Jews, he had already spoken about it in a radio speech of 1939. In the summer of 1941, Hitler ordered the systematic murder of all the Jews in German-controlled lands. The SS-leader Heinrich Himmler, along with a small group working with him, set out to accomplish this plan. Initially, the Jews who had been rounded up by the invading German army were murdered by firing squad. Once Himmler was personally present at the shooting of Jews in Russia, and he himself became ill at the sight. He judged that he could not require German soldiers to solve the "Jewish problem" in this manner. Furthermore, the execution of more than eleven million Jews by firing squad would take too much time, use too many bullets, and be much more expensive than the use of poisonous gas.

The Nazis had already gassed and subsequently cremated the mentally handicapped, the seriously sick, and prisoners of war. The Nazis called freeing themselves of undesirable people "euthanasia". The first mass murder by means of the poisonous gas Cyclon B took place on September 3, 1941, in block II of the Auschwitz camp. On this one occasion, 600 Russian prisoners of war and 298 sick were gassed.

On January 3, 1942, Himmler outlawed Jewish emigration from Nazi-controlled countries. No longer allowed to flee, the Jews were trapped. Then on January 20 a conference took place at 56–58 Wannsee Street in Berlin. Representatives of the various departments of the Nazi high command met to decide on "the final solution" ("*Endlösung*") to the "Jewish problem". The meeting was convened by Reinhard Heydrich, head of the SS (Security Service), whose orders had come from Hermann Göring, Hitler's right-hand man. Adolf Eichmann, who was in charge of Jewish emigration and the confiscation of Jewish property, had already played an important role here.[2]

It is difficult to identify how many Jews died during the Second World War. In 1939, about 8,300,000 Jews lived in Germany and the countries Germany would occupy. By 1945 about 2,000,000 remained. Of these, about 1,000,000 had found safety in the free world. Another million Jews had survived the Holocaust.[3] During the Wannsee Conference, the Nazis

---

[2] See R. Kempner, *Twee uit honderdduizend, Anne Frank en Edith Stein: Onthullingen over de nazimisdaden in Nederland voor het gerecht in München* (Bilthoven, 1969), 51–54.

[3] See P. Lapide, *De laatste drie pausen en de joden* (Hilversum, 1967), 204.

assumed that the *"Endlösung"* would eliminate about
11,000,000 Jews.[4]

"Endlösung" in the Netherlands

The Nazis also estimated at the conference that there
were 160,800 Jews in the Netherlands. This was about
1.6 percent of the Dutch population. After Hitler came
to power in Germany, the number of Jews in the Netherlands increased by about 30,000 refugees. Many of these
fled Germany after the *Reichskristallnacht* (the Reich's crys-
tal night, so called because of the broken windows of
Jewish stores) on November 9 and 10, 1938. During this
night, 267 synagogues were burned and 7,500 Jewish stores
and houses were damaged, some severely. On this occasion, the first Jews were taken to concentration camps.
Jews fled to the Netherlands from countries under German power, not only from Germany, but also from countries such as Austria and Czechoslovakia.

The Nazis implemented the final solution in the Netherlands by sending the able-bodied Jews to the east, where
they would work until they died, and gassing the others
right away.[5] After the war, there were about 22,500 Jews
remaining in the Netherlands. A higher percentage of
Jews perished in the Netherlands—approximately 75

[4] See S. Friedländer, *Pius XII en het Derde Rijk: Documenten* (Amsterdam,
1965), 92; P. Hamans, "Pius XII en de Jodenvervolging", *Emmaüs* 25 (1994):
67–80; D. Dalin, *The Myth of Hitler's Pope: Pope Pius XII and His Secret War
against Nazi Germany* (Regnery Publishers, 2005).

[5] See Kempner, *Twee uit honderdduizend*, 51–54. For participants at the
Wannsee Conference, see p. 52.

percent—than in any other western European country. In France, 25 percent of the Jews were killed; in Belgium and Norway, 40 percent. We can compare these figures with those of Rome during the pontificate of Pope Pius XII. Of the 5,715 Jews there, 4,715 were given shelter by the Church in some 150 Catholic institutions. Some 1,015 Jews were sent to Auschwitz from Rome.[6]

There are various reasons why the percentage of Jews who were murdered was so high in the Netherlands. First of all, the country had a civilian government during the occupation. Because of this, the SS had full authority over the deportation of Jews. Another important reason is that the occupiers in the Netherlands had developed a well-organized system of personal identification. Preceding the deportations, the Nazis organized the official registration of Jews in the Netherlands.[7] According to an order of Wilhelm Harster (leader of the SS in the Netherlands), given on January 10, 1941, all Jews had to be registered. In Germany, the Jewish star had been introduced on September 1, 1941. On April 29, 1942, the wearing of the Jewish star was also prescribed in the Netherlands. The star was yellow—a color of humiliation for the Jews. The word "Jew" was written on it in black letters. Every Jew six years and older had to wear the star on his left breast. The Jewish Council received 569,355 Jewish stars to distribute. The Jews had to buy the star themselves, and this purchase was only possible if they showed their personal identification. From Sunday, May

---

[6] For these numbers, see the Internet. For the numbers about Rome, see *Zenit* 08-29-2006.

[7] See L. de Jong, *Het Koninkrijk der Nederlanden in de Tweede Wereldoorlog*, vol. 5 (The Hague, 1974), 938–1055.

3, 1942, onward, every Jew was required to wear the star. Two and a half months after its introduction, the deportations began. The registration of the Jews was by then nearly completed.[8] In July 1942, Government Commissioner Seyss-Inquart wrote to the executive Nazis that the purpose of the Jewish star was to mark those Jews "who were candidates for deportation".[9] During the 1967 trial against those who had led the "*Endlösung*" in the Netherlands, Harster was asked how it had been possible for the arrests on August 2, 1942, to be so complete. He answered, "That was primarily because of the well-functioning registration."[10]

The Persecution of Jews in the Netherlands

Well before the Jews in the Netherlands were required to register, they were subjected to various humiliating restrictions. Soon after the occupation of the Netherlands began, the National Socialists began to establish measures against the Jews. As early as 1940, all the non-Dutch Jews living in the country were declared "state-less".

Jews could not belong to associations that also had non-Jewish members. They were no longer admitted to particular types of work, such as teaching. They were excluded from the markets and the exchange. They were not permitted in public swimming pools. On particular buildings a sign "prohibited for Jews" was required.

[8] See Kempner, *Twee uit honderdduizend*, 47–48.
[9] L. de Jong, *Koninkrijk*, vol. 5, pt. 2, 1033.
[10] Harster, as quoted in Kempner, *Twee uit honderdduizend*, 103.

As part of the persecution, the government decided on August 29, 1941, to forbid Jews to be taught by non-Jews. School administrations had to report Jews who took instruction in their institutions. This measure was particularly relevant for Catholic schools, especially with respect to Catholic Jewish children. The Most Reverend Jan de Jong, Archbishop of Utrecht (1936–1955), informed Catholic school administrators in a letter of September 13, 1942, that they were not permitted to draw up such a report. He wrote:

> All the baptized who confess the Catholic teaching and who submit to the authority of the Church are members of the Catholic Church and thereby have all the rights and duties of the Catholic faithful. Therefore, they have, without distinction, a right to help from the Church in the Catholic upbringing of their children and, therefore, also a right to a Catholic education.[11]

The Jewish Council

On February 12, 1941, Hans Böhmcker, the representative of the government commissioner for the city of Amsterdam (Beauftragter des Reichskommissars für die Stadt Amsterdam), gave Abraham Asscher, who headed the city's diamond industry, the immediate task of forming a Jewish Council (*Joodse Raad*). The Jewish Council had to

---

[11] The Most Reverend J. de Jong, as quoted in S. Stokman, *Het verzet van de Nederlandsche bisschoppen tegen nationaal-socialisme en Duitsche tirannie* (Utrecht, 1945), 208.

consist of twenty persons. Asscher thought that Professor David Cohen, whom he had known for many years from various committees and commissions, should also be involved in the establishment of this council. As head of the Jewish Refugee Committee since 1933, he had had much contact with the Dutch authorities. Cohen was willing to cooperate in establishing the council, and together they extended a number of invitations on February 12 and 13. Seventeen persons accepted the invitation to belong to this council. Abraham Asscher and David Cohen became co-chairmen. The council consisted entirely of Jews. The Jewish Council had its seat in Amsterdam, at the address Keizersgracht 58.[12]

Unbeknownst to Asscher and Cohen, the Jewish Council had only one goal: to establish a record of the Jews in the Netherlands so that at the right time they could be deported and their property confiscated. Officially, the council had the duty of assisting Jews when they needed help: to find housing for those who were expelled from their homes, to find work for the unemployed, or to distribute food to those in want. The Jewish Council in the Netherlands became the point of contact between the Nazis and the Jews. When Jews had questions about their position in the occupied territory, they could find answers here, too. For all that, the council was exploited by the Nazis to organize the deportation of the Jews and confiscate their possessions. On October 20, 1941, the Jewish Council agreed to cooperate in the creation of a catalogue of all Jews living in the Netherlands. As part of

[12] See L. de Jong, *Koninkrijk*, 5:482–585; 938–1057; *Als een brandende toorts: Documentaire getuigenissen over Dr. Edith Stein (zuster Teresia Benedicta a Cruce) en medeslachtoffers* (Echt: Friends of Dr. Edith Stein, 1967), 32–34.

this registration, the businesses and personal effects of the Jews had to be inventoried. On November 7, it was determined that Jews could no longer travel without permission, and on December 5, all non-Dutch Jews received the order to report for "voluntary emigration". The Jewish Council provided the forms that the Jews had to fill out as well as the brochures containing information about what they could take along in the upcoming "emigration".[13]

Edith and Rosa Stein went to Amsterdam during the middle of March 1942.[14] At the Jewish Council there, they attended to the numerous matters required of Jews, especially the completion of a great number of forms. They stayed there for several days at the Leo Convent of the Sisters of Jesus-Maria-Joseph (Leoklooster van de Zusters van Jezus-Maria-Jozef) on Spaarndammer Street.[15] In Amsterdam, Edith Stein met several people she knew from the past and whom she would see again in Amersfoort and in Westerbork. Among them was Alice Reis, Edith's godchild, who worked as a nurse in a convent in Almelo.[16] Lisamaria Meirowsky[17] also met Sister Teresa Benedicta in Amsterdam. From Westerbork she wrote to her confessor about Edith Stein. She wrote that the Carmelite whom "I met that time in Amsterdam"[18] was also in Westerbork.

By the time the Wannsee Conference was held, much of the preparatory work for the extermination of the Jews

[13] See M. Amata Neyer, *Edith Stein: Wie ich in den Kölner Karmel kam* (Würzburg, 1994), 127–29.

[14] See *Als een brandende toorts*, 46–47.

[15] See ibid., 46.

[16] See ibid., 183.

[17] See ibid., 208.

[18] Dr. Lisamaria Meirowsky, as quoted in *Als een brandende toorts*, 208.

had already been done. The measures against the Jews, however, did not end there. In the Netherlands, no official Jewish ghettos were formed, even though from January 1942 onward, Jews were forbidden to live in certain places or areas. Many Jews, therefore, had to leave home, hearth, and acquaintances. On January 23, 1942, it was ordered that a letter "J" had to be written in the personal identification of all Jews.

As life for the Jews in the Netherlands became increasingly difficult, reports about their mass murder in other countries began circulating. Rosa Stein knew of these reports in the spring of 1942.[19] The following July the systematic deportation of Dutch Jews began. By the end of the month, 12,000 Jews had already been deported. When it became clear that the Dutch Jews were being sent to their deaths, many Jewish people went into hiding. Others fled to Belgium.[20] The weekly deportations in the Netherlands lasted until September 1943. By that time, almost 107,000 Jews had perished.

Certain groups of people were exempt from deportation: Jews married to non-Jews (22,000 persons), workers in a war-related industry (3,500 persons), and workers in the diamond industry (1,200 persons).[21] Those who let themselves be sterilized could also escape death. The Jews in mixed marriages were exempted because the spouse and other family members would not have accepted the deportation of their loved ones, and the Nazis wanted to forestall any possible anger toward the regime. However, beginning on March 27,

---

[19] See Kempner, *Twee uit honderdduizend*, 58.
[20] See ibid., 59–60.
[21] See ibid., 60.

1942, every new mixed marriage became punishable by death.[22]

Interdenominational Consultation

From late 1940 onward, the Protestant religious denominations in the Netherlands consulted with one another about the issues surrounding the German occupation. These meetings were called the Convention of Churches (Convent van Kerken). The following religious denominations participated in these meetings: the Dutch Reformed Church, the Reformed Churches in the Netherlands, the Reformed Churches in the Netherlands in Restored Union, the Remonstrate Brotherhood, the General Baptist Society, the Evangelical Lutheran Church, and the Reformed Evangelical Denomination. The Roman Catholic Church in the Netherlands joined this consultation at the end of 1941. From that time on, this body was called the Interdenominational Consultation (Interkerkelijk Overleg, I.K.O.).[23] Together, these Christian religious leaders were able to give direction to about seven million baptized countrymen, warning them of the Nazis' misleading propaganda.

[22] See ibid., 91.

[23] See A. van der Leeuw, *Die Deportation der römisch-katholischen Juden aus den Niederlanden im Monat August 1942, opgesteld in 1966*, in NIOD, Archive 785, Notes for historical work, inventory no. 136 (Amsterdam, 1966), 1–2; J. Snoek, *De Nederlandse kerken en de joden 1940–1945: De protesten bij Seyss-Inquart, hulp aan joodse onderduikers, de motieven voor hulpverlening* (Kampen, 1990), 76–78.

The Pastoral Letter of Sunday, July 26, 1942

On January 5, 1942, leaders of several Christian denominations met with representatives of the Nazi government to protest illegal arrests, internments without hearing, and the persecution of Jews. They also addressed new government regulations that infringed upon basic human rights with respect to education, the press, the existence of associations, and the practice of religion. A delegation of three representatives of the Interdenominational Consultation met Government Commissioner Seyss-Inquart for a follow-up conversation on February 17, 1942. The delegation consisted of Prof. Dr. W.J. Aalders (Dutch Reformed Church), Dr. J.J.C. van Dijk (the Reformed Church in the Netherlands), and Monsignor F. A. H. van de Loo (Roman Catholic Church, official of the Archdiocese of Utrecht). Seyss-Inquart defended the policy of the National Socialists by pointing to the danger of the Bolshevists. The government commissioner considered mercy toward the Jews out of place because they were a lower race that posed a great danger to the state.[24]

Among the members of the Interdenominational Consultation, there grew a desire to formulate an extensive written protest in response to the actions that the occupying forces had undertaken against the Jews in the previous months. The evening paper of June 29, 1942, had reported that General Commissioner Fritz Schmidt said the following about the Jews: "They should return just as poor to where they came from." This was understood

---

[24] See Kempner, *Twee uit honderdduizend*, 94; Snoek, *De Nederlandse kerken*, 79.

to mean that all Jews would have to leave the Netherlands. In response to Schmidt's speech, the Interdenom-
inational Consultation decided in a meeting held on
July 10 in The Hague to follow the proposal of Monsignor
Felix van de Loo and Professor Dr. H. Kraemer
(Reformed Church) to postpone a lengthy written protest and, instead, to write immediately a telegram in
response to the current situation. This telegram would
be sent to Government Commissioner Dr. Arthur Seyss-
Inquart, General Commissioner for Safety Hans Albin
Rauter, General Commissioner for Special Services Fritz
Schmidt, and the Commander of the Armed Forces (*Wehr-
macht*) Friedrich C. Christiansen. The last mentioned sent
his copy, to which he had added the recommendation of
also deporting those who signed the telegram, to Seyss-
Inquart.[25] The telegram was sent in the name of ten Dutch
religious denominations on July 11. According to the historian Dr. Lou de Jong, the letter was sent in the name
of the greatest number of persons (7 million) who had
ever addressed a letter to the occupying Nazi forces.[26] At
the same meeting, the Interdenominational Consultation
decided that the text of the telegram would be included
in a pastoral letter that would be read in all the churches.[27]

Contrary to its usual practices, and to the astonish-
ment of the religious denominations, the Nazi leadership responded to the telegram. On July 14, the Reverend

---

[25] See Kempner, *Twee uit honderdduizend*, 94; L. de Jong, *Het Koninkrijk
der Nederlanden in de Tweede Wereldoorlog*, vol. 6, pt. 1 (The Hague, 1975),
12–13; Snoek, *De Nederlandse kerken*, 91.

[26] L. de Jong, *Koninkrijk*, vol. 6, pt. 1, 13.

[27] See Kempner, *Twee uit honderdduizend*, 94; L. de Jong, *Koninkrijk*, vol. 6,
pt. 1, 12–13; Snoek, *De Nederlandse kerken*, 91.

Herman J. Dijckmeester was invited by General Commissioner Schmidt for a conversation. This was the day before the first deportation to Auschwitz in the context of the "*Endlösung*" in the Netherlands. To prevent the religious denominations from creating unrest in society, Schmidt informed Dijckmeester that Jews who had been baptized before January 1, 1941, would not be deported. In addition, he said that they were working on establishing more lenient measures against those in mixed marriages.[28] None of the religious denominations had requested this promise. The concern of the religious denominations was, after all, human rights as such, not particularly those of their own members. The religious denominations had intended the telegram to be a quick response to the acute needs resulting from the Jewish persecution and the impending deportation. Still, this promise had a reassuring effect. The Most Reverend Gulielmus Lemmens, Bishop of Roermond (1932–1958), informed the Carmel in Echt and the Poor Handmaids of Jesus Christ in Geleen-Lutterade that Catholic Jews would not be bothered. Archbishop de Jong probably informed the Sisters of the Good Shepherd, where Alice Reis was staying, of the same thing.[29]

The Interdenominational Consultation planned to compose a more fundamental and extensive written protest that would also be sent to the occupying forces. For their part, these forces hoped that their promise would somewhat lessen the negative reaction to the deportations that

---

[28] See Kempner, *Twee uit honderdduizend*, 95; L. de Jong, *Koninkrijk*, vol. 6, pt. I, 13; Snoek, *De Nederlandse kerken*, 91–92.

[29] See letter of Sister Agatha to the Very Reverend J.J. Loeff, in Archives, Archdiocese of Utrecht, no. 76.

would begin on July 15, 1942. In particular, they wanted to prevent the possibility of engendering a widespread protest by the people. Schmidt's promise mollified the Reformed Protestants right away. In the Reformed Synod of July 15, doubt arose as to whether a more extensive protest still needed to be composed at all.

In the weekly staff meeting that Seyss-Inquart had with his closest coworkers on July 17, the government commissioner declared that all baptized Jews would be deported. He had only made the promise of July 14, he explained, so that the churches would keep quiet about the deportation of the Jews. He declared that, "after all the other Jews have been deported, the remaining 'Christian Jews' will be deported at the first politically favorable occasion." His only concern was "by means of this concession, to keep the Christian churches silent about the evacuation of Dutch Jews".[30] General Commissioner Rauter had the task of monitoring religious services on the subsequent Sundays to ascertain whether there were negative reactions from the religious denominations.[31] The Nazis called this pulpit supervision (*Kanzelüberwachung*).

On July 20, the Interdenominational Consultation composed a pastoral letter, which included the entire text of the July 11 telegram. On Thursday, July 23, the letter was sent to the pastors of the various congregations, and on the following day the occupying forces learned of it. The Reverend Dijckmeester was called by Captain I. Gruffke, Schmidt's substitute. Gruffke urged that the text of the telegram be deleted from the pastoral letter. If the

[30] Dr. Arthur Seyss-Inquart, as quoted in Kempner, *Twee uit honderdduizend*, 95.

[31] See Van der Leeuw, *Deportation*, 3; Snoek, *De Nederlandse kerken*, 93.

religious denominations were not willing to do this, he said, dialogue with the occupiers would cease. The Reverend Dijckmeester, however, was in favor of the telegram being read in all the churches. He brought the issue before the Reformed Synod, but the view that dominated was that "among decent people, one party cannot publish a document when the other party is against it." In addition, the members of the Synod feared that "what had now been accomplished for the Christian Jews would then be lost again." [32] The Reformed Synod decided to omit the telegram, though some pastors read it to their congregations anyway. On Friday, July 24, the Synod informed Schmidt and the Catholic archbishop of its decision. [33]

Archbishop de Jong did not want any governmental interference in a pastoral letter. He judged, moreover, that it was impossible to make changes in a letter that had already been sent out. Therefore, the pastoral letter was read in its entirety on Sunday, July 26, 1942, in Catholic churches throughout the Netherlands. [34]

In addition, the bishops announced that those Jews who had been baptized before 1941 would be exempt from deportation. The various Christian denominations each had their own customs regarding the making of important announcements during the services. The version which was read in the Catholic Church read as follows:

[32] Snoek, *De Nederlandse kerken*, 93.

[33] See Petition of the Most Reverend J. de Jong to Seyss-Inquart of August 24, 1942, in Archives, Archdiocese of Utrecht, no. 76.

[34] See Snoek, *De Nederlandse kerken*, 95.

We live in a time of great affliction, both spiritual and material. In recent times two specific afflictions have come to the fore: the persecution of the Jews and the unfortunate lot of those who are sent to work in foreign countries.

All of us must become fully aware of these troubles, and for this reason, they are now brought to our attention as a community.

These afflictions must also be brought to the attention of those who are responsible for them. To this end, the Dutch bishops, in communion with nearly all the churches in the Netherlands, have approached the authorities of the occupying forces concerning, among other things, the Jews, in a recent telegram of Saturday, July 11. The telegram stated the following:

The undersigned Dutch churches, already deeply shocked by the actions taken against the Jews in the Netherlands that have excluded them from participating in the normal life of society, have learned with horror of the new measures by which men, women, children, and whole families will be deported to the German territory and its dependencies.

The suffering that this measure will bring upon tens of thousands of people, the knowledge that these measures are contrary to the deepest moral consciousness of the Dutch people, and, above all, the hostility of these measures against the divine norms of justice and mercy urge the churches to direct to you the urgent petition not to execute these measures.

Our urgent petition to you is also motivated by the consideration that, for the Christian Jews, these measures would make it impossible for them to participate in the life of the Church.

As a result of this telegram, one of the Commissioner Generals, in the name of the government commissioner, has promised that Christian Jews will not

be deported as long as they belonged to one of the
Christian churches before January 1941.

Beloved faithful, when we consider the immense
spiritual and physical misery that, for three years already,
has threatened the entire world with destruction, then
we think naturally of the situation that the Gospel of
today paints for us:

"And when he drew near and saw the city he wept
over it, saying, 'Would that even today you knew the
things that make for peace! But now they are hid from
your eyes. For the days shall come upon you, when
your enemies will cast up a bank about you and sur-
round you, and hem you in on every side, and dash
you to the ground, you and your children within you,
and they will not leave one stone upon another in
you; because you did not know the time of your visitation'" (Lk 19:41–44).[35] Jesus' prediction was literally fulfilled: forty years later, God's judgment over the
city of Jerusalem was accomplished. They had, unfortunately, not recognized the time of grace.

Now, too, everything around us points to a pun-
ishment from God. But, thanks be to God, it is not
yet too late for us. We can still avert it if we recognize
the time of grace, if we recognize what will bring us
peace. And that is only the return to God, from whom
for many years already a great portion of the world
has turned away. All human means have failed; only
God can still bring a solution.

Beloved faithful, let us first examine ourselves with
a deep sense of repentance and humility. Are we, after
all, not partly responsible for the disasters that affect
us? Have we always fulfilled the duties of justice and
charity toward our neighbor? Have we not sometimes

---

[35] All biblical citations are taken from the Revised Standard Version.—TRANS.

entertained feelings of unholy hatred and bitterness? Have we always sought our refuge in God, our heavenly Father?

When we turn to ourselves, we will have to confess that we have all failed. *Peccavimus ante Dominum Deum nostrum*: we have sinned before the Lord, our God.

We also know, though, that God will not spurn a repentant and humble heart. *Cor contritum et humiliatum non despicies.* We therefore turn to him and beg him with childlike confidence for his mercy. He himself tells us, "Ask, and it will be given you; seek, and you will find; knock, and it will be opened to you" (Mt 7:7).

In the Introit of today's Holy Mass, the Church calls to us with the words of the Psalmist, "God is present as my helper; the Lord sustains my life" (Ps 54:4 [53:6]), And the Epistle repeats the very comforting words of the apostle: "No temptation has overtaken you that is not common to man. God is faithful, and he will not let you be tempted beyond your strength, but with the temptation will also provide the way of escape, so that you may be able to endure it" (1 Cor 10:13).

Therefore, beloved faithful, let us implore God, through the intercession of the Mother of Mercy, that he will soon grant the world a just peace. May he sustain the people of Israel, who are being so bitterly tested in these days, and may he bring them to true redemption in Jesus Christ. May he protect those whose lot it is to work in foreign lands and to be separated from their loved ones. May he protect them in soul and body, protect them from becoming bitter and discouraged, keep them faithful to the Christian faith, and may God also strengthen those they left behind. Let us implore him for a solution for all those who are tested and oppressed, for prisoners and hostages, for so many who are threatened by death. *Pateant aures*

misericordiae tuae, Domine, precibus supplicantium: that the
ears of your mercy, Lord, may be open to the prayers
of those who cry to you.

This, our joint pastoral letter, shall be read in the
usual manner next Sunday, July 26, during all the sched-
uled Holy Masses in all the churches and chapels in
our Church Province that have an appointed rector.

Given in Utrecht, the 20th of July of the Year of
our Lord 1942.[36]

For Archbishop de Jong, it was evident that the Nazis
must not be allowed to have any influence on the pastoral responsibilities of the bishops. For this reason, he
neither consulted his brother bishops (not even by telephone), nor did he even inform them of the occupiers'
effort to have the text of the telegram removed from
the pastoral letter.[37] On Monday, July 27, after the pastoral letter had already been read, the archbishop wrote
a letter to his brother bishops, informing them about
the events of the previous Friday. Archbishop de Jong
wrote in this letter, among other things, "I could no
longer ask your advice, but I assumed that you would
also judge that the reading of the letter should certainly
proceed as planned."[38]

On Monday, July 27, there was a meeting at the office
of the government commissioner in The Hague to decide
how to punish the Catholic bishops. Besides Seyss-Inquart,

---

[36] As quoted in Stokman, *Verzet*, 249–51. Cf. a slightly different English
translation of the text in Sister Teresia Renata de Spiritu Sancto Posselt, *Edith
Stein: The Life of a Philosopher and Carmelite*, ed. Susanne Batzdorff, Josephine
Koeppel, and John Sullivan (Washington, D.C.: ICS Publications, 2005), 203–6.

[37] See Snoek, *De Nederlandse kerken*, 95.

[38] Letter of the Most Reverend J. de Jong to the Bishops of the Netherlands, in Archives, Archdiocese of Utrecht, no. 76; L. de Jong, *Koninkrijk*,
vol. 6, pt. 1, 18.

the following people were present: Rauter, Schmidt, General Commissioner Friedrich Wimmer (Internal Affairs and Justice), the commander of the Sicherheitspolizei and the SD [Sicherheitsdienst, the intelligence service of the SS], Dr. Wilhelm Harster. Harster who recorded the minutes of this meeting, dated July 30, wrote:

> Because the Catholic bishops have meddled in this affair [the Jewish persecution] in which they were not involved, all Catholic Jews will be deported (*abgeschoben*) already this week. Interventions will not be honored. General Commissioner Schmidt will publicly respond to the bishops during a party meeting in Limburg on Sunday, August 2, 1942. In the event that the greater number of the Protestant churches also read the telegram to Seyss-Inquart, Protestant Jews will also be placed on the transport. To this end, lists still have to be created.[39]

At the suggestion of Harster, the possible confiscation of the Church's sizable charitable organizations was also discussed.

At his trial in 1967, Harster declared that the reason for the death of the Catholic Jews was "vengeance, retaliation for the position of the Catholic bishops". According to Harster, "The deciding motive of the general commissioner was certainly that he wanted to react to the fact that the Catholic Church did not restrict herself to defending members of her own faith [meant were the Catholic Jews]."[40] The bishops had, after all, spoken about Jews instead of Catholic Jews.

---

[39] A photocopy of this report is printed in Kempner, *Twee uit honderdduizend*, 100; Neyer, *Edith Stein: Wie ich in den Kölner Karmel kam*, 132.

[40] Dr. Wilhelm Harster, as quoted in Kempner, *Twee uit honderdduizend*, 23, 99–100.

Exactly one week after the Sunday on which the pastoral letter was read, a large group of Catholic Jews from all parts of the Netherlands were taken prisoner. On the same Sunday, General Commissioner Schmidt delivered a speech in Waubach, Limburg, on the occasion of the tenth anniversary of the local division of the Nazi Party, the NSDAP. Schmidt said, among other things, the following:

> Last Sunday a letter was read, primarily in Catholic churches, in which the spiritual leaders criticized the measures against the Jews, which have been taken in our effort to protect western Europe against the archenemy. They thought they had to stand up for the Jews, even though at the same time the members of this Jewish race in the east, in the Soviet Union, are the true forces of Bolshevism, destroyers of religion and murderers of priests.
>
> In a number of Protestant churches, a letter in which a similar position was taken was also read. The representatives of the Protestant churches have informed us, however, that the reading of the entire text was not their intention but that, because of technical difficulties, it could not be prevented everywhere.
>
> However, since the Catholic leadership shows not the least concern for negotiations that took place, then we, for our part, are forced to consider the Catholic full-Jews as our greatest enemies and to ensure that they are immediately transported to the east. That has happened. Someday, the Jewish question will also have been solved in the Netherlands.[41]

[41] The speech was printed in the *Deutsche Zeitung in den Niederlanden* on Monday, August 3, 1942. Portions of the text are printed in Dutch in Van der Leeuw, *Deportation*, appendix 2; Stokman, *Verzet*, 116–17; Kempner, *Twee uit honderdduizend*, 100–102; Snoek, *De Nederlandse kerken*, 96.

It had never been the Nazis' intention to exempt the baptized Jews. The Nazi action against the Catholic Jews was most likely aimed at sowing disunity among the Christian denominations, which had proved capable of cooperation in the Interdenominational Consultation. The occupier had the impression that it was successful in creating such disunity within the Interdenominational Consultation. In a secret report of September 24, 1942, Rauter, the highest leader of the SS in the Netherlands, wrote Heinrich Himmler the following about the Jewish extermination in the Netherlands:

> In the meantime, of the Christian Jews, the Catholic Jews have already been deported, because the five bishops, under the leadership of Archbishop de Jonge [sic] of Utrecht, did not comply with the original agreement. The Protestant Jews are still here, and we have indeed succeeded in tearing the Catholic Church from a united front with the Protestants. In a bishops' conference, Archbishop de Jonge declared that he would never again form a united front with the Protestants and the Calvinists.[42]

This last statement was probably more an expression of hope than a reality. The unity within the Interdenominational Consultation was never broken during the time of occupation, and the body remained in existence until the Netherlands' liberation. Rauter was most likely trying to impress his superior in Berlin.

According to the Nazi vision, all Jews had to be exterminated. They gave a promise to exempt the Christian

---

[42] Hans Albin Rauter, as quoted in A. Mohr and E. Prégardier, eds., *Passion im August (2.–9. August 1942): Edith Stein und Gefährtinnen: Weg in Tod und Auferstehung*, Zeugen der Zeitgeschichte, 5 (Annweiler: Plöger, 1995), 19.

Jews, not to protect them from death, but to deter Christian leaders from stimulating unrest among the people when the first Jews were being deported from the country. When the Interdenominational Consultation, with the exception of the Reformed Synod, put no faith in this promise, only the Catholic Jews were arrested in the idle hope of sowing disunity in the united front of seven million Christians. It is possible that the Nazis did not understand the religious denominations in the country and thought that all Protestants in the Netherlands were under the authority of the Reformed Synod, and for that reason they arrested only Catholic Jews.

To repeat, it was the intention to exterminate all Jews, including those who had been baptized. What made the Catholic Jews in the country a special group of martyrs is that they were arrested and murdered because the Nazis wanted to take revenge on the Catholic Church in response to the bishops' protest against the inhumane treatment of all Jews. The occupiers' attempt to prevent the reading of the telegram proves how afraid the Nazis were that Christian leaders could mobilize the people against the planned "*Endlösung*".

The Catholic Jews Who Were Deported on August 2, 1942

As of October 1, 1941, 390 people had registered as baptized Catholic full-Jews of Dutch nationality and 300 of non-Dutch nationality. Thus there was a total of 690 Catholic Jews in the Netherlands. The Dutch Reformed Church included 460 Jews of Dutch nationality and 131 of non-Dutch nationality, making a total of 591. About 600 other Jews belonged to other Protestant denominations. In

the Netherlands there were, therefore, about 1,900 baptized Jews.[43] Most of the Catholic Jews were in a mixed
marriage, that is to say, married to non-Jews.[44]

In July 1942, 722 Catholic Jews lived in the Netherlands. Of these, 213 were taken prisoner on August 2
and, for unclear reasons, were brought to Amersfoort.
There the Catholic Jews received a separate serial number that began with 3000 and ended with 3214.[45] From
the group that had been taken there, 44 were released in
Amersfoort because they were married to non-Jews. On
August 3, there were 169 Catholic Jews in Amersfoort
camp. The next day 97 were brought from Amersfoort
to Westerbork. Of these, 63 left on August 7 for Auschwitz. (Added to this group were 22 of the Catholic Jews
who had been taken prisoner in the district of Amsterdam and brought directly to Auschwitz.)

On August 15, 9 more of the Catholic Jews arrested
on August 2 were sent from Amersfoort to Westerbork.
Of this group, 7 left on August 17 for Auschwitz. The
remaining 63 Catholic Jews were released in Amersfoort.

Also on August 2, in the district of Amsterdam, slightly
over 200 Catholic Jews were apprehended and brought to
the Dutch Theater of Amsterdam (Amsterdamse Hollandse Schouwburg). Of them, 36 were brought directly
to Westerbork,[46] and 32 of these were eventually

[43] See J. Presser, *Ondergang: Vervolging en verdelging van het Nederlandse Jodendom (1940–1945)* (The Hague, 1965), 2:85.

[44] See L. de Jong, *Koninkrijk*, vol. 6, pt. 1, 19.

[45] See NIOD, Bd S, IV, B4, Archive 250 F, port 3, map 12; Frijtag Drabbe Künzel, 80.

[46] See Sister Judith Mendes da Costa, *Sister Judith Mendes da Costa, Dominican Sister of the Congregation of St. Catherine of Siena in Voorschoten, Amsterdam 1895–1944 Auschwitz: Autobiografie*, publication in possession of author (Voorschoten, 2006), 84. See also her biography in this book.

murdered.[47] It is probably no longer possible to determine the exact number of Catholic Jews who were murdered in retaliation for the pastoral letter of July 26, 1942, because too many uncertain factors played a role: numerous lists were created; people were deported on different days and on different transports; some were also brought to other concentration camps. All together approximately 113 Catholic Jews perished because of the response of the Dutch bishops.[48]

There is an observable difference between the treatment of these Catholic Jews and those Jews who were Protestant. Those Jews who were baptized in a Protestant community before January 1, 1941, were arrested, not systematically, but as was opportune, and were interned in Westerbork Camp. Of these, about 350 persons were brought to the Theresienstadt concentration camp (in Terezín, Czech Republic) in September 1944. Most of them were able to return to the Netherlands after the liberation.[49] Catholic Jews, as we have seen, were dispatched more quickly than Protestant Jews.

In the meeting of Nazi leaders in The Hague on July 27, 1942, it was decided that the arrest of Catholic Jews would take precedence over that of Protestant Jews. Since these people had already been inventoried in the previous months, selecting Catholic Jews would be a simple matter. In the week before August 2, the district lists

[47] See Memo of Dr. Erich Rajakowitsch, assistant of the service for the Jews of August 3, 1942, in Edith Stein, *Briefauslese (1917–1942), mit einem Dokumentenanhang zu ihrem Tode*, ed. Kloster der Karmelitinnen Maria vom Frieden, Köln (Freiburg: Herder, 1967), 143.

[48] See Van der Leeuw, *Deportation*, 6–8; L. de Jong, *Koninkrijk*, vol. 6, pt. 1, 19; Kempner, *Twee uit honderdduizend*, 105–6; Snoek, *De Nederlandse kerken*, 97.

[49] See Van der Leeuw, *Deportation*, 9.

were created and were sent to various regions with the order that the people named were to be arrested on the following Sunday. On August 4, 1942, the commander of the security police (Sicherheitspolizei) in Amersfoort used the lists that he had at his disposal to create a new transport list, which included 97 Catholic Jews.[50] Then in Westerbork on August 7, a transport list for the journey to Auschwitz was drawn up. There were 987 names on this list,[51] and, as far as is known, only three persons from this transport survived the war.[52]

Why Did More Catholic Jews Not Flee?

Many rumors circulated among the Jews. According to some of these rumors, it was not the intention to exterminate all Jews. Rather, there was talk that they would be deported to the east, where a kind of Jewish state would be established where they could live in peace. During the time of the Jewish persecutions, this did not seem to be a bad idea. Many Jews, therefore, hoped that through their deportation they would be relieved of the uncertainty and threats that constantly hovered over their

[50] NIOD, Archive 250 F, Amersfoort camp. Inventory no. 14 contains the lists of the persons who were picked up on August 2, 1942. They are organized according to districts. In addition, there are two lists of Catholic Jews who were brought from Amersfoort to Westerbork on August 4. Many of these pieces are also preserved in NIOD, BDC H 213, pp. 1586/1688; one of these is partially printed. See Kempner, *Twee uit honderdduizend*, 106–9. In this file there is also a list created in Amersfoort dated August 15. Nine persons are listed on it, among them Hermine Merkelbach van Enkhuizen-Grünbaum, the mother of the Bock sisters.

[51] See NIOD, Archive 250 I, Westerbork camp, inventory no. 239; cf. Kempner, *Twee uit honderdduizend*, 106, 109–10 (a copy of two of these lists).

[52] See Stein, *Briefauslese*, 146–52; *Als een brandende toorts*, 242–45; Kempner, *Twee uit honderdduizend*, 83–84.

heads. According to other rumors, the Jews were being deported to the east to be brought together there in ghettos and put into forced labor.

Many Jews had become convinced that there was no use in fighting against the Nazi forces because one would lose anyway. In addition, they were all administratively known by the occupier. This fact instilled in many Jews the feeling that they were at the mercy of the Nazis.

In convents, it was thought that everyone who did not cooperate in the arrest of fellow believers would be shot dead. In this way, the religious were frightened into thinking that the occupier would take revenge for hiding Jews by killing other religious, by closing the convent, or by confiscating it. The Jews who were religious were, also for this reason, ready to offer themselves. They wanted to protect their fellow brothers or sisters from what the Nazis threatened to do.

In conclusion, it must also be said that many Jews did, in fact, flee. On the lists of those persons who were to be taken prisoner, remarks such as "does not live at this address", "has left for an unknown destination", or "was not found at this address" are found numerous times.[53]

On the Way to a New Life

Sunday, August 2

The arrest of the Catholic Jews on August 2, 1942, was carried out by the Central Bureau for Jewish Emigration (Zentralstelle für jüdischer Auswanderung). The names

[53] See NIOD Archive 250 F, Amersfoort camp, inventory no. 14.

and addresses of the Jews who were to be picked up had
been known to the occupier for a long time already.
Persons older than sixty years of age were not taken.[54]
Even though it had not been the intention, Jews who
were in mixed marriages were arrested, though many of
these were later released. The action against the Catholic Jews was not begun everywhere at the same time.
The SS arrived earliest at the Trappists (Cistercians) of
Berkel-Enschot (2:30 A.M.).[55] The last to be picked up
were the sisters Edith and Rosa Stein (5:00 P.M.). Most
victims were arrested in the morning between 6:00 and
8:00 A.M.

The arrests were directed by the local German police
(*Ortnungspolizei*), a unit that belonged to the SS. They
had a preprinted flyer that listed the items that the prisoner must or could take along. These were usual things
needed for a journey: food rations for three days, clothing, shoes, a blanket, and so on. In addition, one had to
bring, "all documents concerning capital, possession of
house or land, life insurance, annuities, and so on, stocks,
bonds, and other proof of participation in business ven-
tures". The note further stated that the house one was
leaving had to be locked and sealed. Then a label with
the exact address of the arrestee had to be affixed to the
door key. This key had to be turned in to the police.
Often the name and address of the unfortunate victim
and an arrest number were written by hand on this note

[54] See Kempner, *Twee uit honderdduizend*, 105.

[55] In the village of Berkel-Enschot there are two monasteries: a Cistercian
monastery of men and one of women. Both are Cistercians of the Strict
Observance (*Ordo Cisterciensis Strictioris Observantiae*, O.C.S.O.). The Cistercians are commonly also called "Trappists" because the Cistercian reform
that led to this branch of the strict observance began in the Monastery of La
Trappe in France in the seventeenth century.—TRANS.

of arrest.[56] These details show that the Nazis were concerned about not only exterminating the Jews, but also confiscating their possessions.

Except for some of those apprehended in the district of Amsterdam, all the prisoners were first taken to Amersfoort during the course of the day. That was surely no pleasant journey because it was warm and humid. Toward the end of the afternoon, the storm that had long threatened broke loose.[57] Those Jews who were picked up in Limburg went from their homes to the local commander (*Ortskommandantur*) in Roermond. The 30 prisoners left in two vans at 6:00 P.M. for Amersfoort.[58] A wrong exit was taken, and they wandered through the country. Even though the trip from Roermond to Amersfoort did not need to take more than three or four hours, they did not arrive at the camp until 3:00 A.M.[59] By Monday morning there were 213 Jewish prisoners in Amersfoort.[60]

[56] See NIOD, Archive 250 F, Amersfoort camp, inventory no. 14.

[57] See *Als een brandende toorts*, 157; *Het nevelgordijn opgetrokken: De classis Rotterdam der Nederlandsch Hervormde Kerk tijdens den oorlog* (Rotterdam, 1946), 81.

[58] See Telegram Smole, SS Untersturmführer in Maastricht, to Knolle, SS Obersturmführer, in the Amersfoort camp (Dutch Red Cross, The Hague, War-time Archive Amersfoort, box 6).

[59] See Sister Teresia Renata de Spiritu Sancto Posselt, *Edith Stein: Jodin, geleerde, Carmelites* (Bilthoven, 1952), 251; Mohr and Prégardier, *Passion im August*, 123.

[60] Their arrest had taken place in various districts. Each district left a list of the prisoners it had delivered in the Amersfoort camp. Eighty-six Jews (42 of these were not Catholic) came from the district of The Hague (prisoner nos. 3091–3176); 30 from Maastricht (nos. 3183–3212); 25 from Rotterdam (nos. 3020–44); 16 from Tilburg (nos. 3075–90); 15 from Den Bosch (nos. 3045–59); 15 from Nijmegen (nos. 3060–74); 9 from Eindhoven (nos. 3005–13); 6 from Arnhem (nos. 3014–19); 6 from Enschede (nos. 3177–82); 4 from Breda (nos. 3001–4); and one from Gennep (no. 3183). See NIOD, Archive 250 F, Amersfoort camp, inventory no. 14; Dutch Red Cross, War-time Archive.

Not all the Jews there were Catholic. Of the 86 Jews who were picked up in the district of The Hague, 44 were Catholic. A letter accompanying the arrestees from Rotterdam noted that all 25 were Catholic Jews. The same was also said of the 6 from Enschede.[61]

The Bromberg family, a doctor, his wife, and their son and daughter, were brought to Amersfoort and then to Westerbork.[62] They remained in this camp when the others left on the train for Auschwitz.[63] Richard Bromberg, Sr., was a cousin of Lutz Löb. Richard was a Jew, baptized Catholic in 1927, whose second marriage was with Lucie, who was not a Jew. The Brombergs were probably left behind in Westerbork because they could prove that the Bromberg couple was a "mixed marriage" (that is, a Jew married to a non-Jew). In 1950, Richard Bromberg, Jr., wrote a report about the events of August 2–7, 1942. He explains that in Amersfoort the Catholic Jews were assigned to a special barrack that was separated from the other accommodations with barbed wire.[64] Bromberg recounts:

Notes relevant to the number of Catholic Jews brought into the Amersfoort camp on August 2, 1942, inventory no. 84 (Amersfoort), box 6.

[61] See NIOD, Archive 250 F, Amersfoort camp, inventory no. 14.

[62] The Catholic Jewish married couple Bromberg, their daughter, Ruth (Renée), (born 1927), and son, Richard, (born 1927), were picked up in Roermond on August 2, 1942. Dr. Richard Bromberg, Sr. (born 1886), had been active as a lawyer in the court in Aachen (Germany). In addition, he was a physician. His wife, Lucie Bromberg-Rosenthal (born 1895), had been born in Brussels (Belgium). The family lived at Mgr. Drehmannsstraat 9 in Roermond. See NIOD, Archive 250 F, Amersfoort camp, inventory no. 14; Amersfoort lists (August 4, 1942), Kempner, *Twee uit honderdduizend*, 109.

[63] See Posselt, *Edith Stein: Jodin, geleerde, Carmelites*, 250–51; Mohr and Prégardier, *Passion im August*, 26.

[64] See Posselt, *Edith Stein: Jodin, geleerde, Carmelites*, 252.

As well as one could, one found a place for oneself on the beds. That is, if one could even speak of beds. They were iron frames, stacked two high, without mattresses or straw sacks, so that everyone was forced to rest his tired body on the bare iron frame. We did not get much sleep that night, especially because the light was often turned on when the Germans had to do one or the other inspection. Still, one cannot say that the guards were inhumane. For the SS-ers, one can say that they did not mistreat the prisoners too much, especially not when one considers how they treated prisoners in Amersfoort camp. This is not to say, of course, that they were overflowing with warmth. Even though there was no mistreatment, for the prisoners who were new to this experience, the cold and stern commanding German voice was enough to inspire in them a great fear for the future.[65]

For those who were arrested from the district of Amsterdam, events took a different turn. Sister Judith Mendes da Costa, O.P., recounts in her autobiography that the arrests in Amsterdam began at 4:00 A.M. Police from Bilthoven brought a portion of the group by van to the Dutch Theater in Amsterdam. Sister Mendes da Costa reports that there was a certain freedom and an optimistic atmosphere in the theater, as about two hundred Catholic Jews found themselves together there. Those in mixed marriages and their children were released that same day at 2:00 P.M. Twice, a priest visited the prisoners, and some used the opportunity to go to confession.[66]

---

[65] Richard Bromberg, as quoted in Posselt, *Edith Stein: Jodin, geleerde, Carmelites*, 252.

[66] See Sister Judith Mendes da Costa, 81–92.

Monday, August 3

Back in Amersfoort, the Catholic Jews had heard that their arrest was the result of the letter of their bishops that was read on July 26. A young half-Jewish mother, who was arrested in Maastricht and was in the police car when Sister Mirjam Michaelis was picked up in Mariën-waard, was released from the camp. In the course of the following week, she went to Mariënwaard Convent to tell the local superior what had happened to her and Sister Mirjam. She recounted, among other things, that the leaders of the camp had said to the prisoners who were religious sisters and brothers "You know, after all, that you can thank the bishops for your fate." The religious had answered, "We thank God that we have such bishops, and we gladly suffer for our Holy Church."[67]

In her last letter to her confessor, Father Matthias Frehe, O.P., Dr. Lisamaria Meirowsky writes from the Wester-bork concentration camp on August 6:

> I want to send you a last greeting and to tell you that I am full of confidence and wholly surrendered to God's holy will. Even more, I consider it a grace and election to have to leave under these circumstances and in this way to give witness to the words of our fathers and shepherds in Christ.... I go with courage, confidence, and joy, as do the religious who go with me. We are permitted to bear witness to Jesus, and with our bishops we are allowed to bear witness to the truth. We go as children of our Mother, the Church, and want to unite our suffering with that of our King,

[67] As quoted in *Als een brandende toorts*, 191; Kempner, *Twee uit honderd-duizend*, 23.

Redeemer, and Bridegroom. We want to offer our suffering for the conversion of many, for the Jews, for
those who persecute us: thereby we want to contribute to peace in the Kingdom of Christ.[68]

With the letter to her confessor, Dr. Meirowsky also
enclosed a short letter, in which she wrote, "Would you
please be so kind as to send the enclosed letter to our
Archbishop (de Jong). We are happy to be able to help
him with our sacrifice. He can be at peace and must
never think that we regret his action." [69] In response to
the pastoral letter of July 26, Sister Judith Mendes da
Costa wrote a letter of thanks to Archbishop de Jong. At
least two Catholic Jews from the group in Amsterdam
had done the same in the week before their arrest.[70]

In his account of the experiences of the prisoners, Richard Bromberg, Jr. also notes their support of the bishops.

Monday, August 3, passed with a feeling of fearful
uncertainty. Uncertainty is one of those things that
can make the life of a prisoner in those circumstances
a hell. That morning, after thorough inspections, those
who were baptized Protestant were released as well as
those in a mixed marriage. By means of bed-frames,
the barrack was divided into two sections, where the
men and women stayed respectively. The sisters formed
a closed group, a sort of community, in which the
breviary and rosary were prayed in common. Edith
Stein was considered by all as their superior, since the

[68] Dr. Lisamaria Meirowsky, as quoted in Posselt, *Edith Stein: Jodin, gel-*
eerde, Carmelites, 242–44; *Als een brandende toorts*, 208. Cf. also a slightly different English translation of this letter in its entirety in Posselt, *Edith Stein:*
The Life of a Philosopher and Carmelite, 219–21.

[69] Dr. Lisamaria Meirowsky, as quoted in Kempner, *Twee uit honderddui-*
zend, 132; *Als een brandende toorts*, 209.

[70] See Sister Judith Mendes da Costa, *Autobiografie*, 81, 84.

strength emanating from her quiet being was unmistakable. Neither Cistercian (that is, Trappist) father had, in Amersfoort or Westerbork, the chance to say the Holy Mass or distribute Holy Communion. [Even though it is known that they had taken along hosts and wine, they were apparently forbidden to say the Holy Mass]. They did—secretly—hear many confessions and gave their companions courage. Unarguably, it was a great grace that there were two priests in this strange Catholic transport. It seemed as though all were convinced in the depths of their souls that this would be a journey without return; a journey that, as one of the Trappist nuns had expressed it, would lead to heaven. Even though one could detect little or nothing of external expressions of faith, a certain calm and surrender prevailed among everyone. Never was a single complaint uttered against the policy of the bishops, on account of whose pastoral letter this, after all, had happened. Perhaps this was the case because, at that moment, it was not yet clear that this was the only reason for the arrest.

This day in Amersfoort lasted exasperatingly long. Twice, the entire group was given fresh air, and, for the first time, they were acquainted with the humiliation of being prisoners. On a small piece of land, fenced in by barbed wire, all had to walk around in a circle for ten to fifteen minutes under the watchful eye of the Germans. And when, back in the barracks, one had to use the bathroom, then one had to wait until there were enough people before one was led by armed guards to the appropriate place. This happened even though the barbed wire made escape impossible![71]

---

[71] Richard Bromberg, Jr., as quoted in Posselt, *Edith Stein Jodin, geleerde, Carmelites,* 252–53.

Tuesday, August 4

Early in the morning of August 4, the group from Amersfoort arrived in the Westerbork camp. This camp had
been established by the Dutch government before the
Second World War. At that time, Jewish people who were
seeking refuge from the Nazi regime had been received
there. During the occupation, Westerbork became the
most important temporary camp for Jews being deported.

A total of about 102,000 people passed through Westerbork on their way out of the country. Only a few survived what happened afterward. Because the camp had
been built for refugees, not prisoners, it was at first sight
not such an unfriendly-looking place. It was, however,
surrounded by several meters of barbed wire. Numerous
watchtowers surrounded the camp. On these towers, the
Dutch military police kept watch with machine guns and
floodlights. Once they arrived in Westerbork, the detainees were first brought to an "unpleasant reception hall".[72]

Bromberg writes:

In the night between August 3 and 4, all were loaded
again onto the trucks and brought to the train station
in Amersfoort. No one knew where the ride would
end, and since we were forbidden to open the cur-
tains of the compartments (we were not transported
in cattle cars), the various station names remained
hidden. The strangest rumors were spread about our
destination: from the prison for convicted offenders in
Scheveningen to one of the concentration camps in
Germany. These rumors flew until a good-hearted station master removed all uncertainty by calling out

[72] *Als een brandende toorts*, 157.

with a loud voice as the train was leaving: "All aboard,
direction Assen!" (Even though, by the nature of the
events, no one could board!) Assen, that meant Westerbork. For most of the passengers, this name meant
nothing because our transport was one of the first that
would go to Germany via this camp. But all the rest-
less guesses and conjectures were over when the train
suddenly stopped in the middle of a dike and the doors
were opened. As far as the eye could see, everything
was uninhabited, and there was no sign of a camp. At
the roadside were about twenty men wearing bands
around their arms reading, "Transport group" (*Trans-
portgruppe*). This was a division whose special task it
was to help arriving and departing transports with luggage. They were guarded by about five Dutch military police (as at that time only the commander and
his assistant in the camp were German). After everyone had gotten out, including the sick and elderly,
and all the luggage had been removed, the trip to the
actual Westerbork camp began and lasted about an hour.
The place where the train had stopped turned out to
be Hooghalen.[73]

The trip from Hooghalen to Westerbork was made on
foot by most people. There were a few horse-drawn carts
for luggage and people unable to walk.

Sister Judith Mendes da Costa and her group from
Amsterdam were brought by train directly to the station
in Hooghalen. They arrived there at the same time as
the Catholic Jews from Amersfoort. During the walk from
Hooghalen to Westerbork, Sister Judith prayed the rosary

---

[73] Bromberg, as quoted in Posselt, *Edith Stein: Jodin, geleerde, Carmelites*,
253–54.

out loud. On the way, those who were walking were
passed by the two horse-drawn wagons, and sister Judith
noted that the wagons carried some women religious as
well as many suitcases.[74]

The group of religious sent to Westerbork consisted
of two priests, two brothers, eight sisters, and two Third-
Order members. All wore the habit until Auschwitz. That
made them conspicuous and recognizable.

The camp complex included not only the "living quarters of the commander at the entrance, but also large
buildings for administration, a reading hall, kitchen, linen
room, ironing room, barracks for the sick, as well as streets
lined with small houses".[75] Bromberg describes his stay
in Westerbork:

> Now began one of the worst things that can happen
> to a person in his life: registration. For hours the group
> went from one little table to another to fill out end-
> less lists and papers concerning the most diverse infor-
> mation: from the worth of one's furniture at home to
> possible relatives in the United States or elsewhere.
> This registration took place in a large wooden build-
> ing. All the buildings were wooden except for the
> kitchen. The building used for registration had actu-
> ally served as a theater where there were truly con-
> certs and performances at set times.
>
> The stage was presently being used by the police
> department as a makeshift studio, and all had to take a
> place on a chair to be photographed, holding in their
> hand a sign with their prisoner number. The feeling
> of being imprisoned was very strong here. When this
> was over—all together it had surely lasted about four

[74] See Sister M. Emerentia Peters in *Als een brandende toorts*, 160.
[75] Ibid.

hours—and we were brought to our assigned barracks, it turned out that the men and women were separated without any possibility of contact. One can easily understand what this meant. By means of orderlies—something like errand boys (there were also orphans among these)—who were in service for one or another department in Westerbork, it was possible to smuggle notes, but this could not make up for the separation. Contact was not restored before the Friday of departure.

In the meantime, the sisters in the women's barracks had taken it upon themselves to help the children and the women. The physical work, such as sweeping and cleaning, was done by the non-religious. While the other sisters were busy and talkative, and while they thought of possible missionary work in Germany, Edith Stein was quiet and recollected.[76]

For two full days we were in Westerbork in this way. All efforts to be exempted from the approaching transport on account of illness or other reasons failed because the Jewish leaders in Westerbork—who had the task of setting up the transport list—had received the order to consider no requests for exemption from this special transport. Without exception, all had to be sent on.[77]

Sister Judith Mendes da Costa also tells about her stay in Westerbork. She writes about the arrival at the camp:

We first came into a room where our names were registered. Many men and women sat here at typewriters. We had to show them our personal identification and then received it back. Then we had to wait at

---

[76] Richard Bromberg, as quoted in Posselt, *Edith Stein: Jodin, geleerde, Carmelites*, 253–55.
[77] Ibid., 256.

least an hour in front of the barrack so that a doctor could examine our heads. Those whose "head business" was not in order had to go to another barrack. Outside that barrack, I made the acquaintance of other religious to whom I had waved as they passed by on the high wagons. There were two Trappistine sisters, two Trappist fathers, and one brother, all five from one family; and a Carmelite sister, doctor in philosophy, who came from Germany but had been driven away to the Netherlands. While staying with the Carmelites of Echt, she had been working on a treatise about St. John of the Cross. Her sister, who belonged to the Third Order of Mount Carmel, was with her. Furthermore, there were Dr. Lisamaria Meirowsky, a physician, dressed as a nurse; Sister Mirjam from the Sisters of Trier; Sister Luise Löwenfels from Geleen; Dr. Ruth Kantorowicz; Alice Reis, a godchild of Edith Stein, dressed as a postulant; and a sister from Moerdijk, Sister Charitas.

They had been taken from various houses and were all brought to the camp in Amersfoort. The treatment there had not been that good. The Trappist fathers had been placed against the wall with rifles pointed at them in the presence of the sisters. That was by way of a joke. We decided to stay together for the physical examination, and that worked. It was quickly over. Afterward, the female barrack leader took us to the appointed barrack. There were two large halls and a scullery in the middle. The beds were two high, and a soiled straw sack and a small, dirty pillow lay on the beds. The floor was muddy and dirty, as if it had not been scrubbed in months.[78]

[78] Sister Judith Mendes da Costa, O.P., as quoted by Peters in *Als een brandende toorts*, 160.

In Westerbork, a girl named Els came to Sister Judith. She had been taken prisoner early that day together with her sister, who was diabetic. They had had to leave their old, sick mother behind at home. The mother was not Catholic, but both daughters were. Els was worried about who would now care for her mother. The next day she received a suitcase sent by the pastor containing clothing, towels, blouses, peppermint, aspirin, insulin, soap, toothpaste, and the like. She was happier about the letter from the pastor than about the things, because he wrote "that he would take care of her little mother ...".[79] Sister Judith recounts:

> In the late afternoon the Trappist fathers came to our barrack and walked back and forth outside with their sisters. From one of those fathers, the novice master [Father Nivardus Löb, O.C.S.O.], I received a blessing. The sisters with whom I slept in the barrack approached me and asked if we should not stay together as much as possible, because then we could perhaps pray the Office together. One of the sisters also got our food for us in a large soup tureen, and we came with our plates to her. The others went to the kitchen and could even go there for seconds. We almost always ate *hutspot*,[80] which was well prepared.[81]

Sister Judith did not want to bind herself too much to the group of sisters. It was also clear to her that they could not pray the breviary together, because Sister Teresa Benedicta prayed "the greater Office", and she prayed the

[79] As quoted by Peters in *Als een brandende toorts*, 161.

[80] "Hutspot" is a Dutch dish of mashed potatoes mixed with mashed carrots and onions.—TRANS.

[81] Sister Judith Mendes da Costa, O.P., as quoted by Peters in *Als een brandende toorts*, 161.

"little Office".[82] Sister Judith saw "that the sisters of the other orders took care of the people, and this seemed the appropriate task for us, too."[83]

In Westerbork the religious stayed in barrack 36.[84] The housing was not what Sister Judith was used to. She describes her first night there:

> The first night I could not sleep on account of the fleas. It was also extraordinarily dirty.... I kept my socks on in bed and slept between two woolen blankets so that I would especially not touch the mattress. I had put a clean cloth around the small pillow that was full of moisture stains and spots, and now I could peacefully put my head on it. I slept next to the door. During the night I heard a military policeman who was keeping watch come in. I was not even frightened of it![85]

Wednesday, August 5

Sister Judith tells about her second day in Westerbork:

> In the morning, we sisters rose and went to wash ourselves in the hall at the sink washbasins. Afterward we stood by the door to pray our morning prayer [Lauds],

[82] See ibid. Sister Teresa Benedicta of the Cross and the other contemplative nuns prayed the Divine Office, "the Greater Office", while Sister Judith prayed the Little Office of the Blessed Virgin Mary, colloquially called the Little Office. The Little Office of the Blessed Virgin Mary is a liturgical devotion to the Blessed Virgin, in imitation of, and supplementary to, the Divine Office.—TRANS.

[83] Sister Judith Mendes da Costa, O.P., as quoted by Peters in *Als een brandende toorts*, 161–62.

[84] See Sister M. Teresita Munsters, in *Als een brandende toorts*, 222.

[85] Sister Judith Mendes da Costa, O.P., as quoted by Peters in *Als een brandende toorts*, 162.

the small Hours [Terce, Sext, None], and to make our
meditation. We were not allowed to go out! It was
still too early, and the military police paced back and
forth, on guard in front of our barrack. It was too bad
that we were not allowed out because it was beautiful
weather. Around 7:00 in the morning we were allowed
to walk back and forth, and we could pray. We walked
constantly from the barrack to the barbed wire and
back again. I also lent my Office book to the Polish
physician [probably Dr. Lisamaria Meirowsky].

After we had eaten breakfast—we also got coffee
from the little kitchen—we cleaned the barrack a little. First we dusted, then we wet-mopped. It already
began to look a little different. At midday, it was *hutspot*
again. I will not easily forget that—even after a year,
every time we eat *hutspot* I think of the camp! In the
afternoon, the female barrack leader informed us that
we had to go to the large building near the entrance.
It was a very large hall in which small tables, at which
men were seated, stood some distance from one
another. At the entrance, we were told that we had to
stay behind the chalk lines drawn around the tables (a
meter's distance on each side), so that the men did
not have to worry about being contaminated by Jews!
Everything was taken from us here: first our personal
identification, our documentation card, receipts, our
bank deposit book, money (we were allowed to keep
a small amount), gold, silver, and so on. Every time
we had to sign. At the Dutch Theater I had received
a letter signed by V., in which I was specifically warned
not to sign anything. I therefore wholly refused, and
this caused much delay. I saw that all my companions
signed, and I therefore remained behind alone. Then
I had to go to a man from the Jewish Council, who
asked me why I did not want to sign. I responded,

"Just tell me plainly: we have to sign for our journey
to Germany, but I am sure that I will be freed. They
are working on it, so why should I sign?" No matter
how much they tried to talk to me and convince me,
I kept stubbornly refusing. When I came again to a
small table and papers were once again put before me
to sign, and I refused, I was told: "No one who has
not signed will leave this hall." I was not at all ruffled
by what was said but calmly looked over the large hall
and thought, "Could I not spend the night here?"

A little farther ahead I saw the other sisters busily
signing. What should I do? Inwardly I called upon
the Holy Spirit to ask him for counsel and to enlighten
my mind. I also called my Guardian Angel for help.
In the meantime, I was sent to another little table,
where other papers were placed before me. These concerned possession, houses, transferable securities.

"I do not have those, so why should I sign?" I asked
again. A man came up to us and told the man who
sat behind the little table that I had not signed anything yet. Again I had to tell him the reason for my
refusal. "But even if you have signed, you can still be
released. There have been so many such cases", the
man reassured me.[86]

After being pressured from many sides, Sister Judith
signed after all.

In Westerbork there were little boys who fulfilled the
tasks of orderlies. They were Jewish boys who were about
twelve years old. They wore a star and had an orderly's
cap on their head. One was not allowed to move about
freely in the camp. According to the rules, one always
had to be accompanied by at least one orderly. Sister Judith

[86] Ibid., 163.

asked one of them when they would be going to Germany. He was able to tell her that the departure was planned for the night from Thursday to Friday. In the evening, the names of the prisoners were painted with white letters on their suitcases. For those who needed more luggage, backpacks were for sale.[87] One could even have new soles be put on one's shoes in the camp. Every barrack had a female leader. The administrative employees were also Jews.

Thursday, August 6

Sister Judith was waiting for the definitive decision that she would not be placed on the transport to Germany:

> In the morning around 11 o'clock I had to see the commander again. Many people were waiting together in a small room for their turn. One by one we had to go to the adjoining hall to hear the decision. . . . Every time someone returned, one saw a sad face. The most tragic scenes took place here. A quiet mumbling went through the row of those who were waiting. It sounded full of dismay. All exemptions had been retracted. I prepared myself for the worst. I did not yet know that this only concerned those people who had come here from the Amersfoort camp. I also saw the German Carmelite [Sister Teresa Benedicta]. Her turn came much sooner than mine. Her exemption had also been revoked. She was pale, but looked resigned and still consoled her companions.[88]

[87] See Peters in *Als een brandende toorts*, 165.
[88] Sister Judith Mendes da Costa, O.P., as quoted by Peters in *Als een brandende toorts*, 166.

On Thursday afternoon a lady from Assen came with
suitcases of clothing for the sisters. In another room
of the barrack she distributed them. At the border we
would surely have to take off our religious habit. I
received a black coat and a white shawl because there
were no black dresses left. In addition, I received a
pair of shoes, some white stockings and a white knit-
ted undershirt. We also received apples and peppermint. As I was going to put everything in the suitcase
under my bed, I saw that there were tomatoes on my
plate. Els had brought those. It was a treat from the
Jewish Council.[89]

From Westerbork, the detainees had the chance to make
telephone calls, to telegraph, and to write letters, and
ample use was made of this opportunity. A total of at
least twenty-one letters or telegrams have been saved. They
are dated from Tuesday, Wednesday, and Thursday. The
prisoners asked those at home to send or bring blankets,
clothing, shoes, food (and food vouchers), prayer books,
identity papers, and other necessities. Especially on the
Thursday, numerous visitors or couriers came from Echt,
Venlo, Rotterdam and Meerssen, Tilburg, Moerdijk,
Almelo, and from other places in the Netherlands.

Numerous visitors who went to see those they knew
or to deliver things tell us how such visits in Westerbork
were conducted. Most visits took place on Thursday,
August 6. One had to report to the Dutch police at a
pavilion outside the camp. The prisoners were notified
by an orderly. One could speak with the prisoners in a
special visitor's barrack at the entrance of the camp. By

[89] Ibid., 167.

means of a shrill whistle, the SS informed the prisoners that they had to return to the barracks. Some visitors stayed overnight in Hooghalen or in the area. They wanted to return the next day for a second visit. When they arrived at the camp, however, the prisoners had already left by train for Auschwitz. People from the camp told two visitors from Venlo that about ten to fifteen religious were among the prisoners who had been deported.[90]

Friday, August 7

According to the witness of a woman who stayed in the camp and had been known as Nurse van de Hoff, the Jews were awakened at 3:30 A.M. on the morning of Friday, August 7. A new transport had arrived with people on board who had been picked up on the streets of Amsterdam and who were on their way directly to Auschwitz. Between 5:30 and 7:30 A.M., the prisoners left the camp to go to the train station in Hooghalen. Those who remained behind in the camp gave clothing and food, which they actually needed for themselves, to the departing prisoners. About a thousand remained behind.[91]

Nurse van de Hoff told Mr. H. van Duursen (a courier from Dalfsen who came to bring a package for Sister Charitas Bock from Moerdijk) "that a certain Mrs. Ten Berkel [this is Sophie van Berckel], who had been busy helping the Jews for a long time already, a Catholic lady, who had been repeatedly threatened with imprisonment because she did too much for people, had arrived

[90] For reports about these visits, see *Als een brandende toorts*, 149–56, 191.
[91] See Sister M. Teresita Munsters, in *Als een brandende toorts*, 229.

late yesterday evening. She brought a whole load of blankets and clothing, so that many were helped by it." [92]
Sophie van Berckel wrote to Archbishop de Jong, "I was
happy to have arrived before the deportation and to have
been able to fulfill many of the wishes of the unfortunate ones." [93]

Richard Bromberg wrote:

On the night from Thursday to Friday, the lists with
the names of those leaving on the transport were read.
With the exception of six people (Sister Judith, O.P.,
who was later arrested again and of whom one has not
heard since that time; a very old lady, whose name is
unknown, who was too ill to be placed on the transport and who has since probably died; my parents, sister, and me), all names were read out loud. Early in the
morning of August 7, when the sun had hardly risen,
a long row of men, women, and children was already
formed along the large road that went through the camp.
The religious habits stood out strangely among the luggage consisting of backpacks and duffle bags.

Instead of the military police, the armed SS came,
and, under their snapping commands, the procession
left the camp. Those who remained behind continued
to wave for a long time, and they were the last ones
to see anything from this transport.[94]

At the Hooghalen station, the Jews were placed in live-
stock cars. Every car had an area of $23\frac{1}{2}$ square yards, and

[92] Ibid., 330; Peters, in *Als een brandende toorts*, 167.

[93] Sophie van Berckel to the Most Reverend J. de Jong (August 10, 1942),
Archive, Roman Catholic Archdiocese of Utrecht, inventory no. 76.

[94] Bromberg, as quoted in Posselt, *Edith Stein: Jodin, geleerde, Carmelites*,
255–56.

sixty people were loaded into each one—men, women, and children were mixed. Luggage went in, too. There was no medical care. Volunteers, not the Germans, supplied each car with two buckets: one with drinking water and the other to be used as a toilet. The cars were locked from the outside.[95] They were probably not opened again until the train arrived in Auschwitz.

Saturday, August 8

There is no reliable information about Saturday, August 8. The prisoners probably spent this entire day on the train. The sisters Annemarie and Elfriede Goldschmidt succeeded in sending a postcard to two old acquaintances, Lotte Embacher and Ingeborg Plössner, in Munich (Germany), during the journey to Auschwitz. They let them know, "We are once again back in *Das Reich* [German country] together with very many people." [96]

Sunday, August 9

On Sunday, August 9, exactly two weeks since the letter of the bishops had been read in the churches of the Netherlands, the train that had left from Hooghalen the previous Friday brought 987 Jews to Auschwitz. At the station 464 strong men and women were selected for forced labor.

---

[95] See Snoek, *De Nederlandse kerken*, 99.

[96] Annemarie and Elfriede Goldschmidt, as quoted by Prégardier, in H. Moll, ed., *Zeugen für Christus: Das deutsche Martyrologium des 20. Jahrhunderts*, 2 vols. (Paderborn, 1999), 401.

The remaining 523 men, women, and children were sent to the gas chambers.[97]

Of the men forced into labor that day, there are three known survivors: Jozef van Rijk, Jesaja Veffer, and Maurice Schellekes. All three non-Catholic Jews were questioned by the police in Amsterdam on June 17, 1964, and their report is important for obtaining some insight into what happened at Auschwitz.[98] Auschwitz was the largest of the Nazi concentration camp complexes. It had an area of almost 25 square miles, with three main camps and thirty-nine subsidiary camps. The main camp, Auschwitz-Birkenau, became the extermination camp after the Wannsee Conference. Until the liberation, more than a million Jews, gypsies, and other people who were displeasing to the Nazis were murdered there.

Having reached Auschwitz, the transport of August 7 did not go directly into the extermination camp, Birkenau. As noted, the train stopped at the station in the city of Auschwitz, where the passengers were required to disembark. Among those who were selected for labor, Jesaja Veffer saw a few men in religious dress.[99] Maurice Schellekes estimates that the group chosen for work was about 165 people between seventeen and fifty years of age.[100]

One of Veffer's fellow prisoners overheard a German guard on the platform saying to another that "the women and children would only be registered in heaven."[101]

---

[97] See Mohr and Prégardier, *Passion im August*, 15.

[98] See *Als een brandende toorts*, 242–45; Kempner, *Twee uit honderdduizend*, 112–14.

[99] See Stein, *Briefauslese*, 148–49; *Als een brandende toorts*, 243.

[100] See *Als een brandende toorts*, 244.

[101] Kempner, *Twee uit honderdduizend*, 113.

Veffer later learned that this meant "immediate gassing". Besides the religious, his own wife and child also belonged to this group. They were led away in the direction of the gas chamber.[102]

Jozef van Rijk reported that a number of sisters in religious habit had to board a truck. At the time, he did not know where they were going. Later, he understood that they had been brought directly to the gas chambers, where they most likely were killed immediately.[103] Others went to the extermination camp, Auschwitz-Birkenau, by foot. Once they arrived there, they were brought to a room where they had to remove all their clothing. Afterward, they came to a room that was marked "shower area". The people were made to think they needed to shower. They were pushed close to one another into the shower area, the doors were locked from the outside, and through an opening in the ceiling the poison gas Cyclon B was poured. An SS physician could see through a peephole when all had died. Then the doors were opened, the corpses taken out, and jewelry and gold teeth removed.[104]

Maurice Schellekes was later put to work removing the corpses from the gas chamber and transporting them to the crematorium. At first there were no crematoria. The deceased were placed in mass graves and sprinkled with slaked lime. According to Schellekes' estimation, there are at least 50,000 corpses buried in Auschwitz–Birkenau.[105]

[102] See ibid., 114. The Veffer Family is listed on the transport of August 7, 1942, list A, no. 26 (NIOD, Archive 250 I, Westerbork camp, inventory no. 239).

[103] See Stein, *Briefauslese*, 146–48; *Als een brandende toorts*, 242.

[104] See Kempner, *Twee uit honderdduizend*, 87.

[105] See Stein, *Briefauslese*, 150–52; *Als een brandende toorts*, 244–45.

Not a single document from Auschwitz confirms the death of the Catholic Jews. Those who were murdered there were no longer registered. There is no list, no report of those who died. There is nothing but a deathly silence. For the remainder of the occupation, these victims of Auschwitz were never heard of again. Family members, fellow members of the religious communities, and friends had nothing but the worried hope that they might still be alive.[106]

Rescue Attempts

Already on the morning of August 2, the bishops of the Netherlands had been informed by telephone of the deportation of Catholic Jews. In the course of the following week, Archbishop Jan de Jong also received letters that confirmed which Catholic Jews had been taken away. Some of this correspondence also notified the archbishop that those who were arrested on August 2 were released and had happily returned home.[107]

Archbishop de Jong sent, also in the name of the other bishops, a telegram to Seyss-Inquart on August 2. In this telegram he asked for "mercy for the Christian Jews who, according to reports, have been deported".[108] On the same day, Most Reverend Johannes Petrus Huibers, Bishop of Haarlem (1935–1960), wrote a letter to Archbishop de Jong that included a draft for a telegram to the government commissioner.

[106] See S. Westerholz, "Das Schicksal der jüdischen Nonne Luise Loewenfels aus Trabelsdorf", in *Mesusa*, vol. 4: *Lebensbeschreibungen und Schicksale: Spuren jüdischer Vergangenheit an Aisch, Aurach, Ebrach und Seebach*, ed. J. Fleischmann, 269–309, 306 (Mühlhausen, 2004).

[107] See Archive, Archdiocese of Utrecht, no. 76.

[108] Ibid.

The Archbishop not only wrote the telegram, but through Monsignor van Loo, the Catholic representative for the Interdenominational Consultation, he also brought the matter of the deportation of the Catholic Jews to the attention of this consultative body. In addition, the Archbishop consulted Miss Sophie van Berckel, who often provided him with counsel in matters concerning the Jewish people.

On Sunday, August 23, Archbishop de Jong wrote an extensive letter to Government Commissioner Seyss-Inquart and to General Commissioner Rauter.[109] The archbishop did his best to correct the mistaken notion that had been spread by the occupying forces, that is, that the Catholic Church had agreed to cooperate with them regarding their pastoral letter and had reneged. He stressed that the bishops "in no way, either explicitly or implicitly, either formally or informally, either personally or through one or another representative, promised anyone not to read the telegram in question." The Reverend Dijckmeester had, it is true, informed the bishops on Friday, July 24, that the general synod of his ecclesial community had decided not to read the telegram. "On this occasion, he did not with a single word suggest that he had received the order from the representative of your excellency [Seyss-Inquart] to advise the leadership of the Catholic Church not to read the telegram. We therefore took his statement to be merely informative, without taking this statement to give us any reason to change our own position." At any rate, the reading of the telegram could no longer have been prevented at that moment for

[109] See Letter of the Most Reverend. J. de Jong to the bishops of the Netherlands (August 24, 1942), in Archive, Archdiocese of Utrecht, no. 76.

purely technical reasons. The Reverend Dijckmeester also confirmed once afterward "that in the conversation in question with the representative of your excellency [on July 24] no word was said about the Catholics and the other churches and that he only informed the German government of the decision of his own church". He could not promise the German government anything, because there had not even been a consultation with the other churches, and he had not received a mandate from others for such a consultation. The German government had not even asked him to agree to refrain from reading the telegram. For that reason, under no circumstance can it be claimed that the Dutch bishops did not keep their word. The archbishop therefore asked that the Catholic Jews be treated in the same way as those Jews who were baptized in other religious denominations.[110]

At the encouragement of the archbishop, the Reverend Dijckmeester went to the respective offices in The Hague, inquiring about Archbishop de Jong's petition of August 23. Dijckmeester was told that the answer to De Jong's petition was "negative". Maybe a telegram to the respective authorities could still have an effect. De Jong therefore sent another telegram to Seyss-Inquart and to Rauter on the afternoon of Thursday, August 27. He received no answer. On Sunday, August 29, Archbishop de Jong wrote to his brother bishops that "we can, therefore, as far as we can see, give up all hope."[111] By that time, most of the deported Catholic Jews had already been murdered.

---

[110] See Petition of the Most Reverend J. de Jong to Government Commissioner Seyss-Inquart, in Archive, Archdiocese of Utrecht, no. 76.

[111] Letter of the Most Reverend J. de Jong to the other Dutch bishops (August 29, 1942), in Archive, Archdiocese of Utrecht, no. 76.

The Attitude of the Catholic Jews in a Hostile World

Many of the Catholic Jews who had been arrested on August 2, 1942, had been born in Germany. There they had already been bothered, persecuted, driven away, and robbed of their work, their possessions, and their human rights. They had come to the Netherlands to live in safety and freedom. Once the German occupation began, the Jews in the Netherlands were once again persecuted. They were registered as Jews, had to wear the Jewish star, and were forced to fill out nearly endless amounts of forms. In this way, without their knowing it, the moment of their deportation was being prepared.

The world was aflame. The influence of heathenism and barbarism had deprived society of its human face. Under these circumstances, the faithful who were murdered grew by God's grace to holiness, like unexpected shining pearls on an ugly background. The inhumane Nazi system brought humanity to a worldwide crisis. The martyrs who are presented here show by word and deed that faith, fidelity to God, the following of Christ, and the readiness to sacrifice can make it possible for the human person to fulfill the purpose of his life even in the most difficult circumstances. Auschwitz shows what the human person without God is capable of doing to his fellow man. These martyrs show that the same situation can also be the opportunity for a human being to reach his highest goal—union with God.

Chapter 2

THE STEIN SISTERS

Edith and Rosa Stein were born to Siegfried Stein[1] and Auguste Courant,[2] who were married on August 2, 1871. A total of eleven children were born from this union: Paul (1872–1943), Selma (1873–1874), Else (1876–1956), Hedwig (1877–1880), Arno (1879–1948), Ernst (1880–1882), Frieda (1881–1942), Rosa (1883–1942), Richard (1884–1887), Erna (1890–1978), and Edith (1891–1942). Four of the eleven children died before they were four years old.[3]

The family lived in Prussia, first in Gleiwitz and then in Lublinitz,[4] where Rosa was born. In April 1890, they moved again, this time to the city of Breslau. Edith was born here.

Both parents came from Jewish merchant families. They were practicing orthodox Jews of Prussian nationality. Many of their children adapted themselves to the

[1] He was born in 1843 in Gleiwitz, between Frauenwaldau and Goschütz, Germany. He died in 1893.

[2] She was born in Lublinitz, Germany, in 1849 and died in Breslau, Germany, in 1936.

[3] See S. Batzdorff, *Aunt Edith: The Jewish Heritage of a Catholic Saint* (Springfield, Ill.: Templegate Publishers, 1998), 22.

[4] Both cities are in present-day Poland, but at the time the Stein family lived there, they belonged to Germany.—TRANS.

circumstances of their environment. In Breslau Siegfried
Stein had a lumber business. On July 10, 1893, he suffered heat stroke while inspecting a forest and subsequently died.[5] Auguste Stein, a strong and competent
woman, took over her husband's business. Until that
time the family had not been well off, but under Mrs.
Stein's management, the business flourished, and the family prospered. There were no legal disadvantages for the
family on account of their religion; since 1812, the Prussian Jews had enjoyed the same legal rights as other
citizens.

Saint Teresa Benedicta of the Cross, O.C.D.

[5] See Edith Stein, *Life in a Jewish Family*, trans. Josephine Koeppel, O.C.D.,
ed. L. Gelber and Romaeus Leuven, O.C.D., The Collected Works of Edith
Stein, vol. 1 (Washington, D.C.: ICS Publications, 1986), 41, 73.

Edith Stein[6] was born on the Day of Atonement, October 12, 1891. The house where she was born still stands on Michaelisstrasse 38 in what is now Wrocław, Poland. Edith was not yet two years old when she lost her father. She had no memories of him.

Although her mother remained loyal to her faith her whole life long, the fourteen-year-old Edith made the conscious decision not to pray anymore. She distanced herself from the Jewish faith and from God. She continued, however, to feel that she belonged to the Jewish people, and she made this known when anti-Semitic remarks were made around her.

Edith was a gifted girl, who even at a young age deliberated about what she wanted and how she could accomplish it. She recounts, "As my sixth birthday approached, I resolved to make an end of the despised attendance at the kindergarten. I declared that, absolutely, once that day had come, I wanted to go to the 'big school' and requested that this be my one and only birthday gift; in any case, if I could not have that, I would accept no other gifts."[7] The new semester at the grammar school, the *Viktoriaschule*, began on the day of her sixth birthday. Edith was accepted into the first grade, and after she had caught up with the other children who had already

---

[6] There are many biographies about Edith Stein. The first biography of Edith Stein's life was written by her novice mistress, Sister Teresia Renata Posselt, O.C.D., translated into English as *Edith Stein: The Life of a Philosopher and Carmelite*, ed. Susanne Batzdorff, Sr. Josephine Koeppel, O.C.D., and John Sullivan, O.C.D. (Washington, D.C.: ICS Publications, 2005). This edition is furnished with extensive footnotes and explanatory gleanings. Another excellent general account that cites many primary sources is Waltraud Herbstrith's *Edith Stein: A Biography*, trans. Fr. Bernard Bonowitz, O.C.S.O., 2nd ed. (San Francisco: Ignatius Press, 1992).

[7] Stein, *Life in a Jewish Family*, 78.

been in the first grade for half a year, she became one of the best pupils in the class. Edith describes herself: "As a pupil I was overly zealous. I was apt to skip right to the front of the teacher's desk with index finger raised in order to 'get my turn.' " [8]

Edith attended the *Viktoriaschule* until 1906 and, later, a high school (1908–1911).[9] From 1911 until 1913, she studied at the university in her hometown. After that, she went to the University of Göttingen (Germany) because Professor Edmund Husserl's (1859–1938) *Logical Investigations* drew her to his teaching on philosophy. Edith would remain friends with Husserl for the rest of her life. Husserl was of Jewish background, too, but had been baptized in the Lutheran ecclesial community in 1886.

Edith's attraction to the Catholic faith probably began in Göttingen. She recounts that Husserl's phenomenological method helped to remove rationalistic prejudices. She also became acquainted with the thinking of Max Scheler (1874–1928), who had become Catholic in 1899. There were other people she came to know in this university town who had discovered Christianity, and the consolation that Edith saw Christians find in their faith, even in their deepest sorrows, also pointed the way to the Church.

The married couple Adolf and Anna Reinach were among a group of philosophers whom Edith met in Göttingen. Adolf Reinach together with Theodor Conrad

---

[8] Ibid.

[9] In Germany, as in the Netherlands, there are different levels of high schools. Edith Stein attended a *gymnasium*, the highest-level high school. For the types of schools in Germany, see Sr. Josephine Koeppel's footnote 4, p. 470, in Stein, *Life in a Jewish Family.*—Trans.

were among the founding members of the Philosophical Society. Reinach died in 1917 during the First World War in Flanders (Belgium). Shortly before his death, he and his wife, Anna, had become Lutheran. After Adolf's death, Edith experienced the strength of the Christian faith in the way that Anna accepted her husband's death in union with Christ's Cross.

Edith studied in Göttingen for four semesters (1913–1915). She attended classes in philosophy, psychology, history, and German.[10] In 1915, she concluded her studies for the time being with the state examination (doctoral examination in philosophy). The diploma she earned entitled her to teach introductory courses in philosophy, German, and history.

Toward the end of the winter semester of 1915–1916, at the height of World War I, Edith interrupted her work on her doctoral dissertation to become a coworker for the Red Cross. After completing this service, she returned to Breslau, knowing that she could be recalled by the Red Cross at any moment. In addition to working on her dissertation, she was also a substitute for a sick teacher at her former school from February until October 1916. Next she went to Freiburg im Breisgau (Germany) to complete the oral defense of her dissertation. She went there because Husserl, who was directing her dissertation, was no longer in Göttingen but had become a professor at the University of Freiburg. After she obtained her doctorate *summa cum laude* with a dissertation about the problem of empathy in the knowledge of reality, she

[10] In Germany, one typically pursues university studies in, not one, but several fields.—TRANS.

became an assistant to the already world-famous Professor Husserl.

At the end of 1918, Edith gave up her work for Husserl and returned to Breslau. There she joined the German Democratic Party (Deutsche Demokratische Partei [DDP]), a liberal party that promoted personal freedom and social responsibility and supported the parliamentary democracy of the Republic of Weimar (1919–1933). In the elections of 1919, the DDP obtained 18.5 percent of the votes. For a time, Edith was politically very active. In addition, she began new scholarly activities. She wrote the treatise required for obtaining a teaching position at a university and began to give private introductory lessons on the phenomenology of Husserl at her mother's house. She taught at the adult education school and gave courses for the formation of working women and maids.

From March 1921 onward, she was regularly a welcome guest at the home of philosopher friends, the married couple Theodor and Hedwig Conrad-Martius in Bergzabern in the Palatinate (Germany). In the summer of 1921, Edith read the autobiography of Saint Teresa of Avila (1515–1582) during one of her stays there. The reading of this book was the end of Edith's search for the true faith, and she knew that she wanted to become Catholic. The biography of the woman whose order she would later enter seems to have made it clear to her that the search for God is no mere intellectual exercise. The faith of Saint Teresa gave witness to a relationship of love with God, with Jesus Christ. Knowledge plays a role in this relationship, but it consists primarily in surrender to him.

After studying the catechism and the missal to become familiar with Catholic teachings, Edith Stein was baptized in the parish church of Saint Martin in Bergzabern on January 1, 1922. On this occasion, she added the baptismal name Teresa Hedwig. For her baptismal gown, Edith wore the wedding dress of her friend and godmother, Hedwig Conrad-Martius. On that morning she also received her First Holy Communion. She was confirmed in the house chapel of the Bishop of Speyer, Germany, on the Feast of the Presentation of the Lord, February 2, 1922.

In the homily on the occasion of her beatification, Pope John Paul II said that "she sought the truth and found God." As a philosopher, she sought the first principles of existence and found the foundation of all being, God. Her entrance into the Church did not grow out of her Jewish religious convictions. She had already rejected these beliefs as a fourteen year old. She was not a believing Jew who recognized that Jesus Christ is the long-awaited Messiah. Edith was (at least in practice) an atheist who became Catholic. As a believing Christian, she discovered the roots of Christianity in Judaism. She came to know and appreciate the Jewish faith better as she deepened her Catholic faith.

As a young Catholic, she needed to grow into the faith, into the customs of the Church and the liturgy. Through the intervention of her spiritual director, the Vicar General, Father Josef Schwind, she obtained a teaching position at Saint Magdalena's, the school of the Dominican Sisters in Speyer. She lived in a small room and from there could easily go to the chapel for communal and personal prayer. The intense contact that she had with the Dominican Sisters of the Saint Magdalena Convent during these years were very influential in helping her to grow into the life and culture of the Church. At the same time, the Dominican Sisters attest that Edith Stein's life and example in Speyer had a lasting effect on them.

After the death of her spiritual director in 1927, Edith found her way to the Benedictine Archabbey of Beuron. Archabbot Raphael Walzer became her spiritual director. At this time, Beuron was a center of liturgy, ecclesial culture, and scholarship. From 1928 until her entrance into Carmel, Edith Stein came to Beuron to celebrate all the important feasts of the liturgical year. Archabbot Raphael says of her:

> I have seldom met a person in whom so many and such laudable characteristics were united. At the same time, she remained entirely a woman with tender, almost motherly sensitivities. Mystically gifted, she was unpretentious with simple people, scholarly with scholars, a seeker with seekers, I would almost say a sinner with sinners.[11]

Edith considered that in her new life as a Catholic she had an important responsibility to serve God. She wrote, "I am only an instrument of the Lord.... I would like to lead those who come to me to him."[12]

For eight years, from Easter 1923 until Easter 1931, Edith Stein taught at the school and the Catholic teachers' school of the Dominican Sisters of Speyer. As a teacher, she wanted to communicate more than knowledge. She also sought to help her students, young women and future mothers, to live in the spirit of Jesus. In this

---

[11] M. Amata Neyer, *Edith Stein: Her Life in Photos and Documents*, trans. Waltraut Stein (Washington, D.C.: ICS Publications, 1999), 49.

[12] Stein, as quoted in ibid., 36.

way, she sought to prepare them for both marriage and workplace.

In the letter of reference that Edith Stein received upon leaving Speyer, the director of the school wrote that "in her religious and moral way of life, she was a shining example for her students. She was an excellent guide in the formation of young teachers." [13]

The religious sisters and the students among whom she worked were impressed by her union with God. She not only encouraged them to pray for one another, but also counseled them to practice interior prayer.

Besides her work with the youth, she found time for scholarly activities in Speyer. During this time, Edith translated into German the letters and diaries of John Henry Newman and Saint Thomas Aquinas' *Questiones disputatae de veritate* (*Disputed Questions about Truth*). Besides this, she gave lectures in Germany and abroad on pedagogical themes. Her lectures were often about the vocation of woman and the formation of women. In addition, the topic of liturgical and eucharistic devotion fared prominently in her addresses. Edith Stein once spoke about the role of women in the following way: "Only the most purely developed male and female uniqueness can yield the highest attainable likeness to God. Only in this fashion can there be brought about the strongest interpenetration of all earthly and divine life." [14] Her audiences consisted usually of women who wanted to continue their own formation.

Edith Stein gave up her teaching position in Speyer in March 1931. In the same year, she became a teacher at

[13] Sister M. Scholastica Eiswirth, O.P., as quoted in ibid., 46.
[14] Stein, as quoted in ibid., 41.

the Pedagogical Institute in Münster (Germany). She took up residence in the Collegium Marianum, which was something like a dormitory where sisters from various orders and congregations as well as a number of female students stayed.

She could teach in Münster for only two semesters. By then, Hitler and his National Socialist Party had forbidden Jews to teach, and Edith had to give up her work. She was intelligent enough never to have had any illusions about the Nazis' intentions with respect to their persecution of the Jews and their disregard for the rights of other persons. From the beginning of Nazism, she saw very clearly that their ideology was inimical to God, Church, and the human person. She spoke about this very openly to all who would listen. According to a piece that Edith Stein wrote for her prioress in Cologne, it became evident to her in a conversation with a teacher in Münster in 1933, as she said, "that once again God had put a heavy hand upon His people, and that the fate of this people would also be mine".[15]

Edith therefore planned to travel to Rome to request a personal audience with Pope Pius XI. She intended to ask him to write an encyclical in which he would publicly speak against the Jewish persecution in Germany. But she did not follow through with this plan because, as she herself explains, "Although it suited my nature to make such an overt move, I sensed that this was not yet 'of the essence.' But I did not yet know what this 'essence' really was."[16]

---

[15] Edith Stein, "The Road to Carmel" (December 18, 1938), in Posselt, *Edith Stein: The Life of a Philosopher and Carmelite,* 115.

[16] Ibid.

On her way to Beuron to participate in the liturgy of
Holy Week, Edith stopped first in Cologne. There, she
participated in a holy hour at the Carmel she would later
enter. Edith says that during this time she spoke with
Christ and told him:

> That I knew that it was His Cross that was now being
> placed upon the Jewish people; that most of them did
> not understand this; but that those who did, would
> have to take it up willingly in the name of all. I would
> do that. He should only show me how. At the end of
> the service, I was certain that I had been heard. But
> what this carrying of the Cross was to consist in, that
> I did not yet know.[17]

Even before Edith Stein had entered Carmel, and nine
years before she was arrested in Echt, she had already
given herself wholly to God to carry the cross that she
thought he had placed upon his people and hers. Already
at that time she offered her whole life to God. She "did
not yet know" in what this sacrifice would consist. Perhaps it first became clear to her at the time of her arrest,
when she took Rosa by the hand and said, "Come, we
are going for our people." Perhaps the gift of her life as
expiation was what consciously and mystically motivated
her as she made her way to Auschwitz—and death. Was
this what was "of the essence", the fitting response to
the Jewish persecution that she looked for in 1933? At
that time, it became clear to her that she would not have
an opportunity to speak with the pope in a private audience in Rome during the Holy Year 1933 (the nineteen

[17] Ibid., 116.

hundredth anniversary of Jesus' redeeming death and Resurrection). In consultation with her confessor, she decided not to travel to the Eternal City.

Instead of traveling to Rome, Edith wrote a letter to Pope Pius XI on April 21, 1933. In this letter, she asked the Holy Father to take up a position against the Jewish persecution and the inhumane policy of the Nazi government. With foresight, or may we say with prophetic sight, she concluded the letter, written when Hitler had not yet been chancellor for three months, with the words:

All of us who are faithful children of the Church and who have carefully examined the situation in Germany fear that public estimation for the Church will suffer gravely if the silence continues any longer. We are convinced that this silence will, in the long run, not be able to buy peace from the present German government. The conflict against Catholicism will, for the time being, continue in a quiet and less brutal way than the conflict against Judaism, but it will be no less systematic. Before long, no Catholic will occupy a government position in Germany unless he accepts the new policies unconditionally.[18]

Edith Stein received a confirmation from the Secretary of State, Cardinal Eugenio Pacelli, who later became Pope Pius XII, that her letter had been presented to the Holy Father.[19] Shortly before his death in 1939, Pope Pius XI had been in the midst of preparing an encyclical

---

[18] For the German text of this letter see: *Der Pilger: Bistumblatt der Diosese Speyer* 8 (February 23, 2003): http://www.zenit.org/german/visualizza.phtml?sid=31603.

[19] http://www.3sat.de/3sat.php?http://www.3sat.de/kulturzeit/themen/43295/index.html. [This item is no longer available.—ED.]

against racism and anti-Semitism. There is not sufficient historical basis to connect the writing of this encyclical exclusively to Edith Stein's request of the pope.

Ten days after Edith had returned to Münster from her Easter stay in Beuron, after she learned that, on account of her Jewish origin, she could no longer teach there, she thought, "Might not now the time be ripe to enter Carmel? For almost twelve years, Carmel had been my goal; since summer 1921 when the *Life* of our Holy Mother Teresa had happened to fall into my hands and had put an end to my long search for the true faith." [20]

Since her conversion, Edith had desired to enter Carmel, but in obedience to her spiritual directors, she had not done so. Her spiritual directors discouraged her entrance, first, because she had to grow into living a normal Catholic life, then, because she could not do this for her mother's sake, and, lastly, because her work in the world was an important service for the Church. She had been Catholic for twelve years now, and by 1933, the Nazis had made it impossible for her to continue her work. She could either go abroad or enter Carmel. She thought that her mother would be able to accept the second option better than the first. During her prayer before the exposed Blessed Sacrament in Saint Ludgerus Church in Münster on April 30, 1933, she received, as she describes it, the Good Shepherd's "yes" to enter Carmel. Long before her entrance into Carmel, Edith Stein had made a private vow to ask her confessor's advice in all important matters. Now, too, she asked her confessor's advice and asked

---

[20] Stein, "The Road to Carmel", in Posselt, *Edith Stein: The Life of a Philosopher and Carmelite*, 118.

for his permission. In the middle of May, she received the permission to enter from her confessor, the abbot of Beuron.

On July 15, 1933, Edith left Münster for the last time. After spending some months at home, she painfully said goodbye to her elderly mother and other relatives. On October 13, Edith boarded the train that would carry her from Breslau to Cologne. Of that occasion, she wrote, "I could not feel any wild joy. The scene I had just left behind was too terrible for that. But I felt a deep peace, in the harbor of the divine will." [21]

On the vigil of the Solemnity of Saint Teresa of Jesus, after the first vespers of this Carmelite feast, Edith entered the cloister of the Carmel of Maria Pacis (Mary of Peace) in Cologne-Lindenthal. Later she wrote, "[I]n deep peace I crossed the threshold into the House of the Lord." [22] It was October 14, 1933, and she was forty-two years old.

The Carmel in Cologne had been founded in 1896. (In 1944 it was destroyed in a bombardment.) Edith Stein received a cell with an area of about three square yards. Sister Teresia Renata de Spiritu Sancto Posselt was the novice mistress for her and three other sisters in the novitiate. Edith now had to learn the many little things that every postulant must learn. [23] She who was well-known in the world, who had been admired and honored, now did the simple work every Carmelite does.

[21] Ibid., 129.
[22] Ibid., 130.
[23] The postulancy is typically the first introduction to the religious life for the new member. After this time of introduction, the postulant is clothed or invested and becomes a novice. The novice receives the religious habit and often a new religious name. After one or two years of novitiate, the young sister makes a profession of vows.—TRANS.

She proved to be particularly unfit for every sort of manual work: she was not able to clean, sew, or do other such things well, no matter how earnestly she tried. However, she did everything that she was assigned. It was a school of humility for her. Although Edith intellectually surpassed the other sisters, she so humbly placed her knowledge at the service of the community that, for some time, her fellow sisters did not suspect how learned she was.

For many years before her entrance, it had been Edith's custom to write her mother every week. She received permission to continue this custom in Carmel.[24] Before her entrance, her mother had replied every week. Now she did not reply for a long time. Her sister Rosa, instead, took it upon herself to answer Edith's letters on behalf of the family.

When her postulancy ended, Edith received the religious habit and her religious name on April 15, 1934. Her sister Rosa had bought the white silk material for the bridal dress.[25] This material was later used to make a chasuble, and Pope John Paul II wore it on the occasion of her beatification in Cologne.

Edith was allowed to make a suggestion for her religious name, and the superiors honored her suggestion. Dr. Edith Stein became Sister Teresa Benedicta a Cruce (of the Cross)—Teresa blessed by the Cross. Was this name

[24] The nuns in Carmel did not write often, and Edith Stein requested this exception to the rule for the sake of her mother.—TRANS.

[25] It was a custom in the Carmel (and in many other religious orders) that the postulant dress as a bride on the day of her clothing and that she come so dressed to receive the habit. The wedding dress symbolizes the gift of her whole being to the Person of Christ. This custom is maintained in at least some monasteries.—TRANS.

an allusion to the readiness she expressed on April 1933 to take up the cross of, for, and with the Jewish people and the Church? Many friends and old acquaintances, including her former confessor, Archabbot Raphael Walzer from Beuron, attended her clothing. Her former teacher Edmund Husserl, who had called Edith his best student, sent a telegram.

After her year of novitiate, she made temporary profession on Easter Day, April 21, 1935. One of Sister Teresa Benedicta's friends, Elisabeth Kramer, reports a conversation she had with her shortly after she had made her temporary profession. Elisabeth had remarked that Sister Teresa Benedicta was surely very safe in Carmel. Sister Teresa Benedicta immediately answered, "Oh no, I don't believe that. Surely they will come and take me out of here. In any case I cannot count on being left here in peace." [26]

After Edith's temporary profession, her mother resumed contact with her by adding a few words to Rosa's letters. She called her daughter "Sister Therese". On a nice autumn day, her mother even went by herself to the new Carmel in Breslau-Pawelitz. It was as though she wanted to be close to her beloved daughter in this way.[27] Her mother died on September 14, 1936. She was nearly eighty-eight years old.

In that same year, Rosa was baptized in the church of Hohenlind in Cologne on December 24. Sister Teresa Benedicta was able to be present at the baptism because she was returning home from the hospital that day and

[26] Elisabeth Kramer, as quoted in Posselt, *Edith Stein: The Life of a Philosopher and Carmelite*, 163.

[27] See Posselt, *Edith Stein: The Life of a Philosopher and Carmelite*, 164.

had been given permission to stop at the church. Sister Benedicta had been in the hospital for ten days because she had broken her hand and leg falling down a stairwell in Carmel.[28]

In Carmel, Sister Teresa Benedicta was permitted to continue her scholarly pursuits. In Cologne she wrote, among other things, her metaphysical work *Finite and Eternal Being* (*Endliches und ewiges Sein*). In this work she sought to make a synthesis between the metaphysics of Saint Thomas Aquinas and the phenomenology of Husserl. On September 1, 1936, she concluded this philosophical work, which she had begun before her entrance, under the title *Potency and Act (Potentia et actus)*. The manuscript consisted of 1368 pages. It quickly became evident, however, that no one was willing to publish her work because of her Jewish origin. *Finite and Eternal Being* would not be published until 1948, after her death.

Sister Teresa Benedicta made her solemn profession on April 21, 1938. She received the black veil on May 1 of that same year.[29] Shortly afterward she wrote, "I am confident that the Lord has accepted my life for everyone. I am reminded repeatedly of Queen Esther who was taken from her people precisely to stand before the king for the people. I am a very poor and powerless Esther, but the King who has chosen me is eternally great and compassionate."[30] Sister Teresa Benedicta saw her profession

---

[28] See, ibid., 169–70.

[29] The nuns in Carmel retained the white veil they received at their clothing as novices until they had made their solemn profession. The reception of the black veil took place in a separate ceremony after the solemn profession.—TRANS.

[30] Stein, as quoted in Neyer, *Edith Stein: Her Life in Photos and Documents*, 63.

not only as binding her to the Carmelite Order, but also as an act whereby she surrendered her life to God unconditionally in expiation for others, as an intercessor for her people and for the Church.

Because Edith Stein was a Jew, she foresaw that her life in Germany would be threatened by the Nazis, who rose to power in 1933. After the *Reichskristallnacht* of November 9–10, 1938, this danger drew closer. Motivated by the thought that she might be endangering the lives of her fellow sisters, she requested permission to transfer to a Carmel in another country. The permission was granted.

A friend of the Cologne cloister, Dr. Paul Strerath, offered to bring Sister Teresa Benedicta to the Netherlands. On December 31, 1938, they arrived at the Carmelite Cloister in the Dutch village of Echt. Sister Teresa Benedicta was presented to the community of thirteen sisters. One of them wrote, "What immediately struck us as so pleasant about Sr. Benedicta was her simple, modest bearing, along with her delicate tact and her warmheartedness. . . . Her features were marked by a deep seriousness, that was very noticeable that evening; evidently due to her grief at having to leave her beloved Carmel in Cologne." [31]

On July 1, 1939, her sister Rosa also came to the Carmel in Echt. Both sisters received an official residence permit. Rosa became the portress for the cloister and joined the Third Order of Carmel.

The Carmel in Echt, which was dedicated to the Holy Family and Holy Father Elijah, had been established in 1875 during the time of the *Kulturkampf*, when the

---

[31] As quoted in Posselt, *Edith Stein: The Life of a Philosopher and Carmelite*, 185.

German nuns were expelled from their country.[32] During the first years, only German was spoken there. In 1941, five Dutch women had entered, and from that time, Dutch was spoken, even though most of the nuns understood and spoke German. Sister Teresa Benedicta had to learn this new language, and she did so quickly.

It is sometimes mistakenly thought that Sister Teresa Benedicta received a temporary place to stay in the Carmel of Echt as a refugee. In fact, she became a member of the community there. The chapters of both Carmels voted to approve this.[33] The Cologne Carmel voted on it on November 23, 1941, and the Echt Carmel on December 12. Edith Stein was in this sense, not a refugee, but simply a member of the Carmel in Echt.

In 1976, Sister Ancilla Heggen, O.C.D., published an interview with eight of the nuns who had lived with Sister Benedicta in the Carmel of Echt. They spoke of Sister Benedicta as a harmonious and balanced woman who was unpretentious, warm, simple, and honest. She

---

[32] After the French-German war, the Prussian-German Empire was erected on January 18, 1871, in Versailles, near Paris. It was founded on Lutheran and liberal principles. Otto von Bismarck (1815–1898) became the chancellor in 1871. He considered the Catholic Church, especially as she manifested herself in public life (in, among other things, a Catholic political party called the *Zentrumspartei*), a threat to the unity of Germany. By means of various laws, enacted from December 1871 until April 1875, Bismarck attempted to have the Catholic Church submit to the rule of the kingdom. In 1872 all Jesuits were banned from the country. The so-called May Laws of 1875 banned all religious, except for nursing orders, from the country. Most religious left the country. Even the existence of nursing orders was precarious, and they were under state supervision and subject to expulsion at any time. The nuns from Cologne went to Echt in the Netherlands during the *Kulturkampf*.—TRANS.

[33] A "chapter" is a meeting of the professed nuns of a given Carmel. Certain decisions are made by a chapter vote; that is, the vote of the professed nuns is decisive. The reception of members into the order (to clothing or profession) is a chapter decision.—TRANS.

was reserved and humble when she spoke about the period
of her life when she had studied. Many sisters did not
know much about her background. Sister Benedicta was
at once joyful and serious. She could be very humorous.
Her relationship with her fellow sisters was modest, but
it often also had a fine pedagogical element. She spoke
not only with words, but also with her face or expressions. Toward herself she was strict. When she could help
somewhere, she hurried to do so. The other sisters felt
comfortable around her. She was clumsy in performing
household tasks, but she gladly accepted such duties and
did them as best she could.[34] In choir Sister Benedicta
was very reverent and modest.[35] Sister Stephanie recounts:

> On Sundays and feast days, she used to spend hours
> before the tabernacle. On retreat days, we would find
> her in the choir the whole day long, preferably very
> close to the Blessed Sacrament. During the aerial
> attacks, when we were trembling with fear, she would
> be praying tranquilly with her arms in the form of a
> cross. For everything, she drew her strength from God,
> and that was noticeable on the whole.[36]

So that the sisters would be able to pray the Office
more fruitfully, the prioress of the Carmel of Echt
requested that Sister Benedicta teach Latin. As a novice,
Sister Stephanie learned Latin and tells of the empathetic
way that Sister Benedicta, an excellent teacher, instructed

[34] See Sister Ancilla, O.C.D., "Recollections of Edith Stein by her Sisters", *Carmelite Digest* 3:1 (Winter 1988): 21–24.
[35] See Sister Stephanie, "Herinneringen aan zuster Benedicta", *De Sleutel*
15:5 (1987): 6.
[36] Sister Ancilla, "Recollections", 28.

them. She not only taught grammar, but also recounted many interesting historical details and explained the background of the hymns. Sister Stephanie recalls that Sister Benedicta "was once rather disappointed when she realized that some of us did not know the meaning of the words of the 'Tantum Ergo'. How was it possible to sing it so many years without knowing exactly what one is singing!" [37]

In Echt, too, Sister Teresa Benedicta was assigned scholarly work. Her most important was a study on the life and teaching of the mystic and Doctor of the Church, Saint John of the Cross (1542–1591), which she was asked to prepare in anticipation of the four hundredth anniversary of his birth. Saint John of the Cross was the Spanish Discalced Carmelite who, together with Saint Teresa of Jesus, had reformed the Carmelite Order in the sixteenth century. The title of this last work was *The Science of the Cross*. Even on the morning of her arrest, Sister Teresa Benedicta had worked on it. In a sense, she completed this unfinished work by her own sacrificial death. A fellow sister recounts, "Sister Benedicta applied herself so assiduously to writing this book that she seemed to have had a premonition of what was to happen." [38]

In the meantime, Sister Teresa Benedicta did not forget what was happening in the world. She was prepared to give her life for the sake of peace. On Passion Sunday, March 26, 1939, she wrote a note to her prioress, Mother Antonia. She wrote, "Dear Mother; please, will Your Reverence allow me to offer myself to the Heart of Jesus as a sacrifice of propitiation for true peace: that the dominion

[37] Sister Stephanie, "Herinneringen", 6.

[38] Sister Pia, as quoted in Posselt, *Edith Stein: The Life of a Philosopher and Carmelite*, 192.

of the Antichrist may collapse, if possible, without a new world war; and that a new order may be established? I would like it [my request] granted this very day because it is the twelfth hour. I know that I am a nothing, but Jesus desires it, and surely He will call many others to do likewise in these days." [39]

The Second World War began on September 1, 1939, with the German invasion of Poland. On May 10, 1940, the Germans invaded the Netherlands. When Sister Benedicta came to recreation that afternoon, her first remark was, "Now we [she and her sister Rosa] have seen most of our time here." [40] Sister Benedicta knew that they would no longer be safe in Echt. Steps were therefore taken to make a transfer to Switzerland possible. On Sunday, July 5, 1942, during the month in which the letter of the Dutch bishops—which would lead to the death of many Catholic Jews—was read, the chapter of the only Swiss Carmel in Le Paquier, which was already overfilled, unanimously decided to accept Sister Teresa Benedicta of the Cross. [41] It was arranged that Rosa would have a place to stay, as well. Only the permission of the Swiss Bureau of Aliens was still pending. In a letter of August 3, 1942, the Swiss Bureau of Aliens informed them that neither of the two sisters would be able to obtain a residency permit. It was no longer needed. They were then already on the way to their deaths. [42]

---

[39] Stein, Letter to Mother Ottilia Thannisch, O.C.D., prioress of the Carmel in Echt, as quoted in Posselt, *Edith Stein: The Life of a Philosopher and Carmelite*, 212.

[40] Sister Clara, "Edith Stein, zuster Benedicta", *Samen* 15 (1978): 8.

[41] See Posselt, *Edith Stein: The Life of a Philosopher and Carmelite*, 200.

[42] See ibid., 207. See also p. 275, n. 32: "In fact, according to Secretan, at first a denial of entry permits was issued by Swiss officials on 3 August (see ESGA 3, 579–80), then they reversed themselves and issued a concession of

In order to request a visa, Sister Teresa Benedicta had been required to travel to the Gestapo office in Maastricht. She entered there with the words, "Praised be Jesus Christ!" instead of the required, "Heil Hitler". There were all sorts of complications, and Sister Benedicta and Rosa traveled to Amsterdam in March 1942 to fulfill many formalities. At the Jewish Council and the Gestapo office, they had to fill out numerous forms, which, unbeknownst to them, were a preparation for their already planned deportation and murder. On this occasion in Amsterdam, they met a number of Jewish acquaintances who would become their companions on the way to Auschwitz.

Sister Teresa Benedicta was in silent prayer in the chapel when two men from the Gestapo arrived at 5:00 P.M. on Sunday, August 2, 1942. They said that Edith and Rosa Stein were under arrest and had to come along immediately—they were given five minutes to comply. Useless attempts to negotiate followed. The prioress asked for an extension, because Sister Teresa Benedicta was, after all, already working to obtain a visa and to leave for Switzerland. The SS officers did not respond to Mother Antonia's objections. One of them said, "She can either change into something else or come as she is. Give her a blanket, a mug, a spoon and three days' rations." [43]

Sister Stephanie recounts what happened in Carmel when Sister Benedicta was arrested. It was Sister Benedicta's turn to read at the beginning of meditation in the chapel:

---

entry visas dated 9 September (see ESGA 3, 591–92), a full month after the deaths at Auschwitz-Birkenau of both sisters and their companions."

[43] As quoted in ibid., 208.

She had to interrupt the reading, because Mother Prioress, who had earlier been called to the parlor, came to get her. Shortly thereafter, Sister Benedicta returned. She knelt before the Most Blessed Sacrament, then she turned to us with a red face, but calmly and controlled. Then, leaving the choir, she said with a sad voice, "Bitte, beten Schwestern!" ["Please pray, Sisters!"] Some sisters were also called to leave the choir to prepare the things that Sister Benedicta had to take along.[44]

A sister prepared some scrambled eggs for Sister Benedicta and her sister Rosa, but Sister Benedicta did not want to eat anything. They gave Rosa the eggs with a small spoon. At the moment of departure, Sister Benedicta was calm. Rosa was white as a sheet. Among Sister Benedicta's parting words were, "Greetings to the novices."[45] Sister Benedicta wore her brown habit and black veil when she left Carmel with Rosa. The entire event lasted ten minutes at the most. Both sisters walked across the street to the police van. Miss Delsing heard Sister Benedicta say, "Rosa, komm, wir gehen für unser Volk." ["Rosa, come, we are going for our people."][46] Sister Benedicta's expression again shows her willingness to offer her life. They walked to the corner of the street where the van was parked on the Peyerstraat. Annemarie and Elfriede Goldschmidt, two sisters who had been picked up at the Sisters of Charity of the Precious Blood in Koningsbosch, were already in the van.[47]

[44] Sister Stephanie, "Herinneringen", 7.
[45] Sister Ancilla, "Recollections", 29.
[46] Ibid.
[47] See Sister Teresia Renata de Spiritu Sancto Posselt, *Edith Stein: Jodin, geleerde, Carmelites* (Bilthoven, 1952), 231.

The events caught everyone so much by surprise that no one had the idea of calling the sisters from choir to say goodbye to Sister Benedicta and Rosa. "Those involved were so dismayed that they did not think of it—everything happened so quickly. And that is how she was taken from us without saying goodbye.... We did not know she was leaving." [48]

The prisoners were taken to the local commander (*Ortskommandant*) in Roermond. From there the twenty-seven prisoners from the district of Maastricht left in the evening for the Amersfoort camp in two cars. They did not arrive there until 3:00 A.M. From the moment they entered the Amersfoort camp, the friendly treatment was over. They were scolded and pushed along with rifle butts. The non-Catholic Jews gave the newcomers something to eat. The group spent Monday, August 3, and Tuesday, August 4, in Amersfoort. Richard Bromberg was picked up in Roermond. He was one of the prisoners but was not deported to Auschwitz later on. He wrote, as was already quoted in chapter 1: "By means of bed-frames, the barrack was divided into two sections where the men and women respectively stayed. The sisters formed a closed group, a sort of community, where the breviary and rosary were prayed in common. Edith Stein was considered by all as their superior, since the strength emanating from her quiet being was unmistakable." [49]

During the night of Tuesday, August 4, the prisoners were transported by trucks from the Amersfoort camp to the city's train station. From there, they took a darkened

[48] Sister Stephanie, "Herinneringen", 7.
[49] Richard Bromberg, as quoted in Posselt, *Edith Stein: Jodin, geleerde, Carmelites*, 252.

passenger train to Hooghalen. Before they arrived at the station, they had to disembark from the train. After an hour's walk, the group arrived at the so-called Police Transit Camp for Jews (Polizeiliches Juden Durchgangslager) in Westerbork while Tuesday, August 4, was turning into Wednesday, August 5. There were ten religious in the group, and they decided to wear their habits as long as possible. All wore the Jewish star on the religious habit. The other prisoners were happy that religious and priests were among them because they could find support in their words and prayers. The sisters spent as much time in prayer as possible. Sister Teresa Benedicta, especially, edified the others because of her great calmness and composure.[50] She accepted her fate with equanimity, full of trust and in total surrender to God. But this did not keep her from also lending a hand. She cared for the children whose distraught mothers did not look after them. She washed them, combed their hair, gave them something to eat and drink. Julius Markan, who met Sister Benedicta in Camp Westerbork, asked her, " 'What are you going to do now?' And she answered: 'So far I have prayed and worked, from now on I will work and pray.' "[51]

After days of waiting, a telegram from Westerbork arrived at the Carmel of Echt on Wednesday, August 5. Sister Benedicta asked for a number of things. The sisters in Echt prepared a package of blankets, food, candles,

[50] Account of Julius Markan, quoted in Posselt, *Edith Stein: The Life of a Philosopher and Carmelite*, 214.

[51] Posselt, *Edith Stein: The Life of a Philosopher and Carmelite*, 218; A. Mohr and E. Prégardier, eds., *Passion im August (2.–9. August 1942): Edith Stein und Gefährtinnen: Weg in Tod und Auferstehung*, Zeugen der Zeitgeschichte, 5 (Annweiler: Plöger, 1995), 97.

books, and the like. In cleaning up Sister Teresa Benedicta's cell, the sisters had found a holy card, on the back
of which she had written the offering of her life for the
conversion of the Jews. They put this holy card in the
package, too. The prioress added a note, and two men
from Echt (Piet van Kempen and Pierre Cuypers) brought
the things to Westerbork. The men arrived in Westerbork at 5:00 P.M. on Thursday, August 6. They had to
report to the Dutch police. They showed them the telegram. A Jewish boy was sent to the barrack to get Sister
Benedicta and Miss Rosa. Both men had the occasion to
speak with them. Sister Benedicta wrote at least three
more notes from Westerbork. One note refers to her great
work, *The Science of the Cross*, commenting that "[a] *sci-
entia crucis* [knowledge of the Cross] can be gained only
when one comes to feel the Cross radically." [52] In the
second note she tells her prioress, "Until now I could
pray wonderfully." She asked her to send the next volume of the breviary and a cross and rosary for Rosa. [53] In
one of her notes she asked Mother Prioress to write to
the Ursulines in Venlo and ask them to send the manuscript for her last book to Echt, if they had not done so
already. [54] Sister Teresa Benedicta also wrote to the
Ursulines in Venlo on August 5, 1942, asking them to
send her manuscript to the Carmel in Echt. Even from

[52] Edith Stein, *Self-Portrait in Letters*, trans. Josephine Koeppel, O.C.D., ed.
L. Gelber and Romaeus Leuven, O.C.D., The Collected Works of Edith
Stein, vol. 5 (Washington, D.C.: ICS Publications, 1993), letter no. 330 to
Mother Ambrosia Antonia Engelmann, O.C.D. (December 1941), 341.

[53] See Stein letter to her Reverend Mother (August 6, 1942), as quoted in
Posselt, *Edith Stein: The Life of a Philosopher and Carmelite*, 218.

[54] See Prégardier, in H. Moll, ed., *Zeugen für Christus: Das deutsche Martyrologium des 20. Jahrhunderts*, 2 vols. (Paderborn, 1999), 262.

the camp, she was apparently concerned that this work, *The Science of the Cross*, might be lost.

At Camp Westerbork, Sister Teresa Benedicta told Mr. van Kempen that "if she would have to go [to be deported to work in the Silesian mines], then her prayer would always take first place, no matter what kind of work she was assigned. She wanted to offer her suffering for the conversion of unbelievers, for the Jews, for the blind persecutors, and for all who had lost God from their hearts." [55] The messenger added to his report, "No complaint passed her lips during this conversation." [56] In his report about Sister Teresa Benedicta, Pierre Cuypers writes, "Her deep faith placed her in an atmosphere of heavenly life." [57]

Lucie Bromberg-Rosenthal, who stayed in the barrack with Sister Teresa Benedicta, describes the impression that the Carmelite made on her.

The great difference between Edith Stein and the other sisters lay in her silence. My personal impression is that she was grief-stricken. She was not afraid, but I cannot express it better except by saying that she seemed to carry such a heavy burden of suffering that even when she did smile every once in a while, it made one even sadder. As I write this, the thought occurs to me that she knew what was in store for her and the others. She was, after all, the only one who had once fled also from Germany and who, therefore, knew more than the others—like the Löbs (Trappists), who still

[55] Piet van Kampen, as quoted in *Als een brandende toorts: Documentaire getuigenissen over Dr. Edith Stein (zuster Teresia Benedicta a Cruce) en medeslacht-offers* (Echt: Friends of Dr. Edith Stein, 1967), 152.

[56] Ibid.

[57] Pierre Cuypers, as quoted in *Als een brandende toorts*, 154.

thought of missionary work. Once more, this is my impression: she thought of the impending suffering; not *her* own, for she had long since accepted it, but the suffering that was awaiting the others. Her whole appearance, as I see her in my mind's eye sitting in the barrack, still reminds me of a Pietà without Christ.[58]

Many others also report the notable calm, resignation, and recollection with which Sister Benedicta carried herself in Westerbork and the unmistakable dignity that radiated from her. She radiated a spirit of prayer, a visible union with God. The stay in Westerbork lasted from the morning of Wednesday, August 5, until sometime between the night of Thursday, August 6, and Friday, August 7. Then the group was placed on the train to Auschwitz. On the transport list she is listed next to her sister Rosa under the name "Edith Stein" (list A, number 2).[59] They probably arrived in Auschwitz on Sunday, August 9. On that very day, Sister Teresa Benedicta, along with many other victims, was gassed and buried in a mass grave.

It was not until February 16, 1950, that the first official report about the death of Edith and Rosa Stein was published on a list from the Dutch Department of Justice.[60] Pope John Paul II beatified Sister Teresa Benedicta on May 1, 1987, in Cologne. On this occasion, Cardinal Joseph Höffner said the Carmelite "died as a martyr for her faith in Christ and for her people".[61] The same pope canonized her on October 11, 1998, and a

[58] Lucie Bromberg-Rosenthal, as quoted in Posselt, *Edith Stein: Jodin, geleerde, Carmelites*, 255–56.

[59] NIOD, Archive 250 I, Westerbork camp, inventory no. 239.

[60] See Mohr and Prégardier, *Passion im August*, 15.

[61] As quoted by Neyer in Moll, *Zeugen*, 893.

year later named Saint Teresa Benedicta of the Cross, together with Saint Catherine of Siena (1347–1380) and Saint Bridget of Sweden (1302–1373), patroness of Europe. Some hope that she will one day also be declared a Doctor of the Church.

On October 11, 2006, Pope Benedict XVI blessed a statue of Saint Teresa Benedicta that was placed in the western facade of Saint Peter's in Rome. The marble figure stands next to that of Saint Teresa of Jesus and shows the saint holding a cross and a Torah roll. Rabbis were also present at the blessing of the statue.

Dr. Edith Stein became Sister Teresa Benedicta of the Cross. She consciously and freely united her life to the redeeming death of Jesus Christ, Son of God, Son of the Jewish people. She did this in her baptism, in her dedication to Catholic youth, in the women's movement, and in her scholarship. She did it through her entrance into Carmel and by offering her life for the conversion of the Jews, for the protection of the Jewish people from the Nazi terror, and for the preservation and restoration of peace. In this way, she united herself to Jesus' sacrifice on the Cross and gave herself as he did for the redemption of many.

Rosa Maria Agnes Adelheid Stein was born in Lublinitz on December 13, 1883, eight years before her sister Edith. When Rosa was nearly ten years old, her father died unexpectedly,[62] and it appears that this tragic event left an indelible mark on the child's psyche. She could not concentrate well in school and was sometimes peculiar,

[62] See Stein, *Life in a Jewish Family*, 40.

Rosa Maria Agnes Adelheid Stein in the late 1930s

temperamental, and even maladjusted in the family. Edith recounts that Rosa therefore was nicknamed "the lion". Edith explains:

> It was inspired by her loud roar of rage whenever she was provoked. Of all the children, she was the most difficult to raise. Although in no way lacking talent, she was always a poor student. The most undisciplined boys in the house or in the neighborhood were her best friends. With them she tore through the streets, rang doctors' doorbells, and joined in other pranks boys usually play.[63]

In addition, Rosa had the tendency to bind herself passionately to one or more persons.

[63] Ibid., 50.

Rosa did not know what kind of profession she wanted to pursue, and so it happened that she was sent to her three aunts in Lublinitz for a year. Here she would learn how to manage a household. In this way, too, she was away from the family for a while, so that she could gain stability in a new setting. Rosa had a very happy year with her aunts and returned to Breslau enriched by new experiences. Matured in character and formed in domestic management, she now took over her mother's household. Her mother was then free to dedicate herself more to the family lumber business. Rosa cooked with creativity, generosity, and skill, so that all who enjoyed her food were most satisfied. She was praised highly in this regard by the whole family.[64]

Rosa cared for the household to everyone's satisfaction for more than thirty years. Still, she remained closed and ill-tempered within the family. In contrast, her relationship with outsiders was very different—with them she was actually very loving. Her mother avoided making her wishes known to Rosa. When it was possible, she asked for Edith's help in such matters because it was known that Rosa did not deny Edith anything.[65] Edith recounts that Rosa was good to her time and again:

> As I was always rather pale and anemic, she made me the object of particular solicitude. When I accompanied her to the city on errands, she rarely omitted taking me to a small coffee shop where she saw to it that I had a piece of apple cake with whipped cream or, in the summer, a dish of ice cream likewise topped

[64] See ibid., 51.
[65] See ibid., 114.

with whipped cream. I never begged her for this; but, unintentionally, as we came near our usual haunt (Illgen's Coffee Shop in the *Schmiedebrücke*, where such marvelous things could be had for fifteen *Pfennige*), I would peep at the store window out of the corner of my eyes, and immediately, without saying a word, she would head for the entrance.[66]

Just like her mother and sister, Rosa lived most soberly. She avoided every luxury. She was, nonetheless, an excellent cook, as we have said, who prepared kosher meals, baked the famous *Streuselkuchen* for birthdays, and made sure there was something nice on the Sabbath. Rosa lacked neither feelings of love for neighbor nor empathy. Although she never gave them money, she fed beggars who came to the Stein house during the crisis years of the 1930s. Rosa also cared for a neglected and abused child who was in the class of her cousin Susanne. She even once visited a murderer who was in prison awaiting a death sentence. She explained why she did this by saying that even murderers must know they have not been abandoned.[67]

The relationship between Edith and Rosa grew over time. Edith was the leader in this relationship, and Rosa let herself be guided. The more balanced Edith was a support for her. When Edith left Breslau to pursue her studies, the relationship did not change. At Edith's suggestion, Rosa followed evening classes in literature and art history at the junior college in Breslau. When Edith told her family that she had become Catholic, Rosa was

[66] Ibid., 51.
[67] See Batzdorff, *Aunt Edith*, 158–60.

her support at home. Rosa brought Edith to the train station when she left Breslau for the last time to enter the Carmel in Cologne and subsequently became her contact with the family.[68]

It is not at all clear how Rosa came to the Church. We do know, however, that Rosa followed her sister Edith in baptism. Both sisters saw how much their deeply believing Jewish mother would suffer from both daughters entering the Church. They therefore did everything possible to spare her pain, and Rosa delayed becoming Catholic until after her mother died. Sister Teresa Benedicta wrote to a friend, "My sister Rosa (the only one besides me who never married) has been longing for Baptism for years but, out of concern for my mother, she renounced it so far. But she will soon be taking the preliminary steps, although without the knowledge of our brothers and sisters for the time being, to spare them additional pain."[69] Rosa's inclination toward the Church had not gone unnoticed in the family, however, because her cousin Susanne writes that Rosa already prayed the rosary and went to Holy Mass before she was received into the Church.[70]

Rosa was baptized in the church of the Saint Elisabeth Hospital in Cologne-Hohenlind on December 24, 1936, by Father Johannes van Aacken. Rosa had never before

---

[68] See G. Mesters, "Rosa Maria Agnes Adelheid Stein", in *Getuigen voor Christus: Rooms-Katholieke bloedgetuigen uit Nederland in de twintigste eeuw*, ed. P.W.F.M. Hamans, 562–67 ('s-Hertogenbosch: Liturgical Commission of the Dutch Bishops Conference, 2008); W. Heemskerk, *De heilige Edith Stein en haar tijd* (Sittard, 2005), 93–97.

[69] Stein, *Self-Portrait in Letters*, letter no. 226 to Mother Petra Brünung, O.S.U. (October 3, 1936), 236; *Als een brandende toorts*, 169.

[70] See Batzdorff, *Aunt Edith*, 161.

been so happy. At this most important moment, Edith stood next to her at the baptismal font. Rosa wore her sister's white choir robe as a baptismal gown.[71] This robe was also a sign of the inner bond that united the sisters in life and that would be sealed in their future death.[72] During the midnight Mass that followed, Rosa and Edith went to Holy Communion together. On Pentecost 1937, Rosa was confirmed at Holy Cross Church in Breslau.[73] Rosa attended daily Holy Mass in the cathedral of Breslau, and it is not unlikely that Rosa, like her sister Edith, had a desire for the religious life.

After the *Reichskristallnacht* (November 9–10, 1938), the Stein family prepared to emigrate to America. Sister Teresa Benedicta left the Carmel in Cologne on December 31, 1938, and went to the cloister of the Discalced Carmelites in Bovenstestraat in Echt, in the Netherlands.

Rosa would soon follow her there. In a German newspaper she had read an advertisement placed by a woman looking for members to begin a new religious community of Third Order Carmelites. Rosa contacted the "foundress", and she even went to Roclenge-sur-Geer in Belgium, between Maastricht and Liège, to meet her. An old manor, vacant since the First World War and very dilapidated, served as the house for this new foundation. Rosa had in fact fallen into the hands of a swindler. Thanks to the help of Barbara van Weerts, a relative of one of the Carmelites who corresponded with Sister Teresa

[71] See Posselt, *Edith Stein: The Life of a Philosopher and Carmelite*, 170; M. Linssen, "Edith Stein, Zuster Theresia Benedicta A Cruce O.C.D.", *Een-Twee-Een* 15 (1987): 304–52, 339.

[72] See *Als een brandende toorts*, 169.

[73] See Posselt, *Edith Stein: The Life of a Philosopher and Carmelite*, 172.

Benedicta, Rosa was able to leave Belgium after having stayed there a few months. With only some clothes—she never saw her other possessions again—Rosa traveled to the Netherlands, where the last period of her life would begin. She arrived at the Carmel of Echt on July 1, 1939.[74]

Rosa wanted to enter the Carmel, but this was not immediately permitted. The prioress and the provincial suggested that she first enter the Third Order, wear the habit, and serve as portress for the convent.[75] After being in formation for little more than a year, Rosa made her profession as a Tertiary (member of the Third Order) of the Carmel in Echt on June 25, 1941. She became an extern sister for the Carmel. She had the task of maintaining contact between the sisters in the cloister and the outside world and also took care of the sacristy. As portress, she lived in a guest room. The nuns from Carmel said about Rosa that:

> We never heard her complain.... She had excellent traits for managing a household and, as portress, was well-respected by the people. She, too, had a noble heart. With regard to her own needs and wants, she was unpretentiousness itself, but she was quite generous with others. She had a very healthy judgment, worked with great diligence, rose very early in the morning, and prayed for hours in the chapel. In the evening, too, before going to bed, she had long conversations with Christ in his Eucharistic Presence.[76]

[74] See *Als een brandende toorts*, 174; Batzdorff, *Aunt Edith*, 163.

[75] See Stein, *Self-Portrait in Letters*, letter no. 312 to Mother Petra Brüning (April 26, 1940), 321–22, as also quoted in Batzdorff, *Aunt Edith*, 163.

[76] As quoted in *Als een brandende toorts*, 174.

Upon leaving the convent in Echt, people saw how Sister Teresa Benedicta took Rosa's hand and said, "Come, we are going for our people." [77] During her lifetime Rosa had often found support in her sister. Now Sister Teresa Benedicta took her by the hand as they made their way to their sacrificial death and heavenly goal. During the last days of her earthly pilgrimage, the Tertiary Rosa wore the brown habit of the Carmelites.[78] On the same day as her sister, August 9, 1942, she was gassed and buried in a mass grave.[79]

[77] Ibid., 175.

[78] See ibid., 159.

[79] See Linssen, "Edith Stein", 344. Their names are included on the Department of Justice's list 34, issued on February 16, 1950: no. 44075, Rosa Maria Agnes Adelheid Stein, and no. 44074, Edith Teresa Hedwig Stein.

Chapter 3

DR. RUTH RENATE FREDERIKE KANTOROWICZ

Ruth Kantorowicz was born on January 7, 1901, in Hamburg (Germany), the only child of a Jewish couple. Her father was Samuel Kantorowicz, a physician. Born in 1865 in Posen, presently Poznań, in Poland, he moved to

Ruth Renate Frederike Kantorowicz
Photo: *Als een brandende toorts,* 281.

Hamburg in 1894. From her childhood, Ruth was shy. Her mother, Hulda Hindel Friedheim, once said of her that "if a car comes into another part of the city, then our Ruth already runs from the street into the house."[1]

Ruth received her secondary education at the public high school on the Hansestrasse in Hamburg, and she graduated on February 3, 1922. Her grades show that she did well in the sciences, but for the subject of religion there is a line, not a grade, on her report card. In 1922, she enrolled at the University of Hamburg to study law and government. Because she also wanted to gain some practical experience, in 1923 she worked for the tax authorities and in a branch of the Deutsche Bank. She completed her studies in April 1924, and two years later passed the doctoral examination in economy at the University of Kiel. On October 26, 1926, she enrolled at the Friedrich Wilhelms University in Berlin (Germany). Three years later she discontinued her studies and worked as a volunteer at the *Kasseler Tageblatt* in the editorial office for economy and finances. Probably because she wanted to finish her dissertation, she stopped this work in March 1930. The following July she obtained her doctorate with honors from the Friedrich Wilhelms University in Berlin with a dissertation entitled *Die Wirklichkeitsnähe nationalökonomischer Theorie* (The realistic national-economic theory).

Dr. Kantorowicz became secretary for the headmaster of the new pedagogical academy in Cottbus (Germany). She worked there from March 1, 1930, until the school

[1] Hulda Friedheim Hindel Kantorowitz, as quoted in *Als een brandende toorts: Documentaire getuigenissen over Dr. Edith Stein (zuster Teresia Benedicta a Cruce) en medeslachtoffers* (Echt: Friends of Dr. Edith Stein, 1967), 177.

was closed in March 1932. Next she worked for six months in the library of the pedagogical academy in Frankfurt am Main (Germany). Afterward, she returned to her hometown, where she worked in the public library from October 1, 1932, until September 30, 1933. The previous July the Nazis had ordered that all "non-Arians" be dismissed from civil service positions.

It is not clear how Ruth Kantorowicz came to be Catholic. Her high school report card had a line, not a grade, for the subject of religion, and the reason for this is unknown. Did she not participate in the Christian religion classes because she was Jewish? Did she take them without receiving a grade? Or was she not interested in God and faith during her high school years? The information that would enable us to answer these questions is not available. What we do know is that Ruth Kantorowicz, when she was thirty-three years old, was baptized by Father Joppen, S.J., on September 8, 1934, at Saint Elisabeth's Church in Hamburg. Her mother had already died by that time. It is unknown whether her father was still alive when she was baptized, but we know he supported her decision to become Catholic from a letter that Sister Teresa Benedicta wrote to Ruth. "That your becoming a Catholic gave your dear father joy is a very special grace for you and for him. This joy is, after all, a sign that he himself was very close to the Light and that he went into eternity in the friendship of God. Will you please help to pray for my mother, that her understanding, too, will be enlightened?" [2]

---

[2] Edith Stein, *Self-Portrait in Letters*, trans. Josephine Koeppel, O.C.D., ed. L. Gelber and Romaeus Leuven, O.C.D., The Collected Works of Edith

Edith Stein's sister Else had married the physician Max Gordon. They lived in Hamburg and knew the Kantorowicz family. On the occasion of a visit to Hamburg, Edith had met Ruth when the latter was three years old. Ruth wrote a letter to Sister Teresa Benedicta of the Cross in the Carmel of Cologne (Germany) on October 4, 1934, to inform her that she was joining the Catholic Church. The Carmelite replied:

> Dear Fräulein Dr. Kantorowicz, I was very happy with your kind letter with the good news, which was a surprise to me. I remember very well the little Ruth whom I got to know when she was a three-year-old child: a shy little girl who wanted nothing to do with anyone other than her parents and her aunt. Your good mother was very astounded when, at the Gordons, you made no resistance to my taking you by the hand and leading you into another room. Through my sister (Else) and Ilse (my niece) I have been kept informed of external developments in your life, as you may have learned of mine. . . . Before all else I would like to tell you to lay all care for the future, confidently, in God's hands, and allow yourself to be led by him entirely, as a child would. Then you can be sure not to lose your way. Just as the Lord brought you into his church, so he will lead you to the place in it that he wants you to have.[3]

After her baptism, Ruth wanted to become a religious as soon as possible. In 1934, she celebrated Christmas at

---

Stein, vol. 5 (Washington, D.C.: ICS Publications, 1993), letter no. 181 to Ruth Kantorowicz (October 4, 1934), 185.

[3] Ibid., 184–85.

the Carmel in Cologne.[4] Sister Teresa Benedicta, knowing how to lay a solid foundation for life in the convent,
knew that it was good first to grow more into living
daily liturgical life. She wrote to Ruth: "Use your free
time to get to know and to love God and the church
better: the doctrines of the faith, the liturgy, our saints;
but also the religious institutions and Catholic life in the
present time, along with its shadows, which will not
remain concealed from you in the long run."[5] Ruth
received this letter a few days after the Nazis had dismissed her from her work in the library. Later, she obtained
work in the pencil factory of Max Schüler & Co. in Hamburg. In 1935, she was released from this position, too,
because she was a Jew. Toward the end of the summer of
1935, Ruth moved to Cologne. Now she was free to
visit the Carmel often and to let herself be led by Sister
Benedicta. On November 7, 1935, she received the sacrament of confirmation in Saint Pantaleon's Church in
Cologne. Ruth began to type Sister Teresa Benedicta's
handwritten manuscripts during that year. She trans-
formed thousands of handwritten pages, filled with cor-
rections, insertions, and footnotes, into easily readable
typed texts. It is partly thanks to Ruth that the writings
of Sister Teresa Benedicta have been preserved.

[4] As a lay person, Ruth did not participate in the celebration of Christmas
with the Carmelite nuns inside the cloister. Instead, she participated in the
Holy Mass and the Divine Office from the public chapel. In her letter invit-
ing her to spend Christmas at the Carmel, St. Teresa Benedicta asks Ruth to
come early on the twenty-fourth, so that she could be introduced to the use
of the breviary (see letter 186 of December 9, 1934, to Ruth Kantorowicz).
During this visit, Ruth probably stayed in the convent of Saint Anna near
the Carmel (cf. letter 187 to Ruth Kantorowicz).—TRANS.

[5] Stein, *Self-Portrait in Letters*, letter no. 181 to Ruth Kantorowicz (October 4, 1934), 185.

Ruth wanted to enter Carmel, and she wanted to leave her homeland where the Nazis increasingly antagonized the Jews. With the help of Sister Teresa Benedicta, Ruth entered the Carmel of Maastricht as a postulant on September 15, 1936. She was, however, of such a weak constitution that she could not persevere in the life of Carmel. The prioress and the novice mistress wanted to accept her, but the majority of the community did not,[6] so after ten months, Ruth left the cloister. She had already bought the material for the wedding dress for her clothing.[7] A rose chasuble was later made from this material (for Gaudete Sunday on the third Sunday of Advent and Laetare Sunday on the fourth Sunday of Lent). This chasuble is still in use in the Carmel of Echt. In December 1937, Ruth went to a house for ladies run by the Ursuline Sisters in Venlo. Her stay there was initially paid for by the Carmel in Maastricht. Here Dr. Kantorowicz became a jack-of-all-trades. Later, she served as portress and administrative assistant in the home economics school of the Ursulines.[8]

After Sister Teresa Benedicta came to the Carmel in Echt in 1938, Ruth Kantorowicz took over the typing of her manuscript for *The Science of the Cross*. For this reason, Ruth often came to Echt and had occasion to speak with Sister Teresa Benedicta, with whom she shared a common fatherland, a common Jewish heritage, a common faith, and a common future fate.[9]

---

[6] In Carmel, the decision to accept a member as a postulant into the novitiate or to profession is made, not by the prioress or novice mistress alone, but by the community as whole. The vote of the community in a chapter is decisive.—TRANS.

[7] Cf. n. 25 in chap. 2.

[8] See *Als een brandende toorts*, 180.

[9] See ibid.

On May 10, 1940, the Germans invaded the Netherlands, destroying the relative calm that Ruth had enjoyed
in Venlo. Father Heinrich Hopster, S.V.D., was the confessor of the Ursuline Sisters and came to know Ruth
well. Father Hopster determined that Ruth "was a very
noble, interior soul. She was like a clear mirror that
reflected the life of God in a pure way." [10]

Ruth was very anxious and fearful, and therefore she
gladly confided in Father Hopster. She did not want to
wear the Jewish star and therefore did not go outside.
She kept to her turret room, but the Nazis knew her
whereabouts. Ruth once showed Father Hopster a stack
of forms that she was required to fill out; it consisted of
twenty-four letter-size pages. All manner of possessions
had to be noted: moveable property, real estate, stocks,
valuable objects, and copyrights. It was clear to the priest
that the Gestapo intended to expropriate the Jews' possessions. Sister Anselmo, O.S.U., the superior of the
Ursulines in Venlo, says that it was Father Hopster "who
helped Ruth to overcome her fears and gave her the necessary counsel in case she was taken prisoner". [11]

Ruth Kantorowicz was arrested and taken away from
Venlo at 7:00 A.M. on August 2, 1942. Since it was cus-
tomary for the sisters to receive Holy Communion at
the 9:00 A.M. High Mass, Ruth had not yet received Holy
Communion and had not yet eaten breakfast. While she
quickly packed some clothes, Mère Imelda, the mother
superior, tried negotiating with the SS soldiers. She
attempted to keep Ruth from being taken by saying that
after being baptized, Dr. Kantorowicz ceased to be a real

---

[10] The Reverend Heinrich Hopster, S.V.D., as quoted in *Als een brandende toorts*, 181.

[11] Sister Anselmo, O.S.U., as quoted in *Als een brandende toorts*, 181.

Jew. One of the soldiers replied, "You can pour as much baptismal water as you want over an ox. It will never become a cow. A Jew remains a Jew." [12] When Ruth left the convent, she was very calm. The sister who served as portress said farewell with tears in her eyes. She said, "All for Jesus, right Miss Ruth?" She replied, "Yes, all for Jesus!" [13] She boarded a covered truck.

Ruth was brought to Amersfoort by way of Roermond.[14] The next day she was brought to Westerbork, where the Catholic Jews were separated from the others. The religious were all gathered in one barrack, and Ruth was happy that she was allowed to stay with them. They rose early in the morning and prayed Lauds.

By means of the Jewish Council, a telegram was sent from Westerbork to the Ursulines in Venlo. It read: "Send immediately by courier warm clothes, blankets, medicines for Ruth Kantorowicz at the Westerbork Foreigner Camp near Hooghalen." [15] The sisters in Venlo then took up contact with the Jewish Council of the city. Mr. Cohen had already gathered some things in the event that he himself would be picked up. Now he placed these things at Ruth Kantorowicz's disposal and added a sleeping bag and a container of medicines. On Thursday, August 6, Mr. Alois Schlütter (gardener of the sisters in Venlo) and Mr. Jean Philipsen (owner of a house-painting company

---

[12] As quoted in *Als een brandende toorts*, 181.

[13] As quoted in A. Mohr and E. Prégardier, eds., *Passion im August (2.–9. August 1942): Edith Stein und Gefährtinnen: Weg in Tod und Auferstehung*, Zeugen der Zeitgeschichte, 5 (Annweiler: Plöger, 1995), 123.

[14] R. Kempner, *Twee uit honderdduizend, Anne Frank en Edith Stein: Onthullingen over de nazimisdaden in Nederland voor het gerecht in München* (Bilthoven, 1969), 109. On August 4, 1942, a list was compiled there of the prisoners who would be brought to Westerbork. On this list one reads: "94, Kontowicz (spelled wrong), Ruth, 7.1.01, office clerk."

[15] As quoted in Mohr and Prégardier, *Passion im August*, 126.

in Blerick) went with suitcases to Hooghalen. They arrived there at 5:00 P.M. and met two men from Echt who had come to Westerbork to fulfill a similar task for the Stein sisters. From 5:30 P.M. until 7:00 P.M. they could speak with the sisters in a special barrack near the entrance of the camp. All the sisters wore their religious habit and a Jewish star. It was a moving conversation, during which the sisters, between tears and laughter, related the events that had happened since the previous Sunday.

Even though there were Trappist priests (the Löb brothers), they were not allowed to celebrate the Holy Mass. Ruth was sad about that. She hoped that they would soon be permitted to participate in the Holy Mass every morning. The visit came to an end when the SS let them know by means of a shrill whistle that they had to return to the barracks. Ruth still quickly introduced Sister Teresa Benedicta to both men from Venlo.

The men spent the night in a hotel near or in Hooghalen. Both returned to the camp once more the next morning. When they did, however, they were told that a transport had left for the east and that Ruth Kantorowicz had been among the Catholic Jews on this train.[16] On Sunday, August 9, the train carrying the Jews arrived in Auschwitz. As soon as they disembarked, a number from their group, including Ruth, were immediately taken to the gas chambers.

As a three-year-old child, Ruth had let herself be taken by the hand by Edith Stein. Together they made their last journey to Auschwitz, together they entered the gas

---

[16] See NIOD Archive 250 I, Westerbork camp, inventory no. 239. People outside the camp told the men that there had been ten to fifteen religious in the camp. Ruth Kantorowicz's name is on the transport list of August 7, 1942, under A, no. 15.

chamber, together they died with confidence in the Lord of life. In 1934, Sister Teresa Benedicta had written to the newly baptized Ruth: "Just as the Lord brought you into his church, so he will lead you to the place in it that he wants you to have."[17] This way led through death in Auschwitz to the house of the Lord of life, the Father's house in heaven.

As we have seen, Ruth Kantorowicz typed Sister Teresa Benedicta's handwritten texts. While working on the following passage from *The Science of the Cross*, could she have known of its coming fulfillment in her life?

No human heart ever entered as dark a night as did the God-man's in Gethsemane and on Golgotha. No searching human spirit can penetrate the unfathomable mystery of the dying God-man's abandonment by God. But Jesus can give to chosen souls some taste of this extreme bitterness. They are his most faithful friends from whom he exacts this final test of their love. If they do not shrink back from it but allow themselves to be drawn willingly into the dark night, it will become their leader.... This is the great experience of the cross: extreme abandonment, and precisely in this abandonment, union with the Crucified.... Cross and night are the way to heavenly light: that is the joyful message of the cross.[18]

[17] Stein, *Self-Portrait in Letters*, letter no. 181 to Ruth Kantorowicz (October 4, 1934), 185.

[18] Edith Stein, *Science of the Cross: A Study of St. John of the Cross*, trans. Josephine Koeppel, O.C.D., The Collected Works of Edith Stein, vol. 6 (Washington, D.C.: ICS Publications, 2002), 30–31.

Chapter 4

THE GOLDSCHMIDT SISTERS

Annemarie Goldschmidt was born on January 31, 1922, in Munich (Germany) in the part of the city called Lager Milbertshofen. Her sister, Elfriede, was born in the same city on August 4, 1923. Their parents were well-to-do

Annemarie Goldschmidt (1938)
Photo: Mohr and Prégardier, *Passion im August.*

Elfriede Goldschmidt (1939)
Photo: Mohr and Prégardier, *Passion im August.*

Jews. Their father, Bernhard Goldschmidt, was a businessman. Magda Herzfelder was their mother.

Lotte Embacher came to know the Goldschmidt family in 1935 through Annemarie's participation in the Heliandgroep, a Catholic association for girls led by Lotte. The parents most likely had not yet been baptized. In preparation for entering the Catholic Church, they were still receiving instruction from Blessed Rupert Mayer, S.J. (1876–1945). Both children had already been baptized, however, but probably had not yet received their First Holy Communion. From 1935 to 1938, Annemarie attended the high school[1] run by the English Ladies[2] in

---

[1] The high school she attended was a *gymnasium* (see n. 9 in chapter 2).

Munich-Nymphenburg. It is possible that Elfriede also went to school here.

After the *Reichskristallnacht* (November 9–10, 1938), Bernhard and Magda Goldschmidt, like many other Jewish parents, thought their children would be safer in a foreign country and sent Annemarie and Elfriede to live in the Netherlands. Before both parents were picked up in 1941 to be deported to the east, they gave Lotte Embacher, who by then had married Karl Wilpert, a package of family pictures with the request, "Give them to the children when they return as a remembrance of their parents." [3]

Both daughters arrived in the Netherlands as refugees in the spring of 1939. First they went to Rotterdam (Heyplaat), where they were quarantined. Later, on April 18, they were brought to Eersel in the Dutch province of Brabant. They found lodging in a children's home staffed by the Sisters of Schijndel. From this home, the seventeen-year-old Annemarie wrote to Lotte Embacher on April 23, 1939:

First we were in quarantine. That did not please us so much, of course, but one has to learn to adapt to everything. When the others were often inconsolable, I became more aware what a great consolation we have in our faith. It was very difficult to get to church. We were permitted to go to church every

[2] Englische Fräulein, the Institutum Beatae Mariae Virginis, a community of women founded by Mary Ward (1585–1645) for the education and upbringing of girls.

[3] Bernhard and Magda Goldschmidt, as quoted by Prégardier in H. Moll, ed., *Zeugen für Christus: Das deutsche Martyrologium des 20. Jahrhunderts*, 2 vols. (Paderborn, 1999), 398.

Sunday and the days of Holy Week. And that was, after all, the most important thing. They do not have an Easter Vigil here. We were disappointed about that. During the days of Easter we were alone with sixty Christians. There is very much of a feeling of belonging together.... Now we are in a convent with very nice sisters. We go to Holy Mass and to Holy Communion every day. I have to get used to that again. Every evening we pray the rosary together in Dutch. Every day (it has been five days by now) is a bit often, but one can do everything. We German girls are very spoiled here, especially because we are the oldest.[4]

Annemarie and Elfriede had come to the second convent that Annemarie describes in her letter because the refugees were spread out in the provinces of the southern part of the Netherlands. The housing department in Den Bosch found a place for both Goldschmidt sisters in the convent of the Congregation of the Sisters of Charity of the Precious Blood (Congregatie van de Liefdezusters van het Kostbaar Bloed) located in Koningsbosch, a municipality of Echt. The sisters of this congregation had a boarding house there as well as a number of schools: a kindergarten, an elementary school, a school of advanced primary education (ULO), a home economics school, and a school for training teachers. Both Goldschmidt sisters arrived in Koningsbosch at the end of 1939. They attended the home economics school and learned Dutch there. They felt at home, but in their hearts they missed their parents in Munich.

[4] Annemarie and Elfriede Goldschmidt, as quoted by Prégardier in ibid., 399.

On March 25, 1941, a year after the Germans invaded the Netherlands, Annemarie wrote to Lotte Embacher Wilpert, "It has been almost two years since we left [Munich]. We only hope that we will soon be united with our parents and that everything will be all right." [5] Both sisters wrote to Lotte and her husband, Karl, that they were happy to know the couple visited their lonely parents every once in a while. On December 14, 1941, they wrote to the Wilperts: "Our parents are no longer in Munich. You surely know that. We have not heard any of the details, but we hope to receive news soon." [6] The daughters never again heard anything from their parents. Both sisters must have lived in Koningsbosch in great uncertainty and with serious worries about their parents. They found strength in prayer and in the Holy Mass. With their worries, sadness, and longing for their parents, the two sisters entrusted themselves to our dear Lord, as becomes evident from a prayer of Elizabeth of France that Elfriede copied in a letter to her non-Catholic Jewish friend Ilse Brüll:

My God, what will happen to me today? I do not know. What I do know, however, is that nothing will happen to me without your having known it in advance, without your having commanded or permitted it. Knowing this is enough for me. I adore your eternal unfathomable plans. I submit myself to your

[5] Annemarie Goldschmidt, as quoted in A. Mohr and E. Prégardier, eds., *Passion im August (2.–9. August 1942): Edith Stein und Gefährtinnen: Weg in Tod und Auferstehung*, Zeugen der Zeitgeschichte, 5 (Annweiler: Plöger, 1995), 149.

[6] Annemarie and Elfriede Goldschmidt, as quoted by Prégardier in Moll, *Zeugen*, 399.

plans with all my heart. I want everything, I accept
everything, I offer you everything as a sacrifice, united
with the sacrifice of my Redeemer. I ask you in his
name and through his infinite merits for patience in
my suffering and for the total surrender that I owe
you for everything that you want to happen to me.
Amen.[7]

The official persecution began for both sisters with a
letter of November 15, 1940, that the local commander
(*Ortskommandant*) in Roermond sent to the mayor of Echt.
Mayor Ad Meeuwissen was ordered to inform the local
commander before November 19, 1940, at 6:00 P.M. of
the names, birth dates, birthplaces, former places of residence, and present addresses of all the Jews living in his
municipality. On November 18, the mayor of Echt
responded that five Jews lived in his municipality: Annemarie and Elfriede Goldschmidt, Rosa and Edith Stein,
and the businessman Ernst Max.[8]

On Sunday, August 2, 1942, Annemarie and Elfriede
Goldschmidt were arrested in the convent of Koningsbosch. They were numbers 32 and 33 on the list of thirty-
three Catholic Jews who were to be picked up under the
direction of the police in Maastricht.[9] Sister Hiëronyma
of the Congregation of the Sisters of Charity of the Precious Blood remembers that it was around 4:00 P.M. when

[7] Elizabeth of France, as quoted by Prégardier, in ibid., 399–400.

[8] See *Als een brandende toorts: Documentaire getuigenissen over Dr. Edith Stein
(zuster Teresia Benedicta a Cruce) en medeslachtoffers* (Echt: Friends of Dr. Edith
Stein, 1967), 29–30; M. Amata Neyer, *Edith Stein: Wie ich in den Kölner Karmel
kam* (Würzburg, 1994), 118.

[9] See R. Kempner, *Twee uit honderdduizend, Anne Frank en Edith Stein: Onthullingen over de nazimisdaden in Nederland voor het gerecht in München* (Bilthoven,
1969), 107.

the Gestapo left the convent with both sisters. Without success, the religious sisters had attempted to refuse to let the girls go. Neither Annemarie nor Elfriede had much of an idea of what was in store for them, and they did not protest against having to go along. They even left with a sense of confidence. They were told that the Jews would be gathered in the east, and they probably hoped that they would be reunited with their parents. With many tears they parted. When the superior informed the rest of the sisters, they were very saddened and disconcerted. After a short time, all went to the chapel to entrust "their children" to the Lord. At the time of their arrest, Annemarie was twenty years old and Elfriede was nineteen.

It was not until the next day that it became known in the convent of Koningsbosch that Sister Teresa Benedicta and Rosa Stein had also been picked up.[10] When the Stein sisters were arrested in Echt at 5:00 P.M., Annemarie and Elfriede were probably already in the police van. Together with the Catholic Jews from Limburg, they made their way to Westerbork by means of Roermond and Amersfoort.[11] The four Catholic Jews from Echt had had contact with one another before their arrest. They were not strangers to one another. In a letter that Sister Teresa Benedicta wrote on August 4, from barrack 36 in Westerbork, we read, "The two dear children from Koningsbosch are also with us."[12] The Carmelite told the two men from Echt who had come to bring her things

[10] See Prégardier, in Moll, *Zeugen*, 400.

[11] NIOD, Archive 250 F, Amersfoort camp, inventory no. 14: transport list Amersfoort to Westerbork (transport list A–W) (August 4, 1942); Kempner, *Twee uit honderdduizend*, 109.

[12] Edith Stein, as quoted in Mohr and Prégardier, *Passion im August*, 91.

to Westerbork that "the two girls from Koningsbosch are very pious and full of confidence."[13]

The Goldschmidt sisters sent two telegrams and two letters from the Westerbork camp. On Wednesday, August 5, Annemarie and Elfriede sent a telegram to the convent in Koningsbosch. They asked the sisters to bring them blankets, their warm clothes, and their boots.[14] The following day they sent a second telegram to the convent in Koningsbosch: "Send by express clothes and blankets ... for us."[15] Also on August 6, Annemarie wrote a note to "dear Reverend Mother and all dear sisters" in Koningsbosch:

> [W]e are doing extraordinarily well and cannot complain about anything. We are in good spirits. We will probably leave on Friday morning, but it can always still change.... We are with a whole group. As long as we stay together. Please send very heartfelt greetings to the sisters C[armelites] in Echt from Miss Stein. They are doing very well [the letter suddenly continues here in German]. One says that we will be treated well in the future, and we are therefore in good spirits. We mutually encourage one another. Please continue to pray for all of us. We will send you news as soon as possible. Please do not be concerned.... Heartfelt greetings to the girls (to all of you our prayers). Once more, heartfelt thanks to all, especially you, dear Reverend Mother and Mother Superior, Sister Assistant, Sister Felicia, and Sister Jacqueline.[16]

[13] Ibid., 103.
[14] See Mohr and Prégardier, *Passion im August*, 157.
[15] Annemarie Goldschmidt, as quoted in *Als een brandende toorts*, 236–37.
[16] Ibid., 237–38.

The short letter was written in large part in Dutch, which Annemarie had learned during the two previous years. The letter betrays no sense of panic, and this shows that the group must have been reassured again and again. They probably could not yet recognize that the Nazis were planning to murder them.

Elfriede (Evi) also wrote a short letter in German to the sisters and girls at the convent in Koningsbosch:

> We are in good spirits and stay close to the others in the group. We know, after all, that all of you pray for us. Do not worry too much about us. We have a good Protector. Once more, many heartfelt thanks and many greetings to all: from the kitchen [which was in the basement] to the attic. We met beloved people we knew here. Pray for us.[17]

The telegram from Annemarie arrived on Thursday, August 6, at 6:04 P.M. in Echt. Whatever was contained in the packages that the Sisters of Charity sent, neither of their students received it. Sometime during the night of August 6 or early in the morning of August 7, the two sisters were placed on the transport to Auschwitz.[18]

As was already mentioned in chapter 1, during their journey to Auschwitz, the sisters succeeded in sending a postcard to Lotte Embacher Wilpert and Ingeborg Plössner in Munich. They let them know, "We are once again back in *Das Reich* [German country] together with very many people."[19] They were certainly back in *das Reich*,

---

[17] Elfriede Goldschmidt, as quoted in *Als een brandende toorts*, 238.

[18] See ibid., 236–37.

[19] Annemarie and Elfriede Goldschmidt, as quoted by Prégardier in Moll, *Zeugen*, 401.

but they would not stay there long. By August 9, they had already departed for their heavenly homeland.

Ilse Brüll was placed on a transport from Westerbork to Auschwitz on August 31, 1942. On her last card to the sisters in Eersel, she wrote, "I am on my way to Annemarie and Evi." [20] She, too, died in Auschwitz.

---

[20] Ilse Brüll, as quoted in U. Levy, *De onvoorstelbare jaren 1939 tot 1947* (Eersel, 1995), 24.

Chapter 5

ALICE MARIA REIS

Alice Reis was born on September 17, 1903, in Berlin (Germany).[1] Her father, Martin Reis, was a merchant. Her mother was Franziska Kaufmann. According to the birth certificate, both parents belonged to the "Mosaic religion". Not much is known about Alice's youth. Her father died on August 28, 1924, at the age of fifty-six. Alice was almost twenty-one years old at that time. Her mother was deported from Berlin on March 28, 1942, to Trawniki (Poland), and nothing more was ever heard of her.

In 1927, Alice worked at an orthopedic clinic in Erfurt (Germany) for five months as a secretary and nurse-in-training. After this first period of introduction into nursing care, she became a student nurse in the city hospital of Mannheim (Germany). In September 1928, she passed the nursing examination with the score of "very good". From March 11, 1929, until December 31, 1931, she worked as a nurse in the department of child abuse counsellors in the city hospital of Darmstadt (Germany).

[1] See *Als een brandende toorts: Documentaire getuigenissen over Dr. Edith Stein (zuster Teresia Benedicta a Cruce) en medeslachtoffers* (Echt: Friends of Dr. Edith Stein, 1967), 182–83.

Alice Maria Reis
Photo: *Als een brandende toorts*, 281.

In Darmstadt, she came into contact with Father Alfred Schüler, who was an assistant pastor at Saint Ludgerus' Church. It was to him that she confided her desire to become Catholic, and he gave her instruction in the faith. Alice Reis was baptized in the Abbey of Beuron on December 27, 1930, by Father Gotthard Klocker, O.S.B. The godparents were Mathilde Maria Wissler, a medical doctor from Mannheim, and Edith Stein. In a letter, Edith writes that she was something of a *"causa secunda"* (a secondary cause) in Alice Reis' journey toward the Church.[2]

---

[2] See Edith Stein, *Self-Portrait in Letters*, trans. Josephine Koeppel, O.C.D., ed. L. Gelber and Romaeus Leuven, O.C.D., The Collected Works of Edith Stein, vol. 5 (Washington, D.C.: ICS Publications, 1993), letter 74 to Sister Adelgundis Jaegerschmidt, (December 10, 1930), 76. Cf. also letter 83 to Sister Adelgundis Jaegerschmidt, O.S.B. (January 19, 1931), 82.

In any event, the two ladies must have had enough contact for Alice Reis to ask Edith Stein to be her godmother
at her baptism.

Alice Reis was engaged to the son of a rich Jewish
businessman from Mannheim. When her fiancé's parents
heard that their future daughter-in-law had become Catholic, they threatened to cut off their son's inheritance if
he did not break the engagement. He complied with his
parents' wishes, and this event so shocked Alice that she
suffered a nervous breakdown. She was in the Marien-
hospital in Darmstadt for a long time, and Father Schüler
visited her there often and sought to guide her. During
this time of illness, the desire to become a religious awakened in her. The priest at first discouraged this aspira-
tion, but she came back to it with ever more certainty.
When she left Darmstadt after her recovery, she received
a reference from her workplace stating that she was an
excellent employee. Nurse Alice Reis could handle difficult patients with tact. She had asked for a dismissal
because she wanted to move to Freiburg (Germany), where
she wanted to enter the Lioba Sisters. For unknown reasons, this plan was never realized.

Alice, however, did not give up the idea of becoming
a religious. She turned to the Sisters of the Good Shepherd (Zusters van de Goede Herder). On January 12, 1934,
she entered this congregation. The Sisters of the Good
Shepherd had been founded in Angers, France, in 1829.
These sisters came to the Netherlands in 1860. They
offered help to girls and women in need and had boarding houses. The novitiate for the congregation was in
Leiderdorp in the Netherlands. Alice became a postulant
there. At her clothing on July 19, 1934, she received the

name Sister Maria Benedicta. This name is most likely a
reference to her godmother, Edith Stein, who had received
the habit and the name Sister Teresa Benedicta of the
Cross in the Carmel in Cologne three months earlier.
Alice proved, however, to be unfit for the Congregation
of the Sisters of the Good Shepherd. She suffered from a
severe case of asthma, her overall health was poor, and
her nursing profession did not match the work of this
congregation. On March 13, 1936, she left their novitiate.
Alice then went to work as a nurse at the convent of the
Sisters of the Good Shepherd in Bloemendaal (near
Haarlem).

Presumably Alice had gone to a foreign country to
flee the persecution of Jews in Germany. However, the
Nazis caught up with her when they invaded the Netherlands in 1940. On September 5, Alice received a letter
from the police in Bloemendaal that ordered her to leave
the city before September 9. Enclosed with the letter
was a list of 250 Dutch cities where she, as a Jew, was
not permitted to reside. It was even forbidden for Jews
to visit these places. Alice had less than four days to say
goodbye and to pack her things. Upon arriving at her
new place of residence, she was required to report to the
police within twenty-four hours.[3]

Nurse Alice went to the convent of the Sisters of the
Good Shepherd in Almelo. There she worked in the infirmary of the children's home. In addition, she assisted girls
who needed help and ran errands for the sisters. In the
spring of 1941, she asked to enter the Carmel in Nijmegen.

---

[3] See M. Amata Neyer, *Edith Stein: Wie ich in den Karmel kam* (Würzburg,
1994), 130.

She was not accepted on account of her health and because she could not bring a dowry.[4]

Nurse Alice was a deeply pious soul. Her spirit of prayer edified the religious in the houses where she stayed as a guest. She was in chapel a half an hour before Holy Mass to prepare herself for Mass and for Holy Communion. She went to the chapel numerous times during the day. She prayed the Little Office of the Blessed Virgin Mary daily. She was exact in keeping the Sunday rest. On the Lord's Day, she only did what was strictly necessary in her care for the sick.

Her behavior made clear that she was a gifted woman who had received a good education. In spite of all this, however, Sister Bonaventura, who knew Alice in Almelo, writes of her that "one cannot say that Nurse Alice was happy."[5] She often showed pictures from the past and absolutely wanted no one to speak of her birthday. She did not even allow the girls to sing "Happy Birthday" to her.

She was wholly engaged in her profession as a nurse, but she suffered from poor health, and the pressure of the Nazi threat left her no peace. Slowly, she felt the shadow of persecution and death come closer. The Jewish Council informed Alice on December 18, 1940, that all German Jews living abroad had been declared "stateless". All non-Dutch Jews had to be registered. Thus, Alice Reis had to go to Amsterdam to fill out the many

---

[4] It was a common requirement that those who enter a congregation bring a dowry. After the Second Vatican Council, many congregations changed this custom and no longer require such a dowry.—TRANS.

[5] Sister Bonaventura, as quoted in A. Mohr and E. Prégardier, eds., *Passion im August (2.–9. August 1942): Edith Stein und Gefährtinnen: Weg in Tod und Auferstehung*, Zeugen der Zeitgeschichte, 5 (Annweiler: Plöger, 1995), 137.

forms.[6] From May 3, 1942, all Jews were required to wear
the Jewish star. Alice became ever more melancholy. She
preferred not to leave the convent at all. Long before the
SS came to pick her up, Alice had made preparations.
She had bought boots and warm clothes in case she would
need them.

On Sunday, August 2, 1942, that time had come. At
5:00 A.M., two police officers and two plainclothes officers stood at the convent door. They were admitted into
the parlor. The three sisters who attended to them were
asked to get Alice. She had to come along. They refused
to do so, and for two hours these sisters tried to convince the SS officers not to take Nurse Alice. The officers finally threatened to take measures against the sisters
and the 180 girls.

It was 7:00 A.M. when Sister Magdalena, the superior,
went to Nurse Alice to tell her the terrible news. Even
though Nurse Alice always arose on time and was nor-
mally in the chapel half an hour before Holy Mass began,
she was still in bed on the morning Sister Magdalena
knocked at her door. When she heard that she had to go
with the SS officers, she yelled, "No, no, no!" She threw
herself against the wall and yelled again and again, "No!" [7]
In the end, she accepted her fate. Wholly broken, she
went to the parlor, being led at the arm of the superior.
When she went by the infirmary, Nurse Alice embraced
Sister Magdalena. She asked for forgiveness because she
had often been impossible. It was a heart-wrenching
moment. When she came to the parlor, the SS officers

[6] See letter from Sister Agatha to Mr. Dr. J.J. Loeff, in Archive, Archdiocese
of Utrecht, no. 76.
[7] As quoted in Mohr and Prégardier, Passion im August, 140.

immediately took her outside. She boarded the car, and it left without delay. She was wearing her postulant dress.[8]

Like the other Catholic Jews, she was brought to Amersfoort and subsequently to Westerbork.[9] From Westerbork, Alice had contact with the convent in Almelo three times. She wrote a letter, made a telephone call, and sent a telegram. She informed them that her godmother, Sister Teresa Benedicta, was in the camp. Already knowing that she would be placed on the transport to Auschwitz, she also informed them that she would not stay in the Netherlands. The hygiene situation in the camp was dreadful, and she asked the sisters to send bandages, syringes, medicines, warm clothes, and so on. They immediately sent a trusted person with the requested things, as well as food, to Westerbork. The items were accepted by the camp authorities, but they did not inform the courier that Nurse Alice had already been placed on the train to Auschwitz.[10] She was gassed there and buried in a mass grave. Nothing more was ever heard of her. The convent in Almelo never received the news that Nurse Alice had died.

Alice Reis went to the baptismal font at the hand of her godmother, Edith Stein. Together with Sister Teresa Benedicta of the Cross, she went through death to eternal life.

[8] See *Als een brandende toorts*, 160. Nurse Alice possibly wore such a simple postulant dress during her daily work in the convent, and she would probably have felt safer being dressed as a postulant.

[9] Kempner, *Twee uit honderdduizend*, 108. In Amersfoort, her name was included on the list of prisoners to be taken to Westerbork. Under no. 79, one reads: "Reis, Alice, 9.17.03, nurse."

[10] See NIOD, Archive 250 I, Westerbork camp, inventory no. 239; Kempner, *Twee uit honderdduizend*, 110. On the lists put together on August 7, 1942, in the Westerbork camp in preparation for the transport to Auschwitz, Alice is also noted on list A, no. 2.

Sister Agatha, superior of the boarding house of the Good Shepherd in Almelo, called some of the occupying authorities on August 2 to inquire about Alice Reis. She received only evasive answers. On August 3, she sent an account of the events concerning Alice Reis to Dr. J.J. Loeff in Vught, secretary of the Roman Catholic archbishop in the Netherlands. She also informed the archbishop about what she had done until then and asked what more she could do. In an August 6 letter, Archbishop J. de Jong responded that she had done all that was possible.[11]

[11] See letter of Sister Agatha to Mr. Dr. J.J. Loeff and copy of the reply of the Most Reverend J. de Jong to Sister Agatha, both in the Archive of the Archdiocese of Utrecht, no. 76.

Chapter 6

SISTER MARIA ALOYSIA LÖWENFELS, P.H.J.C.

Luise Löwenfels was born on July 5, 1915, in Trabelsdorf (near Bamberg in Bavaria, Germany) in her parents' home. Her father, Salomon, was born in 1870 in Kaubenheim (near Uffenheim, Germany) and was a butcher and

Sister Maria Aloysia Löwenfels, P.H.J.C.
Photo: Haas, *Luise Löwenfels*.

merchant. The people in Trabelsdorf and Buxheim, where the family later moved, called him the "cattle dealer on a bike".[1] He was also involved in the real estate business. Löwenfels was financially well-off, and his second-place standing on the Trabelsdorf list of the highest taxpayers attests to this. He died suddenly on July 6, 1923.

Luise's mother, Sophia Prölsdorfer, was born in Trabelsdorf in 1875. Her father was also a cattle dealer. Luise's parents' civil marriage took place on July 5, 1898, in Trabelsdorf, and two days later they were married in the city's synagogue.[2] Soon after the *Reichskristallnacht*, on November 28, 1938, Luise's mother emigrated to New York, where she died on November 11, 1940.[3]

The orthodox Jewish faith was practiced in the Löwenfels' home. They prayed together, celebrated the Jewish home liturgy, and kept the Sabbath strictly. Many Jews lived in Trabelsdorf.[4]

The family moved to Buxheim near Ingolstadt (Germany) sometime between 1918 and 1921.[5] They lived in a rented house there, and the father went into the textile

[1] A. de Haas, *Luise Löwenfels: Een "vergeten" martelares* (Geleen, 1998); A. de Haas, in H. Moll, ed., *Zeugen für Christus: Das deutsche Martyrologium des 20. Jahrhunderts*, 2 vols. (Paderborn, 1999), 882–85; S. Westerholz, "Luise Löwenfels und ihre Familie", *Sammelblatt des historischen Vereins Ingolstadt* 11, no. 1 (2002): 189–270, 192, 200.

[2] See Westerholz, "Luise", 200. In Germany, as in the Netherlands, a religious marriage is not recognized by the civil authorities, so that a separate civil marriage must take place.—TRANS.

[3] See S. Westerholz, "Das Schicksal der jüdischen Nonne Luise Loewenfels aus Trabelsdorf", in *Mesusa*, vol. 4: *Lebensbeschreibungen und Schicksale: Spuren jüdischer Vergangenheit an Aisch, Aurach, Ebrach und Seebach*, ed. by J. Fleischmann, 269–309, 307 (Mühlhausen, 2004).

[4] See K. Guth, *Jüdische Landgemeinden in Oberfranken (1800–1942)* (Bamberg, 1988), 301–8.

[5] See Westerholz, "Schicksal", 284.

business. After the death of her husband, the mother and a number of the children moved to Ingolstadt in 1926.[6]

Luise was the eleventh of the twelve Löwenfels children. Two children had died as babies, so Luise grew up as the youngest child in the family.[7] Her father died suddenly on the day after Luise's eighth birthday.[8] Her brother Heinrich was gassed in Auschwitz shortly after Luise herself died this way. The other eight brothers and sisters survived the war in the United States.[9]

Luise was registered as a pupil at the elementary school in Buxheim on May 2, 1921.[10] Beginning in 1926, she attended the convent school, the Gnadenthal, in Ingolstadt, where she completed elementary and high school. On March 17, 1932, she took her final examination.[11] She successfully participated in a business course at the Gnadenthal during the 1932–1933 school year. She probably had a good experience at this school. A few former students recall that "the sisters were pleasant teachers for the Jewish and the non-Catholic Christian pupils. In an effort to avoid the reproach of treating these children unjustly, the sisters sometimes even treated them better than the other students. At least they were more obliging to them."[12] From the reports of the sisters at the school, we know that Luise obtained good grades as a result of her great industriousness. Her very good upbringing, too, was praised by the sisters. However, they also

[6] See Westerholz, "Luise", 223.

[7] See ibid., 200.

[8] See ibid., 223.

[9] See ibid., 263–64.

[10] See ibid., 189.

[11] See ibid., 231.

[12] As quoted in ibid., 223.

said of her that "she gave the impression of being lonely and unstable and was longing for affection." [13]

We cannot determine exactly when Luise was first attracted to the Catholic Church. It is probably a legend that she was already drawn to the Church as a very young girl of somewhere between three and six years of age. There was a synagogue in Trabelsdorf but no Catholic church because the population was largely Lutheran.

The nearest Catholic church was in the town of Priesendorf, a little over a mile away from her parents' house, yet a friend from school is said to remember that Luise would slip into the Catholic church as often as she had the opportunity and that already in her childhood Luise gladly attended Holy Mass and Marian devotions. She was, this friend recounts, very much attracted to these prayers, and it is understandable if her Jewish parents did not like this.

According to another account, Luise's mother waited for her by the church door one day. She took her home, hit her mercilessly, and pulled her by her hair through the room. Her oldest brother, who assumed the position of family head after her father's death, also reacted harshly toward the Catholic inclinations of his youngest sister. When he suspected that Luise had been to the church, he waited for her return home, threw her harshly to the floor, and, placing his foot on her, beat her with a leather belt. Luise, however, felt called by an inner voice to go to the church. Whenever she had the opportunity, she obeyed this mysterious yearning. Long before her baptism,

[13] As quoted in ibid., 224–25; Westerholz, "Schicksal", 285–86.

her family already considered her to be a deserter. She was treated accordingly.[14]

There is no evidence to support the claim that Luise was five years old or younger when these events occurred,[15] so the above-mentioned account may have taken place later, especially since Luise herself spoke of it to others. She told her confidant and godmother, Sister Sanctia Kall from the convent in Mönchenglad-bach-Hehn (Germany), that because of her visits to church she was "pulled by her hair through the house and beaten"[16] by her mother and brother. Luise also told Sister Veronis Rüdel from the Saint Paul Institute in Recklinghausen (Germany) and Father Keuyk from Frankfurt (Germany) the same thing. What she recounted cannot have referred to the time when she was still a young child living in Trabelsdorf.[17] The first verifiable signs of her inclination to the Catholic faith are present no earlier than 1931, when she was sixteen years old and learning to be a kindergarten assistant.[18]

From 1933 to 1935, Luise studied to be an assistant in a kindergarten in Nördlingen (Germany) at the Maria Stern (Mary Star) School, which belonged to the Franciscan Sisters. According to a classmate who after her marriage was called Käte Joseph-Hermann and who knew Luise from the school in Ingolstadt, Luise was already attending catechesis for converts every Saturday and Sunday

[14] See De Haas, *Luise Löwenfels*.
[15] See Westerholz, "Luise", 235–39; Westerholz, "Schicksal", 289–92.
[16] Westerholz, "Luise", 242.
[17] See Westerholz, "Schicksal", 292–93.
[18] See Westerholz, "Luise", 239; Westerholz, "Schicksal", 292.

in Nördlingen during this time.[19] Käte also told her own
parents about this. Her mother, in turn, was thought to
have reported it to Luise's mother, although the latter
was supposedly already aware of the situation.[20]

By 1935, it was clear that Luise wanted to become
Catholic. She had received the religious instruction necessary to take this step. With her diploma, the profession
of kindergarten assistant was open to her. By means of
this position, she could live independently of her family.
Entries from the diaries of her sisters (1935) suggest that
Luise's desire to become Catholic led to a religious break
with her family. Her mother approached Luise after the
family found a crucifix and a religious habit in her bed.
The daughter confessed that she wanted to become Catholic and enter a convent. Consequently, the family members gathered to pray the "shiva", the Jewish prayers for
the deceased, over Luise. By means of this ritual, they
parted from Luise, and she was thenceforth excluded from
the community of the family and the Jewish faith. The
religious break was completed with Luise's baptism. However, the family continued to care about her. A solicitude for Luise can be seen in their efforts to take her
along to America, to notify her in the convent of Geleen
of the death of her mother, and to learn about Luise's
fate after the war.[21]

Luise attempted to enter the Benedictine Sisters in Eichstätt (Germany). Abbess Maria Anna Benedicta Spiegel
von und zu Peckelsheim did not, however, want to accept
her into the community. Luise had not yet been baptized

---

[19] See Westerholz, "Luise", 234.
[20] See ibid., 241; Westerholz, "Schicksal", 292–93.
[21] See Westerholz, "Schicksal", 297–300.

at the time and did not have any experience of living the Catholic faith. It would have been unduly rushed to accept Luise into the Benedictine Abbey at that moment. The abbess did, however, give her a precious rosary. With this present, she probably wanted to encourage Luise on her way to the Church.[22]

Luise now went to Frankfurt am Main, where she worked as a kindergarten assistant in a Jewish children's clinic. On Sundays, Luise and the other young ladies went to the Marian devotions at the Poor Handmaids of Jesus Christ in Schwalbach (Germany). This was Luise's first contact with the congregation she would later enter. The Congregation of the Poor Handmaids of Jesus Christ (Ancillae Domini Jesu Christi) had been founded in 1842 in Dernbach (Germany) by Mother Maria Katharina Kasper (1820–1898), who would be beatified in 1978. The congregation cared for the sick, the elderly, and children.

Sister Alodina, who was the local superior in Frankfurt, brought Luise into contact with the assistant pastor of Saint Boniface parish in Frankfurt-South, Father Richard Keuyk. He worked there from 1929 to 1937. It was to him that Luise first voiced her desire to become a member of the Catholic Church. It was a very difficult decision for Luise to admit her calling to the Catholic faith. The step of joining the Church meant a definitive break with her family, relatives, and Jewish traditions.

On May 30, 1947, Father Keuyk wrote a letter about Luise to the Vicar General of the Poor Handmaids of Jesus Christ. He told her about his relationship with the then already murdered Luise:

---

[22] See ibid., 283.

The first meeting will remain unforgettable. Her personality made a very strong impression on me. With a remarkable calmness of soul, she spoke for two hours about her exterior and interior life. Here was a human child sitting before me, and I had the impression, to use the first words of the Letter to the Ephesians, that she was someone chosen and elected by God in Jesus Christ. It also seemed to me, to continue to speak with Paul, that "in accord with the riches of grace . . . all wisdom and insight" had been lavished upon this noble Jewish girl. Without the least bit of bitterness, she told me about the suffering that filled her life, about what had already been taken from her, and about what she would lose. She then opened her handbag in front of me and showed me the items that were, besides the clothing she wore, the few things she had to her name.

Among these things was a valuable rosary from Jerusalem, which the Abbess of Saint Walburgis in Eichstätt had given her. She also showed me letters from one of her brothers imploring her in an almost shocking way not to become unfaithful to the Jewish Law. Despite the pain she would cause her mother, brothers, and sisters, she was firmly resolved to join the Catholic Church. "I will become Catholic," she said in all humility and equanimity, "even if I have to leave Germany on account of my faith and go to England or America."

After that first meeting, she faithfully came to the lectures I was giving at that time about Cardinal Newman and his religious world. As often as she met me on the street with her Jewish children, for whom she was a faithful guardian, she smiled in a way that showed gain and loss, joy and pain in a wonderful way. She was considered an "apostate" by her family and was not accepted by the abbess of Saint Walburgis in Eichstätt out of fear for the Jewish persecution.[23]

Luise had said farewell to her southern German homeland forever when she went to Frankfurt. In utter poverty, but with her head held high and great strength of spirit, she also left Frankfurt when the position of the Jews became ever more precarious. Her way was truly a "Via Mirabilis" (a wonderful way).[24]

In May 1935, Luise Löwenfels found a new job as a nanny for the Aäron family, who lived in Recklinghausen. The family house was not far away from the Saint Paul Church and the Saint Paul Institute. In Recklinghausen, Luise became firm in her definitive decision to become Catholic. This cost her her job. She sought help from the Sisters of Divine Providence (Zusters van de Goddelijke Voorzienigheid), who were in charge of the Saint Paul Institute in Recklinghausen. Sister Veronis Rüdel especially took Luise under her care, giving her further instruction as Luise made her way to the Catholic Church.

Already before Luise's arrival, the Saint Paul Institute had been placed under the supervision of the Gestapo. Luise could not stay there. The Eppmann family took her in. This family consisted of father, mother, and two daughters, Hedwig and Mathilde. Mathilde was the younger of the two, and Luise befriended Hedwig.

[23] The abbess was a courageous religious, who was not afraid of the Nazis. Luise was not yet Catholic when she came to the abbess. Prudence and common sense demanded that the abbess tell her that it was still too early to admit her to the monastery.

[24] The Reverend Richard Keuyk, as quoted in De Haas, *Luise Löwenfels*, 13–14.

Mr. Eppmann had a sister, Sister Cortonensis, who was a Poor Handmaid of Jesus Christ in Eltville aan de Rijn. Since the Jewish persecution in Germany was ever increasing, it was arranged for Luise to stay in a convent of this congregation, Santa Maria in Mönchengladbach-Hehn.

On November 25, 1935, the Feast of the Holy Martyr Catherine of Alexandria, Luise was baptized by Father Mauritius Demuth, O.F.M., in the parish church of Mönchengladbach-Hehn.[25] She was twenty years old. She chose Maria Aloysia as her baptismal name. Sister Sanctia Kall, a kindergarten teacher Luise trusted very much, was her godmother.[26] On November 26, 1935, Luise received her First Holy Communion.

In the hope of bringing her to safety, the Provincial Superior of the English Province of the Sisters of Dernbach was prepared to accept Luise as a postulant and to take her along to England. But this idea was not carried out.[27] A boarding student, noticing that Luise was Jewish, said, "Luise seems to be Jewish, and if she does not disappear, I will tell." [28] Before October 1937, Luise's brother Bernhard recommended to her that she emigrate to America.[29]

After having been in Mönchengladbach for nine months, Luise returned to the Eppmann family in Recklinghausen. It soon became clear, however, that she could no longer stay in Germany. Mr. Eppmann and his daughter Hedwig took her to the Saint Joseph Convent

[25] See W. v. Bergen, "Bij een grafsteen", *Heemkundevereniging Geleen* 3 (1985): 140–56, 144. Her baptism is recorded in the register of the parish of Mariae Heimsuchung (Visitation of Mary).

[26] See Westerholz, "Luise", 242.

[27] See Westerholz, "Schicksal", 300.

[28] De Haas, *Luise Löwenfels*, 17.

[29] See Westerholz, "Schicksal", 297–98.

of the Poor Handmaids of Jesus Christ in Geleen-Lutterade in the Netherlands. Luise crossed the border legally, and on March 3, 1936, she was registered in the country clerk's office.[30]

Within the context of the congregation's apostolate, Luise was given the task of caring for small children. For additional education in kindergarten child care, she stayed in Groesbeek from June 2 until August 7, 1936.

Luise wanted to become a religious. On December 8, 1937, she began the postulancy in the Congregation of the Poor Handmaids of Jesus Christ. Her giftedness was evident in her capacity to learn quickly. During her postulancy she worked as a kindergarten assistant. In addition, she also passed the examination to be a typing instructor (on February 19, 1938) and the examination to be a stenography instructor in the Dutch language (on April 16, 1938).

On September 17, 1938, she was confirmed. She received this sacrament from the bishop of Roermond, the Most Reverend Gulielmus Lemmens. On the same day, she received the habit of her congregation and her religious name. Thenceforth she would be called Sister Maria Aloysia. The only guest who came for this occasion was her friend Hedwig Eppmann. In a letter to Father Keuyk dated September 2, 1938, the postulant wrote about the sacrament of confirmation that she would receive. "May the Holy Spirit enter me with a rich blessing of grace and enlighten my life's way. The Savior loves his bride!"[31] Concerning her relationship with her family

[30] See Westerholz, "Luise", 247–48.

[31] Sister Maria Aloysia, as quoted in *Als een brandende toorts: Documentaire getuigenissen over Dr. Edith Stein (zuster Teresia Benedicta a Cruce) en medeslacht-offers*, (Echt: Friends of Dr. Edith Stein, 1967), 186.

and her loneliness, she wrote to Father Keuyk, "How happy I would be if you could be here on my day of grace! You can imagine that none of my family will be here. But I will gladly bring this sacrifice for the salvation of their souls ... !" [32]

In the novitiate, Sister Aloysia came to know the spirituality of her congregation. This spirituality corresponded exactly to her own spiritual development. The foundress of her congregation, Mother Maria Katharina, had once written, "God's will is more important than everything in the world. God's will must be done in me, through me, and for me." [33]

Her fellow sisters attest that Sister Aloysia was obedient, conscientious, and faithful in living the rule from the first day in the novitiate. She was gentle, loving, and humble in her relationship with her novice mistress, Sister Hildegundis, and her fellow sisters. During recreation she was full of joy and cheer. [34]

Before Sister Aloysia entered and also during her first years in the convent, she had to supervise the dining room of the girls' boarding school. She cared for the girls with maternal solicitude, even though she had to put up with many youthful pranks from these young ladies. Sister Aloysia felt safe and at home in her congregation.

A fellow sister relates:

Sister Aloysia was a very serious, conscientious, and sensitive woman. She did what was assigned her with an almost scrupulous exactness. She was very humble,

[32] Sister Maria Aloysia, as quoted in De Haas, *Luise Löwenfels*, 19.
[33] Mother Maria Katharina, as quoted in ibid., 42.
[34] See *Als een brandende toorts*, 186.

silent, and did not think of herself. She spoke little about herself, so that even her fellow sisters, who were with her every day, did not know about her past. She was so simple that one truly cannot say anything exceptional or striking about her. She could react energetically against superficiality and injustice.

What I noticed most in her was the way she prayed with full conviction. Her way of praying always made me want to pray with her. She was a very special person. She was very intelligent and made great efforts to learn Dutch. Her Dutch language teacher, who could not understand the difficulty that this posed for her, reprimanded her often. Luise accepted these reproaches in silence.[35]

Her novice mistress writes, "Although she was young in years, she was an interior soul, ripened through the hard and heavy struggle for her faith. She was thankful to the Lord for the many gifts of grace he had given her."[36] On September 12, 1940, Sister Maria Aloysia made her first profession.

When the occupying forces forbad Jews to teach non-Jews, Sister Aloysia could no longer work in the kindergarten. This must have been a great sacrifice for her. She thenceforth had tasks in the convent such as housekeeping and being portress. As the force of Nazi policies expanded, Sister Aloysia, like many others, also had to go to Amsterdam to take care of the formalities required by her status as a Jew. It must have been around May 1, 1942, that she returned from Amsterdam wearing a Jewish star. Sister Aloysia was well aware that the Jewish

---

[35] As quoted in De Haas, *Luise Löwenfels*, 20.
[36] Sister Hildegundis, as quoted in ibid.

persecution was increasing. She feared ever more for her life. She said to one sister, "Now they will soon come to pick me up. I can feel it."[37] A fellow sister relates:

> Sister Aloysia had fearful premonitions about what was possibly in store for her. One could see her more often kneeling in the chapel, offering her prayers—as she herself said—as a sacrifice for her family and her people. Christ was her all, and in union with him she did her work, enjoyed the small joys of life, and offered in silence the suffering that would be—according to her own saying—a prayer.[38]

Another sister recounts: "She was by nature serious and sometimes also a bit melancholic, and this was especially true during the last months before her arrest. She spoke about her premonition, especially after the attempt to go the United States was thwarted."[39]

On July 19, 1942, Sister Aloysia remarked, "I have the feeling that something is going to happen, but I have made my decision and have given myself wholly over to God's will."[40]

A week later, on July 26, 1942, the letter of the Dutch bishops that objected to the persecution of the Jews was read in the chapel of the Saint Joseph's Convent in Lutterade. Sister Aloysia listened with a deeply bowed head, as though she had a feeling that now something would happen soon. In retaliation against the Church's defense

---

[37] Sister Maria Aloysia, as quoted in A. Mohr and E. Prégardier, eds., *Passion im August (2.–9. August 1942): Edith Stein und Gefährtinnen: Weg in Tod und Auferstehung*, Zeugen der Zeitgeschichte, 5 (Annweiler: Plöger, 1995), 165.

[38] As quoted in De Haas, *Luise Löwenfels*, 23–24.

[39] As quoted in ibid., 24.

[40] Sister Maria Aloysia, as quoted in ibid., 25.

of the Jews and humanity, Sister Aloysia would be murdered fourteen days later.

Around 6:30 A.M. on Sunday, August 2, 1942, the bell
rang at the convent. A local policeman and two SS agents
stood at the door. They were led to the parlor, where
the provincial superior, Sister Immaculata, spoke with
them. They wanted to know if Luise Löwenfels lived at
the address because she had to come immediately. Sister
Immaculata went to get her. Together with the sister portress, both sisters went to the parlor. An SS agent asked
Sister Aloysia, "Are you Luise Löwenfels?" She replied
in the affirmative, to which the SS agent responded, "Then
we have to take you along immediately." Sister Aloysia
was very calm. Sister Immaculata cried. She asked for
time to collect some necessary items, and that was allowed.
The Dutch policeman went with the sisters, but the SS
agents stayed in the parlor.

Because it was almost time for Holy Mass, a priest was
already in the house. Sister Immaculata first brought Sister Aloysia to the chapel, where the priest gave her Holy
Communion. It would be for the last time. The policeman stayed reverently at the back of the chapel. Then,
under the watchful eye of the policeman, the necessary
things were packed: two habits, a pair of shoes, food, and
other such things.

In the meantime, Sister Hildegundis, the novice mistress, went to the parlor, where she tried in vain to change
the SS agents' minds. While Holy Mass had begun in
the chapel, Sister Immaculata and the sister portress led
Sister Aloysia outside. Calm and resigned, she said goodbye at the convent door. No one was allowed to accom-
pany her to the police van, which was waiting across the

---

street from the convent fence. She boarded in her religious habit. Then the van drove away. No one knew where Sister Aloysia was being taken. The whole event lasted no more than fifteen minutes. The Dutch policeman returned to the convent and cried while recounting that the SS officers had awakened him that morning. He had been forced to come along to the convent. He had acted correctly and kindly, but he could not do anything else.[41]

It is not clear if the truck then went to Koningsbosch to pick up Annemarie and Elfriede Goldschmidt and then to Echt, where the Stein sisters were picked up. At any rate, it is known that Sister Aloysia left that evening from Roermond with the others who were arrested in Limburg and was taken to the Amersfoort camp. They arrived there in the middle of the night.[42]

The camp leader reported to the convent in Lutterade that they should send Sister Aloysia two woolen blankets, warm clothes, and ration cards for bread. These items were not permitted to be brought by a sister. On Thursday, August 6, a trusted acquaintance of the congregation, Mr. Huub op de Camp, brought the things to Westerbork. Sister Aloysia cried bitterly when she said farewell to Mr. op de Camp. This was Sister Aloysia's last contact with the outside world.[43] The next morning she was on the train to Auschwitz.[44]

---

[41] See convent chronicle, in Mohr and Prégardier, *Passion im August*, 172–73.

[42] See R. Kempner, *Twee uit honderdduizend, Anne Frank en Edith Stein: Onthullingen over de nazimisdaden in Nederland voor het gerecht in München* (Bilthoven, 1969), 108. Sister Maria Aloysia is one of the Catholic Jews whose names appear on the list drafted in this camp. She is no. 86 and comes after Sister Mirjam Michaelis.

[43] See Mohr and Prégardier, *Passion im August*, 174.

[44] See NIOD, Archive 250 I, Westerbork camp, inventory no. 239. On the transport list of August 7, 1942, she is on list A, no. 15.

Luise Löwenfels could have saved her life by going to America with her family, but she gave preference to faith in Jesus Christ and his Church. This choice cost her her life. Because she acknowledged Jesus as the Son of God, she literally had to leave everything to follow him. She left the Jewish setting into which she had been born. In Recklinghausen, she lost both job and housing. And even though she had already parted from her family in holy baptism, as a Jew the loss of her homeland was further required of her. Finally, as a Catholic Jew, she sacrificed life itself in Auschwitz. Her life is a testament to the words of her Lord Jesus Christ, "If any man would come after me, let him deny himself and take up his cross daily and follow me. For whoever would save his life will lose it; and whoever loses his life for my sake, he will save it" (Lk 9:23–24).

In October 1947, Pastor Keuyk wrote about Sister Aloysia, whom he had known since 1935:

> I assume that Sister Aloysia maintained the same attitude that I noticed in her in the days when I came to know her. The reception of confirmation had filled her with such a holy joy in offering sacrifices that I am confident that in the strength of her holy faith, she gave the sacrifice of her young and hopeful life and has entered eternity as a glorious martyr.... May Sister Aloysia obtain for each of us that same heroic fidelity that she showed in her own struggle for the truth and the love "stronger than death" that the deep waters of suffering cannot extinguish (cf. Song of Songs 8:7).[45]

---

[45] The Reverend Richard Keuyk, as quoted in De Haas, *Luise Löwenfels*, 42–43.

What a sight it must have been in heaven when Edith
Stein, Aloysia Löwenfels, and the other sisters were
brought to death in August 1942 in Auschwitz and
elsewhere. They are the heroes who by their death
have conquered the world. Even in their greatest agony,
they rejoiced to suffer and die with Christ. They are
the saints of our day, who have been sent by God to
teach that the essence of our life consists in proving
our faithfulness, and this can only happen in struggle,
suffering, and death. They are the blessed ones of whom
the Lord has said, "Blessed are those who are persecuted for righteousness' sake, for theirs is the kingdom of heaven" (Mt 5:10). The Lord has blessed them
forever and has taken them into his eternal home.[46]

Sister Maria Aloysia paid dearly for her religious convictions. Her choice for the Church brought her to the
gas chambers of Auschwitz at the age of twenty-seven.
On June 28, 2006, a memorial was erected in her honor
at the corner of Geenstraat and De Vaart in Geleen.

---

[46] The Reverend Richard Keuyk, as quoted in *Als een brandende toorts*,
188–89.

Chapter 7

SISTER MIRJAM MICHAELIS, C.S.J.

Else Michaelis was born in Berlin (Germany) on March 31, 1889. Her family consisted of six children. Her father was Adolf Lazarus; her mother was Rosalia Hirschfeld. Else's father worked at an umbrella factory.

Sister Mirjam Michaelis, C.S.J.
Photo: Schilz, *Schwester Mirjam Michaelis*, 28.

Else lost her mother when she was six, and her father when she was sixteen years old. She was then entrusted to the care of a guardian, who saw to it that she was educated in home economics. Afterward, she worked for some time as a nanny and then as a companion for elderly women. Because she wanted to do office work, she followed evening courses that provided her with the appropriate training. She completed courses to become a bookkeeper and worked in this capacity for thirteen years.[1]

On April 19, 1919, at the age of thirty, Else became a member of the Catholic Church. On that day she was baptized in the Corpus Christi Church in Berlin by Father Butz. Two of the parishioners were her godparents: Miss Adelheid Hoheisel and Miss Hedwich Tschirner.[2] She never spoke much about how she came to the Church. When asked how she came to be Catholic, she once said, "That is simply grace. I cannot tell you anything about it."[3] Because she did not consider herself fit to become a religious sister immediately after becoming Catholic, she first became active in the local parish community of Corpus Christi. In addition, she continued her work in the office. She became a valued member of the parish and later became the head of the Catholic business association, Lydia.

During a hospital stay, Else became acquainted with the Sisters of Saint Catherine (Zusters van de H. Catharina).

---

[1] See L. Schilz, *Schwester Mirjam Michaelis: Opfer von Auschwitz* (Trier, 1993).

[2] See A. Mohr and E. Prégardier, eds., *Passion im August (2.–9. August 1942): Edith Stein und Gefährtinnen: Weg in Tod und Auferstehung*, Zeugen der Zeitgeschichte, 5 (Annweiler: Plöger, 1995), 180.

[3] Else Michaelis, as quoted by H. Moll, ed., *Zeugen für Christus: Das deutsche Martyrologium des 20. Jahrhunderts*, 2 vols. (Paderborn, 1999), 885.

These sisters lived in the rectory of the parish, and after her recovery, Else went to live with them. She had actually wanted to become a sister from the time of her baptism. She did not, however, enter the congregation of the sisters with whom she lived. On May 28, 1928, she wrote a letter to Mother Clara, who was then the Superior General of the Congregation of the Sisters of Saint Joseph. She asked to be permitted to enter this congregation. Else wrote, among other things, "How much I would have wanted to give myself to Christ immediately after my baptism and First Holy Communion. But I did not yet feel worthy of this high calling because I was only a beginner; it remained nonetheless my deepest and secret wish." [4] She explains the reason for her desire to become a sister in the congregation as follows: "Since I have a great interest in social work and since your order is well known for its charitable services, I most ardently and humbly ask to be received into the order." [5]

Else Michaelis was an able and independent woman. She did not want to give the impression that she was fleeing to the convent because she could not find her place in the world or because the world could not use her. In the letter of May 28, 1928, in which she asks to be admitted to the congregation, the thirty-nine-year-old Else writes:

Unfortunately, I was until now prevented from realizing my desire due to the years of unemployment. I

[4] Else Michaelis, as quoted in *Als een brandende toorts: Documentaire getuigenissen over Dr. Edith Stein (zuster Teresia Benedicta a Cruce) en medeslachtoffers* (Echt: Friends of Dr. Edith Stein, 1967), 189.
[5] Ibid.

did not want to take the step then because I do not
consider the religious life a "welfare institute". But I
decided that if our dear Lord would give me a good
job, I would then knock at the convent door, where I
could live, work, and pray wholly out of love for God.
Now God has answered my prayers, and on December 8, the Solemnity of the Immaculate Conception,
he gave me a good job.[6]

She was accepted to the Congregation of the Sisters
of Saint Joseph in Trier (Germany) and began her postulancy at the Motherhouse on September 6, 1928. Two
other candidates began the postulancy with her: Sister
Apolonia and Sister Luitgard. Sister Luitgard describes
Else as "a sensitive, humble, pious, and conscientious sister".[7] A year later Else was clothed and was thenceforth
called Sister Mirjam. So it was that she began her novitiate
during this time of crisis for the world. As Nazism gained
influence, Hitler came to power as chancellor on January
30, 1933. Slowly but surely, Germany fell into the grip
of Nazism, with its heathen and inhumane ideology. The
persecution of the Jews increased. Under these circumstances, Sister Mirjam professed her final vows in 1935.

After making her first profession, she was given the
task of portress in the Convent of Saint Gertrude (Ger-
tudisklooster) in Saarland. She fulfilled this task from 1932
until the autumn of 1935. Saint Gertrude was a home
for troubled children. This convent was not far from the
French border, and, in preparation for the war, the convent
was claimed by the Nazis for military purposes.

[6] Ibid.
[7] Sister Luitgard, as quoted in Moll, *Zeugen*, 886.

Sister Mirjam was then transferred to Berlin. There she did the bookkeeping for the Xaverius Institute from 1935 until 1939. The Nazi pressure on the Jews increased. In Berlin, Sister Mirjam suffered through the experience of having her brother George taken prisoner by the SS. After his release, he was able to find safety by fleeing to England. He is the only member of the family who survived the war. One of her sisters, unable to cope with the intimidations and harassment that the Jews suffered, committed suicide by gassing herself.

The still increasing persecution of the Jews in Germany led Sister Mirjam to flee to the Netherlands shortly before the outbreak of the war. On September 1, 1939, the day that Hitler invaded Poland, Sister Mirjam was transferred to the Saint Magdalena Convent in Rotterdam-Overschie. This was a home for unwed mothers as well as a home for children up to six years old. The Sisters of Saint Joseph had worked there since 1936, and Sister Hiëronyma Weinforth was the local superior.

On May 10, 1940, the Germans invaded the Netherlands, and the persecution of the Jews extended also into this country. In September 1940, the occupier determined that Jews could no longer live in the coastal area. As noted previously, there were no less than 250 places in the Netherlands where Jews were not permitted to live. Sister Mirjam had to move. In September 1940, while Sister Hiëronyma was making a retreat with the Franciscans of Nonnenwerth in their Mariënwaard Convent in Meerssen-Limmel near Maastricht, she received a telephone call informing her that the Nazis had ordered Sister Mirjam to leave Overschie. When they heard this, the Franciscan Sisters offered Sister Mirjam a place to live in their convent. The sisters also had a nursing home in Mariënwaard. Sister Mirjam lived there for nearly two years, but not as part of the community of Franciscans. Sister Mirjam lived by herself and served the elderly residents.[8]

In the meantime, she was not protected against the Nazi terror. She repeatedly received orders to go to Maastricht, Eindhoven, Rotterdam, and Amsterdam to be questioned or to fill out the required forms. Before she left for Auschwitz in April 1942, she had been obliged to sign forty-two forms. The superiors of her congregation, foreseeing that she was in danger, looked for a convent in Switzerland where Sister Mirjam could live in safety. The Sisters of Sacré Coeur were willing to take Sister Mirjam, but by then it was already too late.

In the context of her ordinary visitation, Mother Teresia Jungbluth, Sister Mirjam's superior general, came to see Sister Mirjam in Mariënwaard on July 18, 1942. After visitation in Mariënwaard, Mother Teresia went to another convent of the congregation that happened to be located in Amsterdam, where she heard of the Nazis' promise not to deport baptized Jews. She informed Sister Mirjam of this.[9]

On Sunday, August 2, 1942, Sister Mirjam was picked up at 8:30 A.M. from Mariënwaard by two armed Dutch policemen and an SS officer. The policemen guarded the entrance of the house, while the SS officer went inside and asked for Sister Mirjam.[10] He gave Mother Maria, the local superior, the order to have Sister Mirjam

[8] See Mohr and Prégardier, *Passion im August*, 181–82.
[9] See ibid., 187.
[10] See ibid.

ready to leave within half an hour.[11] Mother Maria recounts:

> The Sunday Mass had just ended, and all the inhabitants of the house were eating breakfast. I was called to the door, where a man from the Gestapo asked for Sister Mirjam. I went with him to the second floor, where Sister Mirjam was at that moment helping to serve breakfast. I placed my hand on her shoulder and said, "The cross beckons you." She understood me immediately. The man from the Gestapo had a bayonet in his hand. We went to her room, and the man followed us. He took a notebook from his pocket and read out which articles of clothing she could take along. Within forty-five minutes she would be picked up. I flew down the stairs to get a basket, blankets, and food. All helped. Sister Mirjam did not want to eat breakfast. She remained very calm and composed.
>
> The news of her deportation spread like wildfire through the house. Nearly all the residents stood around her. The man from the Gestapo, a lad no older than twenty, became rather embarrassed. The priest went with Sister Mirjam to the parlor and gave her general absolution. The man from the Gestapo asked me, "Does she also have toothpaste?" I gave him no answer. He was probably embarrassed to see all the residents with tears in their eyes saying such heartfelt goodbyes to Sister Mirjam.
>
> Her last words were, "Now the Old Testament suffers for the New." Someone came to say that the van had come to pick her up. Two Dutch policemen came to the door. They forgot themselves for a minute and

carried the small suitcase for her, the rejected Jew. A truck covered with a canvas stood in front of the door. There was no footboard, no stepping stool to get in. I helped her to climb into the truck. "Look, there is another sister", I called out loudly [this was probably Sister Aloysia Löwenfels from Geleen-Lutterade, who had been arrested before 7:00 A.M. that morning at her convent (Mohr and Prégardier, 183)].... In the truck there were small, narrow benches on which various persons were already sitting. On the first bench were four or five men from the Gestapo. No word was said. I can only remember that this sister was in the truck and a young woman who had one or two small children with her.

One last time I grasped Sister Mirjam's hand, and then the truck drove off. One elderly Dutch man from our home had come to the truck and reproached the Gestapo. They told him, "If you don't keep your mouth shut, we will take you, too." [12]

The sisters from Mariënwaard did not simply accept this arrest. Mother Maria recounts:

Sister Anita and I discussed if we could not free Sister Mirjam through personal intervention. We made our way to the Gestapo office in Maastricht. We were turned away everywhere and had to return home without any success. We called the bishop and asked him if there was not something we could do. He said, "It is sad, Reverend Mother, but we can only pray." [13]

[12] Mother Maria, as quoted in R. Kempner, *Twee uit honderdduizend, Anne Frank en Edith Stein: Onthullingen over de nazimisdaden in Nederland voor het gerecht in München* (Bilthoven, 1969), 135–36.
[13] Ibid., 136.

Mother Maria informed the sisters in Rotterdam-Overschie that Sister Mirjam had been arrested. Mother Teresia, too, who had so recently visited Sister Mirjam in Mariënwaard, was informed on August 2 of her fellow sister's arrest. Mother Teresia was still in the Netherlands.

Sister Hiëronyma, the local superior in Overschie, heard that Sister Mirjam had been taken from Mariënwaard to Roermond and was supposedly in a camp there. In the hope of being able to speak with her, Sister Hiëronyma traveled to Roermond on Monday, August 3. But it was in vain. When she returned to Overschie, she received news by telephone that Sister Mirjam was for the time being in Amersfoort but that she would soon go to Westerbork and that she needed lay clothing.[14]

Mother Maria from Mariënwaard had seen a young mother with two children in the police truck. A few days later they were released. The woman visited Mariënwaard and told them that she was a Dutch "half-Jew". Her husband had remained home with the small children and had done everything in his power to free her. He had succeeded. The mother recounted what had happened to Sister Mirjam after the arrest:

She had been very courageous. Every morning they had read the texts of the Holy Mass and prayed the rosary in a closed circle. (There were five Trappists, among whom were two priests, so that Sister Mirjam was still able to go to confession one more time.) The SS men, especially the younger ones, had mocked the communal prayer and interrupted it with yelling. The older ones were more decent. "Sister Mirjam

[14] See Mohr and Prégardier, *Passion im August*, 189.

resolutely ate everything we were given, even a thin
cabbage soup that I could not get down. Sister Mirjam lay on wooden planks, which stood along the wall
as bunk beds. She had not undressed. You could not
sleep because the SS repeatedly shone floodlights into
the dormitory.

"It was also very awkward to go to the bathroom
that had no door. There was always an SS officer in
front of it." [15]

Sister Hiëronyma traveled to Westerbork, bringing with
her suitcases packed with the necessary things for Sister
Mirjam. She was accompanied by Baroness van Voorst
tot Voorst, one of the residents from Mariënwaard Home
who appreciated Sister Mirjam very much. She insisted
on visiting her with Sister Hiëronyma in Westerbork. They
arrived in Westerbork on Thursday toward the end of
the afternoon. They received no more than about half
an hour to speak with Sister Mirjam. She was very happy
to see them. She informed them that she had not changed
her clothes since Sunday. At their parting she cried bitterly. She said to Sister Hiëronyma, "I offer every suffering and deprivation of life in the camp for our sisters, so
that no sister will be dissatisfied when she lacks something that she thinks is due her." [16] Before they left the
camp, Sister Teresa Benedicta gave the visitors a note for
her prioress, Mother Antonia, in Echt. [17]

From the Westerbork camp, Sister Mirjam wrote a letter to Mother Teresia, her superior general. By the time

[15] As quoted in Kempner, *Twee uit honderdduizend*, 136.
[16] Sister Mirjam Michaelis, as quoted in Mohr and Prégardier, *Passion im August*, 191.
[17] See Mohr and Prégardier, *Passion im August*, 189–91; Moll, *Zeugen*, 887.

the letter arrived by mail at the convent in Overschie,
Sister Mirjam had perhaps already been murdered. The
letter states:

Dearest and kindest Reverend Mother Teresia! I write
you in the hope that you will receive these lines. Now
the good, fatherly hand of God has struck me and a
number of priests and sisters. What has long been feared
has happened. Since Sunday morning I have been in
two camps. On Friday we must travel farther still, probably very far away. Only God knows if we will see
one another again. And his will be done, even if it is
very difficult. Because everything went so fast, I of
course had to leave as I was (i.e., in habit). There are
six other sisters here, all in habit, and therefore I am
happy that I, too, am wearing mine. Two Trappists
priest/brothers are also here in habit.

Until now we have had no lack of food, but otherwise we suffer everything that life in the camp brings
with it. We are about fifty people in one room. Does
this not already provide much to offer the dear Savior? We want to offer our sacrifices for our holy Catholic Church, for all suffering people, and not the least
for our beloved religious communities. It was surely
good of the dear Lord to give us the opportunity to
see one another and talk to one another once more,
wasn't it? The good Mother Maria (superior of Mariënwaard) took care in all haste for the most necessary
things. I owe her and all of you many thanks.

Dear Reverend Mother, I have one more request:
you and all the dear sisters should not be sad or suffer
too much for me, but only pray, pray! We all count
on that. We know and feel that you are praying. Hopefully we—the sisters—can stay together. We do not

know if we will have another opportunity to write later. In any case, we will be united in spirit, prayer, suffering, and sacrifice. Our hardships are offered for everyone![18]

This letter was the last sign of life we have from Sister Mirjam. Like the other Catholic Jews, Sister Mirjam was placed on the transport to Auschwitz-Birkenau on August 7.[19] From the station in Auschwitz she was probably taken directly to the Birkenau extermination camp, where she was murdered in a gas chamber. She is probably buried in a mass grave with the other Catholic Jews.

Sister Mirjam was not arrested unawares. She knew what had been looming over her head. Mother Teresia, who had spoken with her in Mariënwaard only fourteen days before her arrest (on July 18), wrote on August 17, 1942, "Sister Mirjam was prepared for everything, and she went into the future with courage and total surrender."[20] The rector of Mariënwaard, who knew Sister Mirjam well and who had been able to give her absolution shortly before she left, said that "that sister has sanctified herself here and will continue to sanctify herself."[21]

On July 31, 1950, the sisters of Mariënwaard received the written report, legally authorized by the municipality of Meerssen, that Else Michaelis had died on August 9, 1942. She was fifty-three years old.

[18] Sister Mirjam Michaelis, as quoted in Kempner, *Twee uit honderdduizend*, 137; *Als een brandende toorts*, 192; Mohr and Prégardier, *Passion im August*, 193–94.

[19] See Kempner, *Twee uit honderdduizend*, 108. She was no. 85 on the list of Catholic Jews written up in Amersfoort on August 4, 1942.

[20] Mother Teresia, as quoted in Mohr and Prégardier, *Passion im August*, 187.

[21] As quoted in Mohr and Prégardier, *Passion im August*, 191.

In the memorial book of the deceased members of
her congregation, one finds the following text under the
picture of Sister Mirjam: "Lord our God, I praise your
name because you are my helper and my protector. You
have saved my body from destruction, and therefore my
soul will praise the Lord forever."[22]

[22] *Als een brandende toorts,* 192.

Chapter 8

THE LÖB FAMILY

In 1881, Ludwig (Lutz) Löb was born into a liberal Jewish family in Euskirchen in the German region of Eifel. He was just a year old when his father moved to the Netherlands and settled in The Hague, where he ran a clothing store. When he was sixteen years old, Ludwig went to live in Amsterdam, where he attended the higher trade school (Hogere Handelsschool), from which he graduated when he was eighteen. He went to Brussels (Belgium) to pursue an internship and there had his first contact not only with the Catholic faith, but also with socialism and Marxism. The trade business seemed immoral to him, and he asked his father permission to study.

He subsequently went to the city of Delft to study mining. In addition to his regular studies, he read many books on philosophy and religious topics because of a new-found interest in religion. The reading of the New Testament (the *Canisiusbijbeltje* [1906], a version of parts of the New Testament published by the apologetic society of Saint Peter Canisius) settled his calling to the Church. He understood that Judaism had found its fulfillment in Jesus Christ and the Catholic faith. Years later, Lutz Löb recounted "that he could see the present

Judaism as nothing else but the fossilization of the living Judaism of the time of Christ. 'The true Jews from the time of Christ, who remained true to their religion, are the ones who became Christian.' " [1] He once described his entrance into the Church with these words, "Every Jew who truly knows his religion and who wants to confess it according to the Spirit with all its consequences, has, I think, to become Catholic." [2]

During the time that he was studying in Amsterdam, Lutz had become acquainted with Johanna (Jenny) van Gelder, who was born on February 15, 1879, in Naarden. She had grown up in a well-to-do Jewish family in Amsterdam, but her religious upbringing had been minimal. She received piano lessons from Anton Tieri of the Amsterdam Conservatory. [3] During a discussion with his future wife, Lutz responded to her so fiercely that she asked him, "But are you then Roman?" This remark so shocked Lutz that he had to admit that a conviction had grown in him. Together with Jenny he studied the catechism and Catholic customs. [4] This study nurtured the faith that would lead to baptism. [5]

On October 2, 1907, during their engagement, they became members of the Church. The baptism took place in Delft and was administered by the student chaplain,

[1] Lutz Löb, as quoted in R. Bromberg, "Trappisten met davidster", *De Bazuin* 38 (January 15, 1955): 8.

[2] Lutz Löb, as quoted on the website of the Abbey of Our Lady of Koningshoeven.

[3] See Peter Steffen and Hans Evers, *Scheuren in het Kleed: Het joods-Katholleke gezin Löb 1881–1945* (Nijmegen: Volkhof Pers, 2009), 61.

[4] See Bromberg, "Trappisten met davidster".

[5] See R. Kempner, *Twee uit honderdduizend, Anne Frank en Edith Stein: Onthullingen over de nazimisdaden in Nederland voor het gerecht in München* (Bilthoven, 1969), 126.

Father H. Ermann, S.J., who had come to know Lutz during his studies in this city.[6]

On October 31, 1907, they were married in the sacristy of a convent church. Father Ermann was the ecclesial witness to this sacrament.[7] Because their conversion would be a scandal to their Jewish families and relatives, Lutz and Jenny received permission from their spiritual director to live as "crypto-Catholics", which meant that they could externally continue to live as Jews and only had to attend Holy Mass when it was necessary and safe. They later regretted this decision, because it prevented them from living a normal Catholic life.[8] Their reception into the Catholic Church did not prevent Jenny Löb from continuing to be united in a heartfelt way with her Jewish people. Jenny once wrote as follows about Catholics who speak disparagingly about Jews:

> If I had not been so convinced that I had found the true faith, then this disparaging talk might have motivated me to turn back. How little do those who speak this way know about the Jewish people: about their loyalty, their goodness, the solidarity among them, their heartfelt family bonds. How much did I miss all this— the bright humor, the wonderful hospitality—after becoming Catholic. I was so proud of these Jewish characteristics, which were judged so negatively by others. Even though I belong to Jesus with heart and soul, I feel for my Jewish people. I remain united with my people, and I will never deny my Jewish blood.[9]

[6] See Steffen and Evers, *Scheuren in het kleed*, 96.

[7] Ibid., 97.

[8] See Bromberg, "Trappisten met davidster", *De Bazuin* 38 (January 29, 1955): 8.

[9] Jenny Löb, as quoted in Mohr and Prégardier, *Passion im August*, 215.

After his marriage, Ludwig passed his last exams in 1907 and became a mine engineer.[10] The Löb couple had eight children. Lien (1908), their firstborn, came into the world in Rijswijk. On account of Lutz's work in the mines, the couple lived in Hoensbroek for a time, and it was here that their second child, George (Joris), was born in 1909. He was the oldest son. The next son, Rob, was born in The Hague in 1910. By then, the family was apparently already on the way to Indonesia because Rob was baptized there in Padang.

Ludwig received a managerial position in the Ombili mines on the island of Sumatra, Indonesia. In Sawah Loento, Sumatra, the remaining children were born: the twins Wies and Thea (1911), Ernst (1913), Hans (1916) and the youngest, Paula (1919).[11] In 1928, the Löb family also adopted a girl named Deetje, whose mother had died at her birth.[12]

In 1919 the family returned to the Netherlands. Lutz, the father, had accepted a job in the Norwegian city of Spitsbergen. The family settled in The Hague. The Norwegian business went bankrupt, however, and the family became impoverished. Lutz then found a job as a mathematics and natural science teacher at the Roman Catholic high school in Bergen op Zoom. Here he was also active in youth work.[13]

In Bergen op Zoom, Jenny used her musical talent in leading children's choirs. The Löb family also had much

[10] See Bromberg, "Trappisten met davidster", De Bazuin 38 (January 22, 1955): 8.
[11] See Als een brandende toorts: Documentaire getuigenissen over Dr. Edith Stein (zuster Teresia Benedicta a Cruce) en medeslachtoffers (Echt: Friends of Dr. Edith Stein, 1967), 203.
[12] See Mohr and Prégardier, Passion im August, 212, 216–17.
[13] See ibid., 217.

contact with an assistant pastor, Father Anton van Dijk, who entered the Trappists at the Abbey of Our Lady of Koningshoeven on April 25, 1925. His religious name became Father Leo. Father Leo was the Löb family's first contact with the Trappists. From 1926 onward, Lutz went to Our Lady of Koningshoeven for retreat every year. Here he came into contact with Dom Simon Dubuisson, who was then abbot. The Löb family lived intensely from the Cistercian spirituality, and Ludwig lived the spirituality of a Trappist as a layman and a father of a family. It is no surprise that six of his eight children were attracted to this spirituality and entered the Cistercians. Once Lutz invited two of his sons to visit at the abbey during his retreat there. Three of his sons would later enter this abbey: George in 1926, Robert in 1928, and Ernst in 1929.

No Cistercian abbeys for women existed in the Netherlands, and in 1928 the abbot of Our Lady of Koningshoeven took the initiative to found one. Three daughters of the Löb family, therefore, first entered the Cistercian Abbey Our Lady of Peace (N.D. de la Paix) in the Belgian city of Chimay. Lien entered in 1928, Thea in 1929, and Wies in 1930. On July 15, 1937, the three sisters transferred to the Abbey of Our Lady of Koningsoord in Berkel-Enschot, which by then was ready to be occupied.[14]

Neither parent of the Löb family had to experience the German persecution of the Jews. Lutz died "like a saint" at the age of fifty-three on April 6, 1935. Jenny followed her husband in death on September 6, 1938. She was fifty-nine years old.[15]

---

[14] See Archive Koningsoord; *Als een brandende toorts*, 203.
[15] Steffen and Evers, *Scheuren in het kleed*, 188, 326.

On August 2, 1942, two of the Löb sisters, Sister Hedwigis (Lien) and Sister Maria-Theresia (Thea), were taken prisoner at Our Lady of Koningsoord together with Dr. Lisamaria Meirowsky. The sisters were praying Lauds when the Gestapo knocked at the door of the Trappistine Abbey.[16] The arrest did not come unexpectedly. A few days before the sisters were picked up by the Nazis, Sister Hedwigis said to her prioress, "I have put everything in order. I am ready to leave. I only want to take along these books (breviary, missal, New Testament, *Imitation of Christ*), and that is enough."[17] Sister Hedwigis and Sister Maria-Theresia were called away from choir. They went to the abbey infirmary, where the rector, Father Bavo van der Ham, brought them Holy Communion as viaticum, as food for their way to heaven. At first, Sister Hedwigis was beside herself with fear of what could be in store for them. After she received Holy Communion, she soon regained her calm. Her fellow sisters promised her their heartfelt prayers for a quick return. Sister Hedwigis answered, "Oh no, that is not necessary. I have just told our dear Lord, 'I give myself to you, do with me as you will.' "[18]

Sister Maria-Theresia also understood that this parting would be for good. Smilingly she said farewell to all. She thanked everyone and asked forgiveness for her faults. In the meantime, the Gestapo outside were getting annoyed. They pounded impatiently on the door and yelled that

[16] See Kempner, *Twee uit honderdduizend*, 125.

[17] Sister Hedwigis Löb, O.C.S.O., as quoted in the list of deceased members of the Cistercian Abbey of Our Lady of Koningsoord in Berkel-Enschot.

[18] Sister Hedwigis Löb, O.C.S.O., as quoted in Bromberg, "Trappisten met davidster" (January 29).

the sisters should come out soon. When the doors opened, one of the men was surprised. Instead of the fearful and crying people he was used to seeing under such circumstances, he saw how both sisters calmly knelt before Abbess Gertrudis Demarrez to receive her last blessing. With great peace and with smiles on their faces, both sisters came outside. One of the agents said, "I do not understand it at all. It is as though they are going to a feast." Turning to Sister Hedwigis he said, "I think that you are even happy that they have come to get you." The religious responded, "Oh, yes, they can only help us get into heaven sooner."[19] Then both sisters placed themselves under the authority of the Gestapo. They boarded the police van, which soon afterward left through the large gate.[20]

As will be recounted in detail in the subsequent chapter, Dr. Lisamaria Meirowsky had been living at the Cistercian Abbey since 1940. She, too, was arrested. Together with the two nuns she boarded the police van, which drove to the Abbey of Our Lady of Koningshoeven to pick up the two Fathers and one Brother Löb.

Sister Veronica (Wies) Löb was not taken along because she was ill and because the abbess had hidden her.[21]

The Carmelite priest Father Edwin Peters recounts the events of the arrest at the Abbey of Our Lady of Koningshoeven. He belonged to the monastery of Saint Joseph the Worker in the German Essen, but before his entrance there, Father Peters had long been a Trappist in Koningshoeven. Although he later had to leave that abbey for

---

[19] As quoted in ibid.
[20] See a report of Father Anselmus Terstegge from 1962, printed in Mohr and Prégardier, *Passion im August*, 219–22; Kempner, *Twee uit honderdduizend*, 125.
[21] Steffen and Evers, *Scheuren in het kleed*, 365–81.

reasons of health, on that fateful day—August 2, 1942—he was still a Trappist of Koningshoeven and recounts:

> Then that unforgettable night arrived. As always, we had gone into choir at 1:30 A.M. to pray Matins: first Matins and the Little Office of the Blessed Virgin Mary, followed by half an hour of meditation. At 2:30 A.M. we began the great Matins. Ignatius was hebdomadary [a task that changes every week, in this case in the recitation of the Liturgy of the Hours] and had to intone. After he had sung, "*Deus in adjutorium meum intende*" (God come to my assistance), Father Abbot, Dom Simon Dubuisson, was called out of choir by Brother Porter. The Jewish persecution had also come to the peaceful abbey. Shortly afterward, the three Jewish brothers were called from choir. After we had completed the praying of the Office, we heard what had happened. Each of the Löb brothers nobly rejected a fellow brother's offers to help them escape.[22]

A fellow brother advised Father Ignatius to flee. The latter replied, "What will be the consequences for the house? They have threatened to shoot ten priests if we do not come. You will see; we will come back soon." [23] Brother Linus first thought of fleeing. When it was made clear to him what the consequences could be, he asked for prayers, "so that he could persevere".[24]

[22] The Reverend Edwin Peters, as quoted in Kempner, *Twee uit honderdduizend*, 128.
[23] The Reverend Ignatius Löb, O.C.S.O., as quoted in Kempner, *Twee uit honderdduizend*, 128; Mohr and Prégardier, *Passion im August*, 221.
[24] Mohr and Prégardier, *Passion im August*, 221.

Father Anselmus Terstegge, the abbey chronicler, recounts that the Nazis threatened to shoot ten monks.[25] Father Abbot suggested that the brothers celebrate the Holy Mass. It could be their last. Father Ignatius was a bit nervous; he had always been the liveliest. Father Nivardus, on the other hand, was as though lost in God as he offered the Holy Sacrifice. After breakfast they had to pack their things—bed linen, eating utensils, and the like— and then the hour of parting arrived.[26]

After Father Nivardus had offered the Holy Mass and eaten breakfast, there was still some time to spare, so he walked very calmly between the guest house and the gate praying the Office.[27] To a fellow brother Father Ignatius said, "Until we meet again in heaven."

"All said, 'Till we meet again' to the departing brothers. All lied, because everyone knew that we would never see them again. One did not lie: Nivardus. 'Oh,' he said to us, 'do not talk about seeing one another again. This is the first station of our way of the cross. It will also have a twelfth station.' "[28]

In the meantime, Dom Simon was negotiating with the Nazis in the hope of not having to hand over his monks. He called the Bishop of Den Bosch, who told him, "Let them go in God's name, so that nothing worse will happen. Nothing can be done."[29]

When the police van stopped in Koningshoeven and Dom Simon approached it, Sister Hedwigis jumped out of the car, stretched out her arms, and said, "Reverend

---

[25] See the website of the Abbey of Our Lady of Koningshoeven.

[26] See Kempner, *Twee uit honderdduizend*, 129.

[27] See Bromberg, "Trappisten met davidster" (January 29).

[28] Kempner, *Twee uit honderdduizend*, 129.

[29] The Most Reverend Wilhelmus Petrus Mutsaerts, as quoted in Bromberg, "Trappisten met davidster" (January 29).

Father, we are on our way to heaven."[30] After Dom Simon had blessed them for the last time, he said, "Always remain true Trappists."[31] All boarded. The van drove away. The transport of the innocent religious was guarded by six heavily armed men.[32]

The five religious brothers and sisters were brought to Amersfoort Camp by way of Den Bosch.[33] From Amersfoort, their way of the cross led to the train station in Hooghalen. The Löb family went from Hooghalen to Westerbork in a horse-drawn cart.

Some of the details concerning their stay in Amersfoort and Westerbork already recounted in chapter 1 are mentioned again in this chapter. In Amersfoort the guards played games with the monks. The three Löb brothers were placed before the firing squad in the presence of their sisters and many others, and guns were pointed at them. This turned out to be "a joke".[34]

Sister Judith Mendes da Costa mentions the presence of the Löb family in her account of Westerbork. "In the late afternoon the Trappist fathers came to our barrack and walked back and forth outside with their sisters. From one of those fathers, the novice master, I received a blessing."[35]

---

[30] Sister Hedwigis Löb, O.C.S.O., as quoted in Bromberg, "Trappisten met davidster" (January 29).

[31] Dom Simon Dubuisson, O.C.S.O., as quoted in Mohr and Prégardier, *Passion im August*, 223.

[32] See Mohr and Prégardier, *Passion im August*, 223.

[33] See Kempner, *Twee uit honderdduizend*, 108. On the list of prisoners that was written up there on August 4, 1942, in preparation for the transport to Westerbork, Theodora and Lien are noted as nos. 24 and 25; George, Ernst, and Robert follow as nos. 27, 28, and 29.

[34] See ibid.

[35] Sister Judith Mendes da Costa, O.P., as quoted by Peters in *Als een brandende toorts*, 161.

Father Peters said that "both priests had to hear many confessions, while the sisters were angels of mercy for the other detainees."[36] Even though the priests had brought along hosts and wine in their baggage, they could not offer the Holy Mass.[37]

Sister Hedwigis and Sister Maria-Theresia sent a telegram from Westerbork to Berkel-Enschot on Wednesday, August 5, 1942. In this telegram they requested various things they would need for their journey.[38] A similar request, also dated August 5, arrived at the Cistercian Abbey of Berkel-Enschot on Friday, August 7, in the form of a note from Sister Hedwigis. But by that time, they were already on their way to the east. The representative of the Trappist beer brewery in Tilburg, De Schaapskooi (The Sheep Gate), Mr. van Riel, traveled to the Westerbork camp. Perhaps he went to deliver the requested things. He was able to speak with the prisoners.

Early on Friday, August 7, the five religious left from Westerbork for Auschwitz.[39] Both sisters were gassed and buried in a mass grave after their arrival. The three monks were considered healthy enough to work, and they subsequently died from the camp conditions or were gassed sometime that August or September.[40]

[36] The Reverend Edwin Peters, as quoted in Kempner, *Twee uit honderdduizend*, 129.

[37] See Bromberg, "Trappisten met davidster" (January 29).

[38] See Mohr and Prégardier, *Passion im August*, 223.

[39] See NIOD, Archive 250 I, Westerbork camp, inventory no. 239; Kempner, *Twee uit honderdduizend*, 109. In Westerbork, a number of other lists were written up to prepare for the transport to Auschwitz. On list A, no. 17, the five members of the Löb family are listed.

[40] See Kempner, *Twee uit honderdduizend*, 127.

After the death of seven of the Löb siblings, one memorial card was printed for them all. Some of the Scripture passages that were printed on this card reveal the faith-filled attitude with which the Trappists entrusted the fellow members of their order to God. "Truly God is good to the upright, to those who are pure in heart" (Ps 73:1).

"In this life they loved one another; therefore they were not parted in death" (Liturgy). "Behold, I am coming to you in a thick cloud" (Ex 19:9).

> We read these words in the Book of Moses that recounts the Exodus of the Jews. We can apply these words to these chosen souls, who came from that same people to whom God appeared on the holy mountain. The holy mountain is the contemplative cloister. On that mountain, they were praying during the night, when the dark cloud descended upon them. From a purely human perspective, this cloud, ominous and inescapable, would be nothing more than a threat. From this cloud, however, they heard the voice of God. Though each had his own path, they were one in their noble surrender to God's holy will, and they recognized with joy their chosen lot. And we saw them go.

The memorial card concludes with a quote from the book of Wisdom: "In the eyes of the foolish they seemed to have died, ... but they are at peace.... God tested them and found them worthy of himself" (Wis 3:2–5).

As was noted, Louise Löb, who was Thea's twin sister and called Wies, was not arrested with her sisters. She did, however, have to report to the police. She was taken prisoner on April 1, 1943, and brought to Westerbork where she stayed April 9–17, 1943.[41] It is not entirely clear why she was released. Was it because she was sick?[42] Louise, whose religious name was Sister Veronica, did not return to her abbey but went into hiding. Among the places she stayed were the convent of the Sisters of Oisterwijk and the Elisabeth Hospital in Tilburg.

On July 21, 1944, she returned to her own community. She died in the Abbey of Our Lady of Koningsoord in Berkel-Enschot on August 1, 1944, and was buried in the abbey cemetery.[43] The common memorial card says the following about her: "Sister Veronica, the one who quietly endured, died in her cloister after experiencing painful suffering and persecution."

Paula, the youngest, was the only one of the eight children from the Löb family to survive the Second World War. Before the war, Paula had already married Harrie van Broekhoven. In May 1942, their son was born. Separated from husband and child, she went into hiding with a family in Nijmegen until the end of the war. She died in 2004 at the age of eighty-five. The urn with her ashes was placed on the grave of Sister Veronica in the cemetery of the Cistercians in Berkel-Enschot.[44]

Many Jewish families were exterminated by the Nazis. Even those Catholic Jews who had been called to the hidden life of contemplation were not given leave to live in the cloister. Even though they harmed no one, life was denied them because they were Catholic and Jewish.

---

[41] See the Archive of Koningshoeven.

[42] See Mohr and Prégardier, *Passion im August*, 219.

[43] See the Archive of Koningshoeven; Kempner, *Twee uit honderdduizend*, 127.

[44] See Mohr and Prégardier, *Passion im August*, 219.

Sister Hedwigis Löb, O.C.S.O.

Lien Löb was born on March 3, 1908, in Rijswijk and baptized on the same day. Since her parents were crypto-Catholics, the baptism took place in secret. She was confirmed on October 21, 1921, in the parish church of Our Lady of Good Counsel in The Hague.

In 1922, Lien went to the three-year high school in Bergen op Zoom. In September 1923, she transferred to the teacher training school in the same city. In January 1925, she went to the teacher training school of the Sisters of Jesus, Mary, and Joseph (Zusters J.M.J. [Jezus, Maria en Jozef]) in Hoogerheide. On June 11, 1927, she passed the teacher's examination, and on October 5 she became a teacher at the Maria School in Woensdrecht.

Sister Hedwigis Löb, O.C.S.O.

She wanted to become a Cistercian nun. On April 18, 1928, she entered the Abbey of Our Lady of Peace in Chimay. She was twenty years old and was the first Dutch postulant in this convent. On September 4 of that same year, she received the habit of the order and was given the religious name Sister Hedwigis. She made her temporary profession on May 4, 1930, and her final profession on May 4, 1933.

Dom Simon had said to Sister Hedwigis, "I am going to build an abbey for you." When the land for the Cistercian Abbey in Berkel-Enschot was purchased in 1930, Sister Hedwigis co-signed the contract. This was especially noteworthy because she was not yet finally professed at that time. On July 15, 1937, Sister Hedwigis transferred to the Cistercian Abbey of Our Lady of Koningsoord in Berkel-Enschot.

She had many talents: she was musical, played the mandolin, and drew. She was known as a creative, joyful, and spontaneous woman. In the abbey she served, among other things, as portress and librarian.[45]

Sister Hedwigis "had something motherly about her and was wholly absorbed with the thought of sacrifice and penance. Like the others, she lived her religious life for one intention: the conversion of the Jews."[46]

The memorial card describes her as follows: "Sister Hedwigis, the maternally caring one, full of joyful warmth, with a ready spirit of sacrifice and an inner spirit of prayer."

[45] See the website of the Abbey of Our Lady of Koningshoeven.
[46] Bromberg, "Trappisten met davidster" (January 22).

Father Ignatius Löb, O.C.S.O.

George Löb was born on September 25, 1909, in Hoensbroek and was baptized in secret on the same day. He was confirmed in the parish of Our Lady of Good Counsel in The Hague on October 21, 1921. On October 2, 1923, he began his studies in the minor seminary of the Fathers of the Sacred Heart (Priesters van het H. Hart) in Bergen op Zoom. He concluded his secondary studies at the Saint Bernard High School run by the Cistercians in Pey-Echt in Limburg. Afterward, he entered the Cistercians of the Abbey of Our Lady of Koningshoeven in Berkel-Enschot on August 27, 1926.

Father Ignatius Löb, O.C.S.O.

On September 25, 1926, he received the habit and his religious name, Ignatius. He made his temporary profession on September 30, 1928, and his final profession on the same date in 1931. He was ordained a priest on June 6, 1936, by the Bishop of Den Bosch, the Most Reverend Arnold Frans Diepen (1919–1943). On July 20, 1936, he went to the Abbey of Our Lady of Bonnecombe (France) and returned to Koningshoeven on September 1, 1939.[47]

Father Ignatius was drawn more to the practical than to the contemplative aspect of religious life. "He had something of an engineer in him, but he was a man of faith and deeply pious. He had a special devotion to his guardian angel."[48] He was musical, served as cantor, and played the cello in the abbey.[49]

The memorial card describes him with the following words: "Father Ignatius, the warm and exuberant one, ever rejoicing with the joy of the children of God."

Notes about a remarkable but unclear letter about Father Ignatius and Father Nivardus are preserved. In April (or August) 1944, an otherwise unidentified Mr. Israel Polak from Amsterdam wrote a letter to the Abbey of Our Lady of Koningshoeven. Abbot Simon had Father Leo read it. The letter has since been lost, but Father Leo reconstructed its contents from memory on June 18, 1946, in a letter to Father Seraphinus. Father Leo wrote:

Reverend Superior,
    The undersigned has escaped from the Jewish Camp in Poland (Bochnia) a few months ago and after many

---

[47] See the Archive of Koningshoeven.
[48] Bromberg, "Trappisten met davidster" (January 22).
[49] See the website of the Abbey of Our Lady of Koningshoeven.

difficulties has arrived in his homeland. You will be glad to know that I met two priests from your abbey in Poland. They were always very cheerful and friendly to everyone. I spoke numerous times with them about the abbey, and they often spoke of Mary. On June 13 [1943, Pentecost] they were both unexpectedly shot to death. Those killed that day were two Polish priests, two Greek priests with long hair and long beards, and the two religious from your abbey. At the moment of execution, the Father (Nivardus) called out loud, "For the novitiate of Koningshoeven and for its inhabitants!"

I am on my way to England. If it is possible, I will come by to tell you a few details, but you understand that this is very risky. With high esteem, Isr. Polak.[50]

According to this letter, Father Nivardus and Father Ignatius were shot by a firing squad in the Polish concentration camp near Bochnia, between Kraków and Tarnów. However, Mr. Israel Polak never appeared at the abbey, and it was therefore assumed that this was a Nazi scheme whose purpose was to elicit a response providing grounds for further arrests.[51] If, however, this information is authentic, then the date of death for both priests would need to be corrected.

Brother Linus Löb, O.C.S.O.

Rob Löb was born on October 15, 1910, in The Hague. He was not baptized until January 22, 1911, in Padang, Indonesia. Father H. C. Verbraak, S.J., administered the sacrament to him. He was confirmed in the parish church

---

[50] The Reverend Leo, O.C.R., as quoted in the Archive of Koningshoeven.
[51] See the Dutch Red Cross: File EU 141.026.

Brother Linus Löb, O.C.S.O.

of Our Lady of Good Counsel in The Hague on October 21, 1921.

From February 26, 1924, until February 26, 1925, he attended the minor seminary of Saint Joseph run by the Marianist priests in Hulst. He later entered the Capuchins in Udenhout on October 18, 1926, and received the habit three days later. His religious name was Benjamin. On July 13, 1927, he began the novitiate. He left the Capuchins on March 25, 1928, and on the same day entered the Trappists of Koningshoeven. He received the religious habit on September 26, 1928, and the religious name Brother Linus. On March 19, 1931, he made his temporary profession, which he renewed on March 11, 1934. Brother Linus made his final profession on March 19, 1937.[52]

---

[52] See the Archive of Koningshoeven.

According to a report of the International Tracing Service (Bad Arolsen) from 1990, Robert Löb died at 4:20 P.M. on September 6, 1943, from a weak heart and poor circulation. However, the official date of death remains September 30, 1942.[53]

His fellow brothers described Brother Linus as follows: "He had a light-hearted and cheerful nature and liked to make a joke out of everything. One could not call him an example of observance of the rule, but he was persevering and faithful, and that is what counts in the end."[54]

As a lay brother, he worked mainly on the farm. He was creative and technically adept. At the beginning of the war he had secretly made a radio (the occupying forces did not allow the possession of radios), for which the abbot who was making a visitation admonished him.

From Amersfoort, he wrote a letter to the community in which he asked forgiveness for the "bad example he had given and that he hoped to be able to make up for much of it."[55]

The memorial card describes Brother Linus with these words: "Brother Linus, the cheerful and carefree one, who deep in his heart was movingly loyal to Jesus."

Sister Maria-Theresia Löb, O.C.S.O.

Dorothea (Thea) Löb was Louise's twin sister. She was born in Sawah-Loento on October 22, 1911, and was baptized by Father J., Erftemeijer, S.J., in the city of her

---

[53] See the Dutch Red Cross: File EU 141.029.
[54] As quoted in Bromberg, "Trappisten met davidster" (January 22).
[55] As quoted in Bromberg, "Trappisten met davidster" (January 29).

Sister Maria-Theresia Löb, O.C.S.O.

birth. She was confirmed on October 21, 1921, in the
parish church of Our Lady of Good Counsel in The
Hague.

Thea and Wies studied together at the Franciscan Sisters' school in Etten en Leur from September 1924 until
March 1925. They took part in the course required for
admittance to teacher training school. Thea was only seventeen years old when she entered the Cistercians of Our
Lady of Peace in Chimay on April 12, 1929. She received
the habit on the following October 20 as well as the
religious name Sister Maria-Theresia. She made her temporary profession on April 21, 1931, and her final profession on May 13, 1934. On July 15, 1937, she transferred
to the Abbey of Our Lady of Koningsoord in Berkel-
Enschot. At this abbey, Sister Maria-Theresia had the task

of sewing and taking care of flowers, insofar as her weak health permitted.

"She had the piety and the strong faith of her parents. She, too, wanted to give her life for the conversion of the Jews." [56]

The memorial card describes her as follows: "Sister Maria-Theresia, a devoted child of Mary, who was ardent in honoring the Mother of God."

Father Nivardus Löb, O.C.S.O.

Ernst Löb was born in Sawah-Loento on October 29, 1913, and was baptized by Father Dionysius Pessers, O.F.M.

Father Nivardus Löb, O.C.S.O.

[56] Website of the Abbey of Our Lady of Koningshoeven.

Cap., on January 15, 1914. Ernst completed his entire secondary education at the Saint Bernard High School in Pey-Echt (September 6, 1926, until July 26, 1929). On August 20, 1929, he entered the Abbey of Koningshoeven in Tilburg. He received the habit and his religious name, Nivardus, on September 27 of the same year. He made his temporary profession on September 29, 1931. He renewed his temporary profession on October 21, 1934, and made his final profession on September 29, 1935. The Most Reverend A. F. Diepen, Bishop of Den Bosch, ordained him a priest on June 3, 1939.[57]

Father Nivardus was exceptional in the fulfillment of the duties of the religious life. He lived in the continuous presence of God. His fellow brothers said about him, "His name was Ernst,[58] and he was seriousness itself; that is, he had a wholly supernatural outlook. With all his dignity, he was always friendly and attentive, truly lovable. Every once in a while, the heavens shone forth from his big, shining eyes." [59]

One of Father Nivardus' former brothers in the Abbey of Koningshoeven, the Carmelite Father Edwin Peters, recounts:

> Father Nivardus Löb was my assistant novice master. We loved him very much, because he was the "deepest" Löb. Since we, as is typical in all novitiates, were not permitted to have contact with the professed, I knew Father Ignatius and Brother Linus only by sight, but I knew Father Nivardus from our daily life together. Father

[57] See the Archive of Koningshoeven.
[58] The Dutch word "ernst" means "seriousness".—Trans.
[59] As quoted in Bromberg, "Trappisten met davidster" (January 22).

Nivardus had had the desire to be a martyr from his childhood onward. In a personal conversation with me, he once said that it would not be at all difficult for God to make a martyr out of a Trappist. When the order came that the Jews had to wear the star, he sometimes pinned it on as a joke when we had to go to work.[60]

On the afternoon of Saturday, August 1, (1942), we novices had to prepare the vegetables for Sunday. As usual, Father Nivardus was with us, and he had once again put on his star. As we were working, he suddenly said, "Who will eat from these vegetables tomorrow? Perhaps there is one among us who will no longer eat them." Then he laughed over the seriousness of his interjection and the tension it had caused.[61]

Neither Father Nivardus nor his brothers ever ate those vegetables.

The memorial card says of him: "Father Nivardus, the serious one, the monk through-and-through, who penetrated ever more intensely the thoughts of God and the immense love of Jesus."

Hans Jozef Löb

Hans Löb was born on October 11, 1916, in Sawah-Loento. On October 22, 1916, he was baptized there by Father Rupertus Verbruge, O.F.M., Cap.

From January 30, 1928, until July 28, 1932, Hans attended the Saint Bernard High School in Pey-Echt.

---

[60] Since the Cistercians are contemplative and never went outside the abbey, they did not need to wear the Jewish star. This is the reason that Father Nivardus pinned the star on as a joke.—TRANS.

[61] The Reverend Edwin Peters, as quoted in Kempner, *Twee uit honderdduizend*, 128.

Hans Jozef Löb

Beginning in 1932, he continued his secondary education at the Catholic high school in Bergen op Zoom, where his father also taught. On June 26, 1935, he passed the final examination.

Hans was the only one of the Löb brothers who never became a monk. On June 13, 1936, Hans moved to Berkel-Enschot, where he became a technical artist for the Tempofoon British Import Company in Tilburg (from April 1, 1937, until September 20, 1938). On December 13, 1939, he moved to Monster to work for Paul Löb in The Hague.

He attempted to escape the Nazi persecution by going into hiding.[62] On December 30, 1942, his name was

---

[62] See Mohr and Prégardier, *Passion im August*, 219.

removed from the register of Monster with the comment "unknown destination".

Despite his attempt to keep a low profile, Hans was nonetheless arrested and taken to Westerbork on August 28, 1942. From there he left for Auschwitz on August 31. The twenty-six-year-old man was selected for forced labor in the area of Auschwitz. As a prisoner, the number 177886 was tattooed on his arm. He was put to work in the Blechhammer labor camp.[63]

As the Russian troops came through Poland heading west, Hans Löb was put on a transport going the same direction. On February 10, 1945, he was taken from the Gross-Rosen concentration camp to Buchenwald. On the way there both his feet froze, and he died from this on February 18, 1945.[64]

The common memorial card states the following about Hans: "Their brother Hans was released from his earthly suffering on February 20, 1945, in Buchenwald. We have the firm confidence that he has received the reward for his steadfast faith."

On October 25, 1946, the Polish Tomas Wictor, wrote a letter about his experience in the concentration camp in Blechhammer. In his letter, he speaks about Hans Löb, who was a fellow prisoner in Blechhammer:

"It was in 1943. Hans sold his portion of food, in order to use the money to have a Mass offered for the repose of his father's soul. It was truly a heroic deed.

[63] See the Archive of Koningshoeven; Kempner, *Twee uit honderdduizend*, 131.
[64] See documents of the Red Cross, in Kempner, *Twee uit honderdduizend*, 127, 131.

Happy the parents who have raised such a son! The whole time that I knew him, he went to confession in writing twice a year. Although I tried, I did not succeed in bringing him Holy Communion.... In the end, justice shall be victorious, because no one can conquer God." [65]

[65] Thomas Wictor, as quoted in Steffen and Evers, 425.

Chapter 9

DR. LISAMARIA MEIROWSKY

Lisamaria Meirowsky was born on September 7, 1904, in Grudziądz, near the Vistula River. From 1772 until 1920 this area belonged to Prussia. Her father, Professor Dr. Emil Meirowsky (1876–1960), was born in Guttstadt in Eastern Prussia. He studied medicine at Königsberg

Dr. Lisamaria Meirowsky
Photo: © Kommission für Zeitgeschichte, Bonn, Germany

(Kaliningrad) and specialized in dermatology. He had his practice in Grudziądz until he moved to Cologne-Lindenthal (Germany) in 1908. His brother had already lived there for a long time. Lisamaria's brother, Max Arnold, was born in 1910. They were a well-to-do family. In Cologne, Emil opened a practice, where he also had a laboratory. He later became a professor at the university and the head of the board of physicians in Cologne.

On November 24, 1933, Professor Emil Meirowsky was forbidden to teach at the university; in February 1936, he was divested of his academic titles; in 1938, he was forbidden to practice his profession; and in 1939, he fled with his wife and son to England. In 1947, he left England for the United States.[1]

Lisamaria attended the girls' high school[2] in Cologne. A diocesan priest from this city, Father Wilhelm Neuss, taught religion and mathematics there. After her graduation in 1923, Lisamaria went to Bonn (Germany) to study medicine at the Friedrich Wilhelms University. Here she came into contact with Father Wilhelm Neuss once again, because he had in the meantime become a professor at the university. It was to him that she first spoke about joining the Church. He also gave her religious instruction. From 1925 until 1927 she studied in Munich (Germany). Afterward, she returned to Bonn in order to take her last examinations there in 1929. In a letter of August

---

[1] See A. Mohr and E. Prégardier, eds., *Passion im August (2.–9. August 1942): Edith Stein und Gefährtinnen: Weg in Tod und Auferstehung*, Zeugen der Zeitgeschichte, 5 (Annweiler: Plöger, 1995), 197; Prégadier, in H. Moll, ed., *Zeugen für Christus: Das deutsche Martyrologium des 20. Jahrhunderts*, 2 vols. (Paderborn, 1999), 310.

[2] Lisamaria attended a *gymnasium*.—TRANS.

18, 1927, to Father Neuss, Lisamaria expressed great doubt about whether or not she wanted to become Catholic. She was grateful that the Church had helped her to come to know God, but she realized that it is not sufficient to know God. She writes that "one has to search for God again and again; otherwise, one loses him".[3]

In April 1933, she obtained her doctorate with a dissertation in the field of dermatology. She had always had poor health, and after obtaining her doctorate, she became so ill that she was in danger of dying. After her recovery, she once again took up contact with Father Neuss. He referred her to Father Josef Könn, parish priest at Holy Apostles church in Cologne, for religious instruction and further preparation for reception into the Church. On the Solemnity of the Assumption of Our Lady, August 15, 1933, the twenty-nine-year-old Lisamaria was baptized in the chapel of the Hospital of the Knights of Malta in Bonn. Father Neuss administered the sacrament that freed her from original sin, gave her God as Father, and made her a member of the Catholic Church. Her father and mother did not oppose her baptism.

After her baptism, Lisamaria went once more to Munich, where she became a scientific assistant at the university. As a Jew, she was soon restricted in her scientific work by Nazi officials. Perhaps this was the reason that she left for Rome. Here, too, she studied medicine and obtained a second doctorate. It is possible that this dissertation pertained to pediatrics, because she is more than once referred to as a pediatrician. In Rome she met Father Franciscus Stratmann, O.P. (1883–1971), who had

---

[3] Lisamaria Meirowsky, as quoted by Prégadier, in Moll, *Zeugen*, 309.

fled from Germany. He wanted to found a congregation of Dominican sisters with the name Pax Christi in regno Dei (Peace of Christ in the Kingdom of God). They would be called the Dominican Sisters of Christ the King. His idea was inspired by the Pope Pius XI's encyclical *Quas primae*, about Christ the King, issued on December 11, 1925. Father Stratmann, O.P., came to know Lisamaria "as a childlike and pious soul, who surpassed many cradle Catholics in faith, hope, and charity."[4] In the cell where Saint Dominic had lived near the church of Santa Sabina, Lisamaria Meirowsky was invested as a Third-Order member of Saint Dominic. She received the name Maria Magdalena Dominica.[5]

In 1938, Father Stratmann and Lisamaria Meirowsky went to Utrecht in order to dedicate themselves to assisting Jews who had fled from Nazi-controlled areas. Professor Schmutzer had established an organization to this end. After the invasion of the Germans on May 10, 1940, Father Stratmann and Dr. Meirowsky had to go into hiding. The former found refuge in a Belgian convent of Dominican sisters. Lisamaria was lovingly received by Cistercian nuns on August 14, 1940. She was permitted to live in the gatehouse of the Abbey of Our Lady of Koningsoord in Berkel-Enschot (not far from Tilburg). She made herself useful there as portress, physician, and nurse. She also worked in the garden.[6]

---

[4] The Reverend Franciscus Stratmann, O.P., as quoted in *Als een brandende toorts: Documentaire getuigenissen over Dr. Edith Stein (zuster Teresia Benedicta a Cruce) en medeslachtoffers* (Echt: Friends of Dr. Edith Stein, 1967), 207.

[5] See Mohr and Prégardier, *Passion im August*, 197–99; Prégardier in Moll, *Zeugen*, 310.

[6] See *Als een brandende toorts*, 160; Mohr and Prégardier, *Passion im August*, 199.

She maintained regular contact with Father Stratmann by mail, sending letters to him via a convent in Lier (Belgium). He received her last letter on August 9, 1942, the day on which she probably died.[7] In this letter Lisamaria relates a story that speaks of her readiness to suffer and also her readiness to accept suffering in place of others. She recounts:

At the beginning of the war, I read a true short story. An old farmer, who was a passionate smoker and whose only son was at the front, laid his pipe in the cabinet. With this sacrifice, together with his prayers, he wanted to beg God to preserve the life of his son. Soon afterward, news came that his son had been the first one in the infantry to die. When someone remarked to him that his sacrifice had been in vain and that God had not heard his prayers, he replied full of faith, "I am sure that the dear Lord has accepted my sacrifice and that he helped my boy to die a good and holy death. And now," the farmer continued, "I will no longer touch this pipe as long as the war lasts, and I will bring this sacrifice for another soul."[8]

In response to the Dutch bishops' protest against the persecution of the Jews, Dr. Lisamaria Meirowsky was arrested early on the morning of August 2, 1942. Together with the two sisters Sister Hedwigis Löb and Sister Maria-Theresia Löb, she was taken from the Trappistine Abbey of Berkel-Enschot and brought to Amersfoort by way of the Cistercian Abbey of Our Lady of Koningshoeven.

---

[7] See F. Stratmann, *In der Verbannung: Tagebuchblätter 1940–1947* (Frankfurt, 1962), 194.

[8] Lisamaria Meirowsky, as quoted in Stratmann, *Verbannung*, 253–54.

On the evening of August 2, sixteen Catholic Jews from
Tilburg and its environs arrived in Amersfoort.[9]

On Tuesday, August 4, the prisoners were brought to
Westerbork. Together with the other religious, they were
housed in barrack 36.[10] Dr. Meirowsky, as a medical
expert, was put to work in caring for the arrestees. She
was, therefore, dressed as a nurse and wore a Red Cross
armband for the duration of her detention in the camp.
Despite her work, she found the opportunity to be in
written communication with the home front. On August
5, she wrote a telegram, a postcard, and a letter to the
Cistercian Abbey in Berkel-Enschot from Westerbork. She
asked the nuns to send all manner of necessary things by
means of a courier, especially clothing, a bag with bandages, food vouchers, her certificate of birth and baptism, and the certificate that permitted her to practice
her medical profession. For her spiritual life, she asked
for a number of books: the Dominican breviary, the
Roman Missal (*Missale Romanum*), the *Manual of Christianity* (*Manuale Christianum*), Prayers of St. Gertrude (*Pre-
ces Gertrudianae*); Garrigou-Lagrange, *Three Stages of the
Spiritual Life* (*Trois âges de la vie intérieure*), *Captivated by
the Trinity* (*Im Banne der Dreieinigkeit*); Bernadot, *Our Lady
in My Life* (*Notre Dame dans ma vie*). In her letter, she
asked them to save all her other things.[11]

---

[9] See R. Kempner, *Twee uit honderdduizend, Anne Frank en Edith Stein:
Onthullingen over de nazimisdaden in Nederland voor het gerecht in München*
(Bilthoven, 1969), 105 and 108. In the list that was drawn up there on August
4, 1942, Lisamaria Meirowsky is no. 26, coming after the two sisters and
before the three brothers of the Löb Family.

[10] See Prégadier in Moll, *Zeugen*, 142.

[11] See Mohr and Prégardier, *Passion im August*, 202–5; Prégadier in Moll,
Zeugen, 311.

On the Feast of the Transfiguration of the Lord (August 6, 1942), Lisamaria Meirowsky wrote, in pencil, an impressive farewell letter from the Westerbork camp to her former confessor, Father Matthias Frehe, O.P. (who died in 1967). This priest had also been the spiritual director of Sister Judith Mendes da Costa, O.P., a fellow detainee of Lisamaria's in Westerbork. Dr. Meirowsky writes to Father Frehe:

> You surely know that we are here and that we are awaiting our departure to Poland. Tomorrow morning we will leave to go there. With me are two Trappistine nuns, two religious priests, and a lay brother from the abbey. All of us were picked up early on Sunday morning and brought to the Amersfoort camp. On Tuesday, the Feast of our Holy Father Saint Dominic (August 4), we were taken to Westerbork near Hooghalen. I know, good Father, that in everything and with everything, you empathize with us. Your spiritual child, Sister Judith, is also here, as is the Carmelite from Echt whom I met that time in Amsterdam. For exactly this reason, I want to send you a last greeting and to tell you that I am full of confidence and wholly surrendered to God's holy will. Even more, I consider it a grace and election to have to leave under these circumstances and in this way to give witness to the words of our fathers and shepherds in Christ.[12]

The circumstances to which Dr. Meirowsky refers is the July 26, 1942, letter of the Dutch bishops, in which they protested against the Jewish persecution. She considered

---

[12] Lisamaria Meirowsky, as quoted by Stratmann in *Als een brandende toorts*, 208. See also Posselt, *Edith Stein: The Life of a Philosopher and Carmelite*, 219–21, for a slightly different English translation of the entire letter.

it "a grace and an election" to be a prisoner and to endure whatever would come for the sake of the bishops' actions, for the faith, and for the way of life corresponding to it. As a Catholic, she considered it an honor and election that she was allowed to suffer for the Church; and with conviction, she placed her very life at her disposal.

Her letter continues:

Even if our suffering has increased somewhat, the grace we receive from God has increased doubly, and a wonderful crown is prepared for us in heaven. Rejoice with me: I go with courage, confidence, and joy—as do the religious who go with me. We are permitted to bear witness to Jesus, and with our bishops we are allowed to bear witness to the truth. We go as children of our Mother, the Church, and want to unite our suffering with that of our King, Redeemer, and Bridegroom. We want to offer our suffering for the conversion of many, for the Jews, for those who persecute us: thereby we want to contribute to peace in the Kingdom of Christ.

In case I do not survive, would you be so good as to write my beloved parents and brothers later and tell them that the sacrifice of my life was for them? May God grant them the light of faith and eternal and temporal happiness, if it is his will. Please convey to them all my love and gratitude, and tell them that I ask forgiveness for all the wrong I may have done and the suffering that I may have brought them. Please also tell them that my mother's sisters and my father's twin sisters left for the camps in Poland filled with faith, confidence, and surrender. Please also greet my sister-in-law and my little nieces. I pray for their souls with all my heart.

There is little that I need to convey about my spiritual father, Father Franciscus Stratmann. He will be able to remain calm when he hears that I am happy to be able to bring this pure sacrifice, that I accept in advance everything that may still come by way of suffering, and that I offer it as a holocaust of love to the Most Holy Trinity. By this offering, in union with my Redeemer and Bridegroom, may I adore, praise, and give thanks for God's grace, do penance for all our sins and those of others, and beg for a holy death—both for ourselves and those to whom God will grant it. I offer all for peace with God, peace on earth, and the spread of the Kingdom of Jesus through Mary. Please tell that good and very dear Father that he need not be sad but, on the contrary, should thank God with me and join me in singing a *jubilant Magnificat*. The work that we began together will be accomplished when, where, and how God wills. Thus, I will cooperate in it in the most fervent and best possible way, be it through my small suffering—which is nothing in comparison to the joy of eternity that awaits us—or be it through my assistance from above.[13]

If you have the opportunity later, can you go or write to the abbey in Tilburg and tell Father Willibrordus van Dijk that I always pray for him with gratitude? I will personally still write to Mother Abbess and Father Chaplain [of Berkel-Enschot], who was my confessor. All our good friends and acquaintances participate in our prayers and sacrifice. Please also write Mrs. Schmutzer in Utrecht. In a special way, I ask for extra prayers for the good Dr. Lazarus, who is in the

[13] Ibid., 208–9.

camp in Amersfoort (he had not worn the star). I pray much for him myself.

In conclusion, I thank you once more for your goodness to me and for your more than merciful love of neighbor. You have so often encouraged me. Now we no longer have even Holy Mass or Holy Communion. This is the worst part. But if Jesus does not want it, then I do not want it either. He lives in my heart and goes with us to give us strength. He is my strength and my peace. As soon as I can write again, you will hear from me. Would you be so kind (if you agree with it, that is,) to write me on a postcard prestamped for international mail (but not with a prepaid reply)? May Mary protect you and may God's love continue to sanctify you. Once more I humbly ask for your prayers and your priestly blessing.

In Jesus and Mary,
your Sister M. Magdalena Dominica (in the world Meirowsky, physician)[14]

As remarked in chapter 1, Dr. Meirowsky included a note for Archbishop de Jong in which she declares herself "happy to be able to help him with our sacrifice" and that he "can be at peace and must never think that we regret his action."[15]

Abbot Simon from the Cistercian Abbey of Our Lady of Koningshoeven sent Mr. van Riel, representative of the Trappist brewery, the Sheep Gate (De Schaapskooi), to Westerbork on August 6. He was the courier who

---

[14] Sister Teresia Renata de Spiritu Sancto Posselt, Edith Stein: Jodin, geleerde, Carmelites (Bilthoven, 1952), 244. The entire letter is printed here in another Dutch translation, see 242ff.

[15] Lisamaria Meirowsky, as quoted in Kempner, Twee uit honderdduizend, 132.

brought the things requested by the prisoners. He succeeded in speaking with the priests and sisters from Berkel-
Enschot as well as with Lisamaria Meirowsky.[16] While
waiting for the train at the station in Hooghalen on Friday, August 7, to return to Tilburg, it became clear to
him that the prisoners had already been put on a transport for the east during the night.[17]

Upon arriving at the train station in Auschwitz, Dr.
Lisamaria Meirowsky was probably brought directly to
the gas chamber, together with the majority of the religious. After she was murdered there, she was probably
placed in the same mass grave where Saint Teresa Benedicta of the Cross, along with the others, was buried.

Because Father Stratmann had received no mail from
Lisamaria Meirowsky for an extended time, he asked about
her at the Trappistine Abbey in Berkel-Enschot through
a Dominican prioress. The abbey sent him the response
through a nun who had had much contact with Lisamaria Meirowsky. On March 10, 1943, she wrote to Father
Stratmann concerning how Dr. Meirowsky was deported
on August 2, 1942, along with two "non-Arian" nuns
from the community. The Trappistine nun writes with
uncertainty about their fate:

Our Reverend Mother sent me to the parlor from time
to time to speak with Lisamaria. This past summer, I
was impressed by the seriousness with which she

---

[16] See Prégadier in Moll, *Zeugen*, 311.

[17] See NIOD Archive 250 I, Westerbork camp, inventory no. 239; Kempner, *Twee uit honderdduizend*, 109. On list A that was drawn up in Westerbork
on August 7, 1942, in preparation for the transport, Lisamaria's name is no. 17
and is listed before the Löb family. Her date of birth appears incorrectly on
this list.

considered the possibility of her own death. She asked
me to tell her everything I knew about death that could
be consoling, and she committed these things to memory. I had the impression that God was preparing her
for a great sacrifice. May my impression not become
reality![18]

From Lisamaria's letters to Father Stratmann, it had
likewise become clear to him that she had been preparing for her death during this last year. She collected
prayers on this topic, for example, and wrote them out.
One of those prayers was about uniting oneself with all
the Holy Masses that would be celebrated at the moment
of one's own death (one had calculated that worldwide
about four Holy Masses per second were celebrated).
This was probably a prayer used by the movement of
the Eucharistic Crusade. In her second-to-last letter, she
disclosed that she spent five minutes daily preparing herself for death. She wrote that her concern with the "last
things" was taking more of her time. Father Stratmann
thinks that she was preparing herself for death because
she felt inspired to do so by the Holy Spirit.[19] In this
way, God was preparing Lisamaria for the great sacrifices that lay in her future: being arrested; being torn
away from the religious atmosphere where she felt so at
home; being unable to participate in the Holy Mass; no
longer being able to receive Holy Communion or the
sacrament of penance; being treated as one ostracized;
and, lastly, having to give the sacrifice of her life in the
gas chambers of Auschwitz-Birkenau.

[18] As quoted in Stratmann, *Verbannung*, 195–96.
[19] See ibid., 196.

As her spiritual father, Father Stratmann had an inner bond with her. In his diary, this Dominican writes about Lisamaria Meirowsky in May 1943:

> I have known very few people in whom the super-natural disposition was so developed. Her nature was not immaculate, but this does mean that she did not have beautiful gifts, such as a great generosity. But she was sufficiently humble—humility was her strongest virtue—to recognize her own deficiencies and to work to overcome them. She was so intensely directed to the supernatural that she lost nearly all interest in other things. Her passionate nature, her genuine childlike-ness and awareness of her own weaknesses, together with God's help and her devout love for Jesus, laid the foundation for her sanctity. If she is no longer alive, I have lost my dearest child as well as a most promising coworker in the apostolate. But I can hardly mourn over her. She is probably already enjoying eternal bliss; and since her love and her suffering will have already burned away any deficiencies, purification in the here-after will hardly have been necessary. The planned founding of a congregation of Dominican nuns (Pax Christi), which I had wanted to accomplish with her, has now most likely become unfeasible. But I am sure that she will help me from heaven as she would have on earth.[20]

The letter that Dr. Meirowsky sent to her former con-fessor, Father Frehe, from Westerbork on August 6, 1942, was also sent to Father Stratmann. He copied it and sent it to her parents in the United States, accompanied by a

[20] Ibid.

ten-page letter informing them about their daughter.[21] Her father, who had no faith, wrote to Father Stratmann: "It is almost impossible for us to get over this blow. All our thoughts, day and night, are of her, and all our own worries and difficulties have lost their meaning. We have spiritually and physically collapsed, and for us there is unfortunately no consolation. It is truly a miracle how much strength the faith gave her. Her last letter to Father Frehe is a shocking document of her inner perfection and purity."[22]

[21] See ibid., 253.
[22] As quoted in ibid.

Chapter 10

THE BOCK FAMILY

Besides father and mother, the Bock-Grünbaum family consisted of three daughters: Edith, Resi, and Leni. They lived in Vienna (Austria). The father, Samuel, was born on August 17, 1875, in Wazau (Moravia) and was an attorney or legal advisor. The mother, Hermine Merkelbach, was born in Leobersdorf (Austria) on September 29, 1886.

The three daughters were all born in Vienna. Edith, the oldest, was born on August 23 (or 29), 1907. The second daughter, Thérèse or Resi Bock, was born on June 13, 1909. The third and youngest daughter, Helene (Leni) Louise, was born on June 25, 1912. The parents' marriage was not harmonious and ended in divorce.

After the divorce, Hermine moved to the Netherlands in 1920. On July 31, 1922, her three daughters left Vienna to join their mother in Rotterdam. On August 29, 1922, Hermine and her three daughters were baptized in Saint Elisabeth's Church in Rotterdam. The Most Reverend Augustinus Josephus Callier (1903–1928), Bishop of Haarlem, confirmed the four of them on October 16, 1922, in the same church where they had recently been baptized. Nothing is known about the way that the family came to the Church. It is clear that there was a longer period of preparation for their baptism, which in the mother's case must have taken place or at least been completed in the Netherlands. For the daughters, the majority of their Catholic formation must have taken place in Vienna. After her baptism and still that same year, Hermine married Willem Merkelbach-Van Enkhuizen.

Edith attended the teacher training school of the Sisters of Roosendaal (Zusters van Roosendaal) in Breda. From 1922 onward, Resi and Leni attended a boarding school run by the Sisters of the Sacred Heart (Zusters van het H. Hart) in Moerdijk. Leni attended the primary school, and Resi followed a course of studies in preparation for the teacher training school and then began the teaching courses proper.[1]

Sister Charitas Bock, S.S.C.J.

Resi Bock interrupted her studies at the teacher training school in Moerdijk in order to enter the Sisters of the Sacred Heart as a postulant on February 17, 1927. This congregation had been founded in Moerdijk in 1886, and the sisters had apostolates in teaching and nursing. In August 1927, Resi began her novitiate. On this occasion she received the habit and her religious name, Sister Charitas. From August 1927 until August 1928, she completed her canonical novitiate year, and on August 15, 1928, she made her first profession of vows.

Immediately afterward, she resumed and successfully completed her studies at the teacher training school. On

---

[1] See Sister Maria Theresita Munsters in *Als een brandende toorts: Documentaire getuigenissen over Dr. Edith Stein (zuster Teresia Benedicta a Cruce) en medeslachtoffers* (Echt: Friends of Dr. Edith Stein, 1967), 210–11.

Sister Charitas on the day of her final profession, August 15, 1931.
Photo from her congregation.

June 28, 1929, she received her diploma and was immediately assigned to teach at the primary school of Hazerswoude Rijndijk.[2] This school had been entrusted to
the Sisters of the Sacred Heart, and Sister Charitas
belonged to the community of St. Liduïna's Convent in
Hazerswoude.

On August 15, 1931, she made her final profession of
vows. On the remembrance card of her profession, she
wrote: "God alone as witness; Jesus Christ as example;
Mary as support, and then nothing, nothing except love
and sacrifice. Lord, in order to fulfill your request, I ask
you: Give your light to the poor heathens; and since the

[2] See ibid., 211.

harvest is so great, multiply the number of your laborers who work in the fields of your Church." [3]

From 1929 until 1940, Sister Charitas worked in Hazerswoude as teacher and youth minister. She could use her natural gifts of "firmness, handiness, imagination, and creativity" [4] in this work. Her sister Edith, who had in the meantime become a teacher in Rotterdam, supported her sister with suggestions for activities in teaching and in youth work.

Sister Charitas describes her own appearance as being "of medium height, oval face, black hair and grey eyes". [5] A few testimonies about her character have been preserved. The director of the teaching training school, Sister Theresia-Hermus (who died in 1955), describes Resi before her entrance to the congregation as "a quiet and serious girl, who thought more than she spoke". [6] Sister Charitas' correspondence also reveals her character. She is "a healthy woman without problems, a skilled practical woman, who worries little or not at all about herself and who reacts most soberly to the events of life. She appears to be all action and initiative, knows no rest, and daily drinks fully from the life that is given to her." [7]

As the war approached, her unrest increased. Because she was Jewish by birth, Sister Charitas' work permit was revoked on November 22, 1940, and she was no longer

[3] Sister Charitas Bock, as quoted in ibid., 212; A. Mohr and E. Prégardier, eds., *Passion im August (2.–9. August 1942): Edith Stein und Gefährtinnen: Weg in Tod und Auferstehung*, Zeugen der Zeitgeschichte, 5 (Annweiler: Plöger, 1995), 236.

[4] Munsters in *Als een brandende toorts*, 212.

[5] Sister Charitas Bock, as quoted in *Als een brandende toorts*, 211.

[6] Sister Theresia-Hermus, as quoted in *Als een brandende toorts*, 212.

[7] Ibid., 213.

allowed to work in the school, nor was she allowed to tutor. Sister Charitas writes about this: "That we have been ousted from our profession in this way! That is a cross that you feel every day anew."[8]

Early in December 1940, she was transferred to the convent in Moerdijk, where she was assigned work in the house. She was portress and assisted in caring for the boarding school girls.

On November 25, 1941, the Bock sisters, along with all other foreign Jews, were declared "stateless" when their citizenship was revoked.[9] Since their mother had married a Dutch man, she retained her Dutch nationality.[10]

Sister Charitas saw the danger of the Nazis approach very clearly. It did not escape her notice that she, as a Catholic Jew, was not safe from their inhumane plans. In Moerdijk, Sister Charitas once asked a fellow sister if she were afraid of the Germans. This sister responded in the negative. Sister Charitas responded, "You do not have to be afraid. . . . But I. . . . If it has to be, I will give my life for the preservation and blossoming of Catholic education in the Netherlands."[11] Her uncle, Wilhelm Grünbaum, her mother's brother, had been in a concentration camp but had escaped. From him, Sister Charitas knew how the Nazis could deal with people.[12]

In the context of the mass registration of the Jews, Sister Charitas also received numerous forms to complete. Although she was required to go to Amsterdam to

---

[8] Sister Charitas Bock, as quoted in *Als een brandende toorts*, 213.
[9] See ibid., 214.
[10] See Archive 250 F, Amersfoort camp, inventory no. 14.
[11] Sister Charitas Bock, as quoted in *Als een brandende toorts*, 215.
[12] See Mohr and Prégardier, *Passion im August*, 233.

complete formalities at the Jewish Council and the Gestapo office, she excused herself with a doctor's report indicating that she had stomach problems that were being treated. This was truly the case. Mr. F. Teulings from Vught, who served as episcopal liaison with the Jewish Council, arranged these matters for Sister Charitas.[13]

Sunday, August 2, 1942, was the first day of her annual retreat.[14] At 5:45 A.M., a local policeman from Hooge en Lage Zwaluwe rang the bell at the door of the Convent of the Sacred Heart in Moerdijk. There was no sign of life yet at the house. Since it was a Sunday during the school vacation, the Sisters had been permitted to sleep in.

After the portress had answered the doorbell, the policeman informed her that Sister Charitas had to come along to Breda. The portress informed Sister Hermus of the policeman's message. Sister Hermus went to Sister Charitas' room. She recounts, "When she saw me her first words were, 'Do I have to go?'"[15] The sisters fruitlessly attempted to avoid Sister Charitas' arrest. The policeman explained that he was personally responsible for her arrival in Breda before 7:00 A.M. Sister Hermus also called various authorities to ask for advice. Mr. Teulings from Vught, the legal advisor of the congregation who had put Sister Charitas' papers in order with the Jewish Council and other authorities, could not be reached. She called the bishop's house in Den Bosch. The Most Reverend Wilhelmus Petrus Mutsaerts (1943–1960) (who had only been ordained a bishop on June 29, 1942) was not home.

[13] See Munsters in *Als een brandende toorts*, 215–18.
[14] See J. Buitkamp, *Moerdijk van bezetting tot bevrijding* (Moerdijk, 1979), 13.
[15] Sister Theresia-Hermus, as quoted in *Als een brandende toorts*, 219.

His secretary advised her "to let the sister go, because there was no way to avoid it. I (that is, Sister Theresia-Hermus) asked if we could send along a second sister. Yes, that was good, because it is our custom always to have the sisters travel two by two when possible." [16]

Sister Hermus also informed the Diocese of Breda that the Catholic-Jewish Sister Charitas had been picked up. Before she left the convent, Sister Charitas had time to go to confession with the retreat master. She also received his blessing, and then she courageously said goodbye to her sisters.[17]

At the request of the superior, Sister Ignace de Bruin accompanied Sister Charitas. Sister Ignace, who had recently fled from Finland, recounts what happened after she and Sister Charitas left the convent:

Sister Charitas was perfectly calm. She quickly dressed in her habit.

> The men in the car made all sorts of excuses for what they had to do. Police vans with heavily armed soldiers were at the Kasteelplein [the castle square] in Breda when we arrived. We first had to go upstairs to an office where various old people were sitting. . . . At the office we were all snapped at terribly, and then all who were called had to go into the police vans. . . . Sister Charitas said to me, "Just act normal. Do not cry or anything like that. We cannot give them reason to have fun on our account", and she kept talking very much.
>
> I first wanted to go along. "Aber dann kommen Sie nicht mehr zurück" [but then you will not return], they said. And Sister Charitas did not want it either.

[16] As quoted in ibid.

[17] See Buitkamp, *Moerdijk*, 13.

"One is enough", she said. She did not yet know that her whole family had been picked up in the same way. And then they drove away, amidst the show of power from the soldiers with their weapons. And there I stood alone at the Kasteelplein, and a German officer then said to me, "This is the fault of your bishops who had that letter read in the churches." [18]

In the large police van that left from Breda, there were three other prisoners besides Sister Charitas: an older married couple and a young father who had had a Jewish grandmother. The young father had married a non-Jewish wife. They had two small children, but mother and children did not have to come.[19]

Sister Ignace realized that she would never again see Sister Charitas. She went to the bishop's residence in Breda, where she spoke with the Most Reverend Petrus Hopmans (1914–1951), Bishop of Breda. She told him what the German soldier had said. The bishop then called Archbishop J. de Jong. Sister Ignace concludes her account with the words, "Perhaps it was one of the first reports that Archbishop de Jong received about Seyss-Inquart's merciless retaliation measures." [20]

On August 3, a physician wrote a report in which he declared "that Sister Charitas has been in treatment for a year and a half already, that she must lead a very calm life, and that she must rest much".[21] With the intention

[18] Sister Ignace de Bruin, as quoted by Munsters in *Als een brandende toorts*, 220.

[19] See Buitkamp, *Moerdijk*, 13–14.

[20] Sister Ignace de Bruin, as quoted by Munsters in *Als een brandende toorts*, 220.

[21] As quoted in ibid.

of giving this physician's report more weight, the mayor from Zevenbergen also signed it.

From Westerbork Camp, Sister Charitas wrote her Mother Superior on Tuesday, August 4. She recounted what had happened after her arrest. From Breda she had been brought to Amersfoort.[22] There she met her mother, two sisters, and two other acquaintances from Vienna, as well as many unknown Jews, among whom were the Löb family and six or seven other women religious. The treatment was "*optima forma*", and the food was good. In Amersfoort she met Father R. Hegge. He had been arrested in January 1941, together with Father J. Galama and Father van Rooyen. The three priests had been taken from their parish in 's-Heerenberg. Father Hegge was the brother of one of Sister Charitas' fellow sisters, Sister Mansueta.

Her mother was not among the prisoners taken to Westerbork; rather, she stayed in Amersfoort. The group arrived in Westerbork on Tuesday, August 4, at 2:00 A.M. In her letter, Sister Charitas stated that she was exhausted and was in need of much sleep.[23]

In two telegrams from Wednesday, August 5, and a non-dated note, Sister Charitas asked her convent in Moerdijk for food, clothing, shoes, and medicines. She gave the following as the mailing address: "Barrack 36, Room 4, Lager Westerbork".[24] On Wednesday, August

[22] See R. Kempner, *Twee uit honderdduizend, Anne Frank en Edith Stein: Onthullingen over de nazimisdaden in Nederland voor het gerecht in München* (Bilthoven, 1969), 107. On the list that was written up in Amersfoort in preparation for the transport to Westerbork on August 4, 1942, we read, "2, Bock, Theres, 6.13.09, religious."

[23] See Munsters in *Als een brandende toorts*, 221–22.

[24] Ibid., 222.

5, at 11:45 A.M., she also wrote a long letter to her superior. "Here one is a number." By that time she already knew of her probable deportation to the east on the following Friday. The priests lived in the men's barrack. Once she received a blessing from one of them. "Last night it was very cold. I threw my coat over Leni. I have two thick blankets. Yes, you have taken good care of me",[25] she wrote. She rose at 5:45 A.M. and prayed from 6:00 to 7:00 A.M. There was plenty to eat. Once a day there was a warm drink, and once a day a warm meal. It tasted good, she said, although she had stomach problems.[26]

The Superior General, Mother Vincentia van Schendel (who died in 1967), and her Vicaress Sister Theresia-Hermus traveled, together with Toon van Kinderen, from Moerdijk to Westerbork on Wednesday, August 5, to deliver the things that Sister Charitas had requested. They met Sister Charitas in a small office shortly after 9:00 P.M. The conversation was brief, and Sister Charitas was afraid that she would return too late to her barrack.

The next morning (Thursday, August 6) both sisters returned to the Westerbork camp. This time they could speak with Sister Charitas and both her sisters. In 1950 Sister Hermus wrote that Sister Charitas "was very brave. Our Lord strengthened her."[27]

Sister Teresa Benedicta of the Cross gave the two sisters from Moerdijk a note, which they mailed in Amersfoort on August 6, 1942. Sister Teresa Benedicta wrote, "A Mother Superior from one of the convents arrived

[25] Sister Charitas Bock, as quoted in ibid., 224.
[26] See ibid., 224.
[27] Sister Theresia-Hermus, as quoted in ibid., 225.

last evening with some suitcases for her child and now offers to take some short letters along."[28]

On Thursday, August 6, Mr. H. Van Duursen, a resident teacher at the convent of the Sisters of the Sacred Heart in Dalfsen,[29] brought a package of food to Westerbork on behalf of the convent. It was enough food for ten persons for several days.[30] This courier's visit to the camp made a great impression on him. On August 7, 1942, he wrote to the Mother Superior how heartwrenching it was to see "dozens of people (visitors) crying and with broken nerves" staring at the barracks of the prisoners in the hope of seeing them and being able to give them something.[31] When the prisoners received permission to meet with visitors, Sister Charitas walked in front. Mr. van Duursen admired her strength of spirit. In his estimation, she was "a heroine".[32] He could speak with her at length. She was in good spirits. She did not want to remove her religious clothing unless it was commanded. Sister Charitas assumed that she would be away for a long time, but she did not exclude the possibility of a return. There is no sign that she suspected that she would be murdered.[33]

Mr. van Duursen left Westerbork at 3:30 P.M., so that he would still be in time to board the train to Dalfsen.

[28] Stein, Letter to Mother Antonia, as quoted in Sister Teresia Renata de Spiritu Sancto Posselt, *Edith Stein: The Life of a Philosopher and Carmelite*, ed. Susanne Batzdorff, Josephine Koeppel, and John Sullivan (Washington, D.C.: ICS Publications, 2005), 218; Munsters in *Als een brandende toorts*, 224.

[29] See Munsters in *Als een brandende toorts*, 231.

[30] See ibid., 226–27.

[31] Ibid., 227.

[32] See ibid.

[33] See ibid., 228.

From one of the train stations on his way home, he called the superior in the convent in Dalfsen, Sister Godefrida, to tell her what things Sister Charitas had requested. When he arrived in Dalfsen that evening, a whole package had already been prepared and was ready to be brought to Westerbork on the following day.

On the morning of Friday, August 7, Mr. van Duursen once more left Dalfsen for Westerbork. Once in Westerbork, the military policemen informed him that "all Catholic Jews" had been placed on a transport to Germany early that morning.[34] Between 5:30 A.M. and 7:30 A.M., the prisoners had left the camp to go to the train station in Houthalen.[35]

The people who remained behind in the camp gave those who were leaving clothing and food, even though these were things they themselves needed. A thousand people remained in the camp.[36] Nurse van de Hoff, a nurse in Westerbork, attempted to relieve the plight of the prisoners and told Mr. van Duursen "that a certain Mrs. Ten Berkel,[37] a Catholic woman who had for a long time already helped the Jews and had been threatened with arrest numerous times because of it, arrived last night with a whole load of food, blankets, and clothing, so that many could still be helped." Van Duursen left the package with the things intended for Sister Charitas at

[34] See ibid., 229.

[35] See NIOD, Archive 250 I, Westerbork camp, inventory no. 239. Her name, together with that of her sister Edith, is in fact on the transport list of August 7, 1942 (as no. 7 on list A). Her sister Helene is on list A, no. 8.

[36] See Munsters in *Als een brandende toorts*, 229.

[37] This is probably Sophie van Berckel. Her activity in Westerbork is evident, among other things, from the Archive of the Archdiocese of Utrecht, no. 76.

the camp for other prisoners.[38] He brought the money back with him. The prisoners were, after all, not allowed to keep money.[39]

Nurse van de Hoff had the suspicion that those who were deported would be murdered. Mr. van Duursen writes the following in his letter, "Therefore, Reverend Mother Superior, pray for her [Sister Charitas'] eternal happiness. It is severe for me to say it this way, but today I cannot be anything but straightforward, because I have been touched by it too deeply."[40]

Before her departure, Nurse van de Hoff had talked with Sister Charitas and had said goodbye to her.

> Sister Charitas had been courageous, even though she was somewhat pale from emotion. She was courageous and full of confidence. This is the last I heard of Sister Charitas. But I recall that the people in the camp say that they thought she had been given the name "Charitas" because of her work among her fellow prisoners!!! I cannot say it more beautifully, and I conclude with her own words to me, "Oh, for me it does not matter. What can happen to me? But for the laity."[41]

Sister Charitas' congregation made numerous efforts to have contact with her after her arrest. The Nazis intimated that there was hope of contact or even of Sister Charitas' return. Once they even said, "It all looks good for her."[42] When, even after the war, there was no sign of life from Sister Charitas, her mother, or sisters, the

[38] See Munsters in *Als een brandende toorts*, 230.
[39] See ibid.
[40] Mr. van Duursen, as quoted in ibid.
[41] Nurse van de Hoff, as quoted in ibid., 230.
[42] Ibid., 233.

Sisters of the Sacred Heart had a funeral Mass celebrated for their fellow sister in their chapel in November 1946.[43]

After Mr. Merkelbach had been informed by the Red Cross of the probability of his wife's death, he wrote to the superior of the Sisters of the Congregation of the Sacred Heart on December 24, 1946:

> It is terrible!!! I am sorry that I must forward such reports to you, but to be honest, we did not expect differently, after everything we have heard and read. Perhaps we can cling to the belief that gassing is still the most painless death and that they were thereby spared from even more horrendous mistreatment.
>
> This past November, I requested information from the Dutch Vatican Mission, and I am still waiting for a definitive answer from there. One never knows, perhaps a miracle has still happened. The only thing we can do is pray and hope that they are all with our dear Lord.[44]

On December 20, 1948, the sisters received a definitive death report for Sister Charitas from the Red Cross. The report says that Thérèse Bock "was deported on August 7, 1942, from Westerbork with the destination of Auschwitz.... Since nothing else has been heard of her since the deportation, ... it must be assumed that the aforementioned Thérèse Bock must have died in or around Auschwitz from illness, exhaustion, or gassing after August 7, 1942, and at the latest sometime during September 1942." [45]

[43] See ibid., 234.
[44] Mr. Merkelbach, as quoted in ibid., 234–35.
[45] Red Cross report, as quoted in ibid., 235.

Edith Bock

Edith Bock attended the teacher training school of the Sisters of Roosendaal in Breda, where she obtained her diploma. She found work as a teacher in Rotterdam, and she was also active in youth ministry. Edith was not married. She gave her sister, Sister Charitas, all manner of suggestions for her craft and music classes and for theater activities.[46]

The Bock family was not without worries in the 1930s. The mother, Hermine, Edith, and Leni were the breadwinners. It is not clear whether Hermine's husband was unemployed or handicapped. Hermine was also sick for

Edith Bock

[46] Munsters in ibid., 212.

extended periods of time. The family experienced finan-
cial difficulties and became impoverished. As a consequence of the anti-Semitic regulations of the day, Edith
lost her job as a teacher, and that meant the loss of the
primary breadwinner's income. After Edith was dismissed from her position, she devoted herself to teaching
Jewish children. Her youngest sister, Leni, was often sick,
and her stepfather seemed not to have been able to take
care of the costs.

Edith was arrested with Leni and their mother in their
home at the address of Katendrechtselagedijk 231A in Rotterdam on Sunday, August 2.[47] In Amersfoort they met
Sister Charitas.[48] During the night between Monday and
Tuesday, they went from Amersfoort to Westerbork. Edith
was a stronger person than Leni. In Westerbork, she and
Sister Charitas were a support and encouragement for many
who needed help.

In the report that Mother Vincentia and Sister Theresia-
Hermus wrote about their visit to Camp Westerbork on
Thursday, August 6, it says that "Edith was courageous
and brave. Leni, the youngest, was very sad. Edith and
Sister Charitas wanted to make their stay there apostol-
ically fruitful. 'We can still do so much good here,' she
[Sister Charitas] said, 'if we keep everything in order and
are brave.' "[49]

Most likely, Edith Bock, together with both her sisters and the whole group of Catholic Jews, arrived in

[47] See NIOD, Archive 250 F, Amersfoort camp, inventory no. 14.
[48] See Kempner, *Twee uit honderdduizend*, 107. On the list that was written
up there in preparation for the journey to Westerbork, we read under no. 7:
"Bock, Edith, 8.29.07, teacher."
[49] Sister Charitas Bock, as quoted in *Als een brandende toorts*, 225.

Auschwitz-Birkenau on Sunday, August 9, was gassed and buried in a mass grave.

Helene Luise (Leni) Bock

Leni was the youngest member of the Bock family. In 1922, as already mentioned, she and her sister Resi went to the boarding school of the Sisters of the Sacred Heart in Moerdijk, where Leni attended elementary school.[50]

After she had left Moerdijk, Leni went to work in an office. Sister Charitas described her sister's fiancé to her uncle (her stepfather's brother), Louis Merkelbach-Van

Helene Luise (Leni) Bock

[50] See ibid., 210–11.

Enkhuizen, as "a respectable and religious boy with about the same cultural and social education as Leni." His first name was Jan, and they dated for six and a half years. They were not yet married when Leni was arrested in 1942.[51]

As far as health and character go, Leni makes a less stable impression than her other sisters, as the excerpt from Sister Charitas' letter suggests, when she writes that she threw her coat over Leni out of concern for her. After her arrest on Sunday, August 2, 1942, Leni, together with Edith and her mother, went to Amersfoort.[52] She was brought to Westerbork together with the whole group.

When Mother Vincentia and Sister Hermus visited Camp Westerbork on Thursday, August 6, Leni was very depressed.[53] Leni's fiancé also traveled to Westerbork. He came from Rotterdam with clothes for both sisters. When Jan arrived in Westerbork, he did not yet know that Sister Charitas was also a prisoner. He appeared incredulous when he heard that Sister Charitas was also there.[54]

Leni went to her death with the other Catholic Jews.

Hermine Merkelbach-Van Enkhuizen-Grünbaum

On Sunday, August 2, three Catholic Jews were picked up from their house at Katendrechtselagedijk 231A in Rotterdam.[55] On that same day, Mr. Willem Merkelbach

[51] See ibid., 212.

[52] See Kempner, *Twee uit honderdduizend*, 108. The list of August 4 records her name under no. 8: "Bock, Helene Louise, 6.25.12, office clerk."

[53] See Munster in *Als een brandende toorts*, 225.

[54] See ibid., 227.

[55] See NIOD, Archive 250 F, Amersfoort camp, inventory no. 14.

Hermine Merkelbach-Van Enkhuizen-Grünbaum
and Willem Merkelbach-Van Enkhuizen
Photo: Mohr and Prégardier, *Passion im August*, 242.

wrote to his priest brother, Louis Merkelbach, who was
then chaplain for the Franciscan Sisters of the Guest-
house in Etten. He wrote:

> Early this morning at 4:30 A.M., Herma, Edith, and
> Leni were taken away. They had to take along blan-
> kets, etc., and food for three days, and then they were
> transported in a large police van to I know not where,
> though one suspects the concentration camp in Amers-
> foort. I immediately went to the rectory of the Capu-
> chin fathers, who would inquire into the matter. Now
> it appears that the Jews who have become Catholic
> have been picked up throughout the whole country
> in retribution for the letter of the bishops. I con-
> tained myself for a long time this morning, but now I

am broken. . . . I think it is so terrible for them. They never deserved such a thing—on the contrary. And they had had so much hope of remaining free on account of that letter of the bishops, Edith still hoping to become a teacher at a school for Jewish children. Terrible! One can only hope that the dear Lord will spare them further suffering, because otherwise they will not survive it. I do not know what do to with myself, but more about that later. I long to know where they are; even more would I have them home this evening. Too bad that we are so far apart.

Today—Monday—everything went so differently from what I had thought, and I have not yet sent this letter. Your letter just arrived with the 7:00 A.M. mail. Thank you for that, Louis. Yes, will the bishops still be able to do something? One can only hope so! This afternoon I received a telephone call from Moerdijk asking if I knew where my wife and children were and if I knew anything about Sister Charitas. Unfortunately I did not learn anything new today.[56]

Mrs. Merkelbach was married to a non-Jew. This is probably the reason that she remained behind when her three daughters were taken to Westerbork on Tuesday, August 4. Many in mixed marriages were initially released. Hermine Merkelbach's case was different.

Willem Merkelbach traveled to Amersfoort twice in the attempt to free his wife. It seemed that his efforts would be crowned with success, because the officials also agreed with him that the papers were in order. On August 15, 1942, however, she was brought from Amersfoort to Westerbork with eight other Catholic Jews. Of this group

[56] Willem Merkelbach letter to Louis Merkelbach, as quoted in *Als een brandende toorts*, 221.

Chapter 11

ELVIRA MARIA JOSEPHA SANDERS-PLATZ

Elvira Platz, also known as Elviere or Elvi, was born on September 15, 1891, in Cologne (Germany) into a Jewish family with many children. The first wife of her father, Jonas, had died, and he was left behind with a number of young children. He subsequently married Ida Heimbach, and Elvira was the youngest of the four children

Elvira Maria Josepha Sanders-Platz

from this second marriage. The family lived in the center of the city at the address Moltkestrasse 84.

Elvira's brother Alfred was married to a daughter of the owner of the Gerzon fashion clothing store. This business had a branch in Leiden on Breestraat. During the First World War, the Gerzon family brought Elvira and her sister Selma to Leiden. Selma was entrusted with the management of the store, and Elvira became head of the hat production department.[1] Elvira's future husband, Joseph Franciscus Xaverius Sanders, was a Catholic from a well-to-do family in Leiden. He was born in this city on May 30, 1876. His father was Aloysius Petrus Willebrordus Sanders, and his mother was Anna Louisa Geertruida Wensveen. They lived in Leiden. Mr. Sanders had a successful soap factory called Sanders & Co., which Xaverius took over in 1911. Xaverius Sanders served four terms as a councilman of the Roman Catholic political party in Leiden (from 1920–1927). During this same time period he was also alderman of finances twice.[2]

Xaverius Sanders often sat in the study of his house on Breestraat. This room looked out onto Elvira's workplace, and something began to grow between these two young people. Later Elvira once said, "Love began to blossom behind those windows."[3] Before they made the

---

[1] See "Recollections" of daughter Anna Sanders of her mother, Elvira Sanders-Platz, written for her oldest daughter, Nitha, part 7 (1997), 12; A. Mohr and E. Prégardier, eds., *Passion im August (2.–9. August 1942): Edith Stein und Gefährtinnen: Weg in Tod und Auferstehung*, Zeugen der Zeitgeschichte, 5 (Annweiler: Plöger, 1995), 25, 280–81; interview with Dr. N.M.E. van Oosten-Neuwahl, granddaughter of Elvira Sanders-Platz, Leiden.

[2] Information about Xaverius Sanders: http://www.janvanhout.nl/pluche2/pers/plup_sander_1204.htm.

[3] Sanders, "Recollections", pt. 7, 12.

decision to share their lives, however, Xaverius wrote Elvira a respectful letter in October 1917. In this letter, he raised the question of their different religious convictions. He pointed out that this difference could mean that family and friends would reject them if they were married. Her future bridegroom asked Elvira to let him know as soon as possible whether she would be willing to become Catholic, in order to marry him. If her reply was positive, Xaverius wrote, "I wanted to suggest that you go to Cologne for a time and consider the matter without seeing me and without speaking to me. Find a venerable Catholic priest there, and tell him what is on your heart, tell him what the concern is, let him advise you, and do not make a decision in the matter of religion before you have become truly convinced." He thought that she would need three months time for this.[4]

Elvira chose Jesus Christ and his Church. After the usual preparation, she was baptized on March 30, 1918, at the Convent Huize Duinzicht in Oegstgeest. On June 25, 1918, they were married at Saint Peter's Church in Leiden.[5] "Their love and their faith were the foundation of their common life."[6] The couple went to live at Witte Singel 40 in Leiden. In 1926 they moved to number 68 on that same street. They had happy years. Their only child, Anna (Anneke), was born on June 2, 1919. Elvira was well-accepted in her husband's family. Her daughter confirms that "my mother became Catholic with heart and soul."[7]

---

[4] See ibid., 8.

[5] See ibid., 9.

[6] Prégardier in H. Moll, ed., *Zeugen für Christus: Das deutsche Martyrologium des 20. Jahrhunderts*, 2 vols. (Paderborn, 1999), 326.

[7] Sanders, "Recollections", pt. 7, 9.

Every Sunday the whole family went to church. Mother and daughter then went to Holy Communion. Father received Holy Communion only on Christmas and Easter. Elvira's relationship with her Jewish family also remained good. Her mother regularly spent some days with them and loved Xaverius.[8] Her sister Selma married Fritz Hecht, and they lived in Amsterdam.[9] Upon being married, Elvira became a Dutch citizen.[10]

Times changed when the Nazis came to power in Germany. Elvira's husband broke relationship with friends who were too pro-German. With the assistance of a lawyer, he was able to bring his German family members to the Netherlands after the *Reichskristallnacht* (the night of November 9 and early morning of November 10, 1938). He allowed them to stay in his home in Leiden. Shortly before the German invasion of Poland on August 17, 1939, Xaverius died at the age of sixty-three in Leiden from *angina pectoris*. Elvira was then forty-seven years old. On one occasion, upon waking from his coma, Xaverius predicted the future suffering of his beloved wife. He said, "You will no longer have a roof over your head."[11] After her husband's death, Elvira dedicated herself to the Church more than she had in the past. She undertook charitable works in her parish. Among other things, she helped with the annual triduum for the sick. She also participated in classes to deepen her faith.[12]

The German invasion of the Netherlands on May 10, 1940, would have a great impact on Elvira Sanders' life.

[8] See ibid.
[9] See ibid., 12.
[10] See NIOD, Archive 250 F, Amersfoort camp, inventory no. 14.
[11] As quoted by Prégardier in Moll, *Zeugen*, 326.
[12] See Sanders, "Recollections", pt. 7, 11.

After Mass on July 26, 1942, Elvira called her daughter, Anna, who had by that time married the economist and manufacturer Dr. Heinz Neuwahl and who lived in Alphen aan de Rijn. Elvira asked, "Did you hear the letter of the bishops in church? Now everything is fine, and I no longer need to worry!" She would, however, never again step foot into a church on Sunday for a Holy Mass. Because Elvira Sanders-Platz was a Catholic Jew, she was arrested on August 2, 1942. On Sunday morning, the Gestapo arrived at her house at Lorentzkade 8 in Leiden at 7:30 A.M.[13] She was taken prisoner and brought to Amersfoort. From there she went to Westerbork.[14] At this time, her daughter, Anna, was expecting her first child. She did not learn of her mother's arrest until the late afternoon of August 2. With the help of her lawyer, she learned that her mother was in Westerbork. She wanted to travel to the camp to bring her mother the necessary things for her journey, but she was strongly advised not to do this, because she ran the risk of being taken prisoner herself. Family members went to Westerbork. They were permitted to turn in the suitcases at the gate but were not able to speak with Mrs. Sanders.

At 2:30 P.M. on Thursday, August 6, Elvira Sanders-Platz wrote her last letter from Westerbork. This letter shows that she did not expect to return alive. In it, she entreats her daughter, "Do not forget Dad, Anneke, but pray for me, too. Be happy together. God bless your child." Addressing her sister-in-law next, the letter of farewell continues, "You know my will: Holy Masses, and the cemetery plot is now for you. I will probably not rest

[13] See ibid., 2; NIOD, Archive 250 F, Amersfoort camp, inventory no. 14.
[14] See NIOD, Archive 250 F, Amersfoort camp, inventory no. 14. On the transport list of August 4, she is listed as no. 74.

with my dearly beloved husband." She also asked for "Many Holy Masses, pray, pray." [15]

Elvira Sanders-Platz also knew of the relationship between the pastoral letter of July 26, 1942, and her arrest and deportation to the unknown east. She, too, saw this as a calling to share in the redemptive suffering of the Messiah. In her letter of farewell, she writes, "The Catholic Jews will surely stay together! We are the sinners; if we had not been baptized, we would be free. This is therefore my election: to participate in the suffering of our dear Lord. I hope to continue to live in this spirit." [16] This last sentence was also cited on her obituary card.

Elvira left Westerbork by train on August 7.[17] On August 9, 1942, she arrived at Auschwitz with the other Catholic Jews. She was probably gassed and buried with them on that same day. She was fifty-three years old.

On what would have been her fifty-sixth birthday, September 15, 1947, her family received the message from the Dutch authorities that Elvira Sanders-Platz had died.[18] On Monday, October 6, 1947, a Requiem Mass was celebrated for her at 7:30 A.M. at the church where she had been married, Saint Peter's Church in Leiden. Elvira's daughter, Anna, survived the war by going into hiding. She died in 2001 at the age of eighty-two.[19]

---

[15] Elvira Sanders-Platz, as quoted in Sanders, "Recollections", pt. 7, 15.

[16] Ibid., 16.

[17] See NIOD, Archive 250 I, Westerbork camp, inventory no. 239. On the transport list from Westerbork, she is on list A, no. 7.

[18] See the Dutch Red Cross: File EU 100.605.

[19] Interview with Dr. N.M.E. van Oosten-Neuwahl, granddaughter of Elvira Sanders-Platz, Leiden.

Chapter 12

THE HAMBURGER FAMILY

Salomon (Sallie) Herman Hamburger[1] (referred to as Herman) came from a Jewish merchant family. His parents were Herman Salomon Hamburger and Sara Cohen Schavrien. Herman was the youngest child and had an older brother and an older sister. He grew up in a strong

The Hamburger Family

[1] Born in Woerden in 1898; died in Amsterdam, Schiphol, in 1946.

Calvinistic environment in the old polders[2] around the Dutch river IJssel.

As a convinced pacifist, Herman refused to go into military service during the First World War and was therefore sentenced to two years in prison in 1918.

On March 19, 1924, Herman married Eva Jeannette Maria Kalker, who had been born in Rotterdam. Eva Jeannette was baptized together with her first child in 1925 and was thus received into the Church. Herman was baptized on Holy Saturday of 1927 in Vianen. Two famous Dutch Catholics, Pieter van der Meer de Walcheren and his wife were the godparents.[3] The couple had five sons and three daughters. One boy died in infancy.

Although he was a successful businessman, Herman later devoted himself entirely to writing. His first book was *Aardebanden* (Earthly bonds) in 1922. His novel *Het wassende water* (The cleansing water), written in 1925, is considered to be his masterpiece. Herman's literary work was awarded numerous prizes, and he became well-known especially as the author of regional novels. He also worked as a journalist for various magazines. His penname, Herman de Man, was at first only a pseudonym, not his legal name.

The family moved often. From 1930, they lived in the house called Vrededaal (Valley of Peace), at the street address Beekveld A 19 in Berlicum. The family would later provide shelter here for Jews who had fled from Germany.[4]

---

[2] A polder is a piece of land surrounded by dikes. In the case of the polders of the IJssel in the Netherlands, these polders of land were recovered from the water of the IJssel by human effort.—TRANS.

[3] See Peter Steffen and Hans Evers, *Scheuren in het kleed: Het joods Katholeeke gezin Löb 1881–1945* (Nijmegen: Volkhof Pers, 2009), 196–97.

[4] See A. Mohr and E. Prégardier, eds., *Passion im August (2.–9. August 1942): Edith Stein und Gefährtinnen: Weg in Tod und Auferstehung*, Zeugen der

When the Germans invaded the Netherlands on May
10, 1940, Herman de Man was in his little house in the
French Alps. He had withdrawn there in the beginning
of 1940 to finish a book. After the invasion of the Germans, he could no longer return to the Netherlands. He
tried to return to his family, but he was then caught in a
bombardment in Paris. He was not injured in the bombardment, but he was nevertheless advised to return to
the Alps. At first he did so.

He later fled to London via Spain and Portugal. During his stay in London, he worked for the Government
Information Service and Radio Oranje.[5] On September
9, 1943, his pseudonym "de Man" became his legal name
by royal decree.

Being of Jewish origin, the Hamburger family was among
those arrested by the Gestapo in response to the letter that
the Dutch bishops had read in churches on July 26, 1942.
On Sunday, August 2, 1942, the Nazis were at the door of
the Hamburger residence in Berlicum. Very early that
morning—at 1:00 A.M.—the mayor of the town had received
word to "take the family away", but he had not done anything about it. At 6:00 A.M. the local police, together with
the Gestapo, arrested all the inhabitants of the house: the
mother, Eva, was thirty-seven years old; Anneke, thirteen;
Jochie, eleven; Magdaleentje, ten; Pieterje, nine.

The mother was completely surprised by this event.
No one had warned her between 1:00 A.M. and 6:00 A.M.
This would have been enough time to flee. With the

Zeitgeschichte, 5 (Annweiler: Plöger, 1995), 25; 261–69; G. Vaartjes, *Herman
de Man: Een biografie* (Soesterberg, 1999).
    [5] Radio Orange was the radio station for the Dutch people from their
government-in-exile, which was in London. The Queen, also, was in London during the time of the occupation.—TRANS.

police already in the house, the mother called her family doctor, Dr. Hofmann, for help. He was allowed into the house, but he could not prevent the deportation.[6]

Five members of the family were loaded onto a farmer's wagon and left the town in the direction of Vught. From there they were brought to Amersfoort. On the list that was written up at this camp, the family is found under the name "Hamburger". About the mother, the following is noted: Eva Jeannette Hamburger-Kalker, born April 10, 1905. Housewife. Only the children's name, "Hamburger", and their ages: thirteen, eleven, ten, and nine years old,[7] are indicated. From Amersfoort the family went to Westerbork.

On Friday, August 7, 1942, they were placed on the transport to the east.[8] They were in the same train as other Catholic Jews who were brought to Auschwitz. Richard Bromberg, who was himself a prisoner, writes about the Hamburger family. "The wife of the author Herman de Man and her children belonged to this transport."[9] They arrived in Auschwitz on August 9. They were probably gassed and buried in a mass grave on that same day.[10]

The Gestapo also tried to arrest the other three Hamburger children. Jan, the oldest, was attending boarding

[6] See Mohr and Prégardier, Passion im August, 264.

[7] See R. Kempner, Twee uit honderdduizend, Anne Frank en Edith Stein: Onthullingen over de nazimisdaden in Nederland voor het gerecht in München (Bilthoven, 1969), 108.

[8] See NIOD, Archive 250 F, Amersfoort camp, inventory no. 14; Archive 250 I, Westerbork camp, inventory no. 239. On the transport list bearing this date, the mother, Eva, her sons Petrus and Joachim, and her daughters Magdalena and Anna are on list A, no. 13.

[9] Richard Bromberg, as quoted in Sister Teresia Renata de Spiritu Sancto Posselt, Edith Stein: Jodin, geleerde, Carmelites (Bilthoven, 1952), 251.

[10] See the Dutch Red Cross: File EU 101.453 up to and including 457.

school in Zuidhoorn House at the street address Rotter-
damscheweg 1 in Rijswijk. He was arrested there. He
was taken with the group of prisoners from The Hague
district to the Amersfoort camp. He is listed on the transport list of August 7, 1942, on list A, number 17 as
Johannes W. Hamburger.[11] Jan therefore went to Auschwitz on the same train as his mother, brothers, and sisters.

The seventeen-year-old Jan was not gassed, however,
but selected for forced labor. He worked in a mercury
mine in Upper Silesia. According to certain accounts, he
succeeded in escaping and wanted to go to his father in
France. Upon arriving in France, however, he unknow-
ingly entered an SS post and was immediately arrested
and shot to death. He was nineteen years old.[12]

The fifteen-year-old son, Joost, had been studying at the
minor seminary of the Fathers of the Holy Ghost (Paters
van de H. Geest) in Weert since September 1941. The
Gestapo went to arrest him there on August 2, 1942.
The prefect told the police, however, that Joost was on
vacation. In that way, the boy could, with the help of
the Fathers of the Holy Ghost, go into hiding.

On May 21, 1943, Joost Hamburger, who was now
called Jos, was brought to the family of Joseph and Ada
van der Heijden in Someren-Eind. Joseph had two missionary brothers in the Congregation of the Holy Ghost.
The Fathers of the Holy Ghost had come to Joseph van
der Heijden and asked him if the Jewish boy could stay

[11] See NIOD, Archive 250 I, Westerbork camp, inventory no. 239; Kempner, *Twee uit honderdduizend*, 109.
[12] See Mohr and Prégardier, *Passion im August*, 264.

with him. The family was warned that they could receive the death penalty if the boy were discovered. Van der Heijden agreed to take the boy, and that same day Jos was brought there. Joseph van der Heijden describes this initial encounter:

> Jos was a small young man of fifteen. His face was as white as a sheet. I asked the superior who was with the boy if he had brought me a TB patient. The answer was negative. He had been examined regularly and was as healthy as a horse. He had, however, spent the last six weeks in a chair in an attic room and had barely moved. Should he become ill and die, then I would have to bury him in my yard and not talk about it to anyone. They left him entirely in my care.[13]

Joost stayed with the family until the end of the war. Later, too, he maintained regular contact with them.

On October 1, 1947, he continued his studies with the Missionarii Opificum (M.O.) in Argenteuil, Belgium. This congregation had been founded in 1894 by Theofiel Reyn. Joost completed his novitiate in the Andenne (Belgium) and studied theology in Louvain (Belgium). On August 7, 1955, he was ordained a priest by the Most Reverend J. Kerkhofs, Bishop of Liège (Belgium), in the church of the Franciscan Fathers in Sint-Truiden. On August 14, 1955, he celebrated his first solemn Holy Mass in Someren. Until 1963 he worked in Belgium. Afterward he went to Brazil, where he

---

[13] Joseph van der Heijden, as quoted in W. Joosen and M. Kooistra-Kruyf, eds., *Geschiedenis van Someren in de Tweede Wereldoorlog* (Someren, 1984), 107.

died suddenly on June 19, 1981, in Contagem-Belo Horizonte.[14]

During his last vacation in Europe he visited Auschwitz. His memorial card reads: "[T]here he united himself with the Risen Lord in the Eucharist and, thus, also felt united with those who died there. It was a moving event for him." [15]

Marietje (Maria Elisabeth, born May 14, 1926, in Vianen) was the third oldest child. She was about sixteen years old in August 1942. Marietje was not home when the other members of her family were arrested, because she was staying with the De Winter family in Den Bosch. This family lived in the house of Dr. Diamant. They were Jews, and Mr. De Winter was the chairman of the Jewish Council of Den Bosch. At that time, it was still thought that his membership to the Council gave a certain security.

On August 2, 1942, the Gestapo also attempted to arrest Marietje in Den Bosch, but the threat of danger had already been heard from Berlicum. Marietje had a slight case of flu, and to mislead the Germans they pretended it was a serious illness. She was admitted to the Carolus Hospital for several weeks. The Germans did not pick her up there.

During the remainder of the war until the liberation on November 17, 1944, she went into hiding in Helden

---

[14] See J. Coenen, *Hertog Jan en de Zummerse mens: Een overzicht van de geschiedenis van Someren en Lierop* (Someren, 2001), 448.

[15] Archives of the Congregation of the Holy Ghost, Gemert; Mohr and Prégardier, *Passion im August,* 265; Joosen and Kooistra-Kruyf, *Geschiedenis van Someren,* 107–8.

where she stayed initially in the rectory of Father A. R. J. Thomassen (1913–1944) and his sister. Marietje married William Boserup, and the couple had two children, Annemarie and Eva. In the 1950s the family moved to Denmark, and in 2006 she still lived in Lyngby.[16]

After the war, Herman de Man returned to the Netherlands. He then learned what had happened to his family: that his wife and four of his children had been gassed by the Nazis and that his son Jan had been shot to death in France. Herman was wholly distressed when he heard this news. He moved into a rental house in Eindhoven with his two remaining children. He was a broken and bitter man. The text from the memorial card for his wife and children reveals the embitterment. The sentence that introduces the names of his beloved dead reads, "On Sunday morning, August 2, 1942, the following people were deported from Berlicum by the enemy, who were assisted by fellow countrymen. . . ." After the war, the mayor of Berlicum had to resign his office because he had failed to act in the case of the de Man family.[17]

In Eindhoven, Herman de Man opened a car dealership together with a business partner. On November 14, 1946, as he was returning from a business trip to London, his airplane, a KLM-Dakota, crashed during the landing at Schiphol Airport because of bad weather. All twenty-six passengers lost their lives. Herman de Man

---

[16] See Archive of the Congregation of the Holy Ghost, Gemert; interview with Mr. Hoogbergen (September 9, 2006); Mohr and Prégardier, *Passion im August*, 263–65, 269 (where they mistakenly speak of The Hague instead of Den Bosch).

[17] See Mohr and Prégardier, *Passion im August*, 264–66.

was forty-eight years old. At his own request, he found his last place of rest at the Catholic cemetery in Oude-water on November 19, 1946. His funeral drew much public attention, reported as it was in the news shown in the movie theaters.

Chapter 13

BROTHER WOLFGANG ROSENBAUM, O.F.M.

Fritz Rosenbaum's parents were strict, believing orthodox Jews. His father Louis (Ludwig) was a well-to-do
textile merchant who owned numerous houses, and his
mother was Elly Markus. Fritz, an only child, was born
on May 27, 1915, in the German Witten along the Ruhr.

Fritz Rosenbaum before his entrance into the Fransiscan order.
Photo: Mohr and Prégardier, *Passion im August*, 272.

Fritz received a thorough religious upbringing at home, and his mother played an especially important role in this matter. In addition, he attended the Jewish elementary school. At a very young age, Fritz showed an extraordinary interest in the Catholic faith. Even before going to school, he was good friends with a neighbor boy who was Catholic, and he remained friends with him until high school.

This neighborhood friend received religion lessons at his elementary school, and Fritz visited him regularly to ask what he had learned. The district postman, Zurhast, who often came to visit the family, was a fervent Catholic. He, too, played a role in Fritz's journey toward Jesus Christ and his Church. The pastor, Father Johannes Rechmann, often invited Fritz along when he went for a walk. The conversations they had during these times were frequently about the faith; in this way, Fritz grew in his faith and his enthusiasm for Jesus Christ.

Fritz was seventeen when he told his father that he was considering becoming Catholic. His father's answer was brief and clear: "If you become Catholic, you will be disinherited." [1] In 1930, Fritz left school and went to work in one of his father's textile stores in Dortmund (Germany). [2]

He was eighteen years old when he decided to become Catholic. The friend from his youth presented him to

---

[1] Louis Rosenbaum, as quoted by E. Kutzner in H. Moll, ed., *Zeugen für Christus: Das deutsche Martyrologium des 20. Jahrhunderts*, 2 vols. (Paderborn, 1999), 764.

[2] See A. Mohr and E. Prégardier, eds., *Passion im August (2.–9. August 1942): Edith Stein und Gefährtinnen: Weg in Tod und Auferstehung*, Zeugen der Zeitgeschichte, 5 (Annweiler: Plöger, 1995), 273.

the pastor, Father Rechmann, for the necessary catechetical instruction in preparation for baptism. It soon became clear that he did not have much more to learn. Against the will of his father, Fritz was secretly baptized in the parish church of Saint Joseph (now Saint Francis) in Witten on September 15, 1933. His godfather was Franz Koch.[3] On October 8, 1933, the auxiliary bishop, the Most Reverend Augustinus Baumann, confirmed him. Pastor Rechmann describes Fritz's journey to the Church. "I will never forget the catechism lessons for Fritz Rosenbaum. I never knew a soul who hungered so much for truth and for love of the Savior. How filled he was with love for God after his baptism! How often he said to me, 'Now everything, truly everything is all the same to me, as long as I love Jesus.' "[4]

Fritz now went to Holy Mass and Holy Communion daily. In the summer of 1934, he spent a number of weeks vacationing with a friend in the area of Bitburg (the German Eifel). The rural Catholic life of this area pleased him so much that he wanted to become a farmer. In the spring of 1935 he began to work on a farm. Without complaint he accepted the sometimes very heavy labor, to which he was not accustomed. He was highly regarded by his coworkers. He worked on the farm for a half a year.

His father, who had already been attacked by the SD (Sicherheitsdienst, the security service of the Nazis) in 1934, was not equal to the constant pressure that the ever more powerful Nazis exerted against the Jews or to their

---

[3] See ibid., 274.
[4] The Reverend Rechmann, as quoted by Kutzner in Moll, *Zeugen*, 764.

anti-Semitic propaganda. In 1935 he took his own life.[5] For the sake of his lonely mother, Fritz once again moved to Witten. He was steadfast in his practice of the faith. Under his influence, his mother also found her way to the Church. She was baptized on December 20, 1936, in Witten. She was confirmed on October 3, 1939, in the Saint Paul's Church in Cologne (Germany), because at that time she was living in a Jewish residence there. In Cologne, a Franciscan priest regularly came to visit her. He advised her to go to another country. Elly Rosenbaum did not take his advice because as a Catholic she considered herself a fallen-away Jew and was thus afraid of other Jews. In the late autumn of 1942, she was deported to Minsk (white Russia).

After his baptism, the calling to leave the world and to give himself wholly to the Kingdom of God in the religious life grew in Fritz. He went to the Franciscans and asked to be received into the order. The provincial, however, had his reservations. Times were difficult under the Nazi yoke for the Franciscans, too.

The Franciscan province was already dealing with the legal implications of "currency smuggling" charges—an accusation made by the Nazis because the priests financially supported their fellow brothers in other countries. Public moral accusations were also made against priests and religious with the goal of placing the Church in a bad light. (Those who were condemned were rehabilitated after the Nazi period.) A burden of taxation was imposed on the order, and in 1935 the provincial was placed in a concentration camp because he had worked

[5] See Mohr and Prégardier, *Passion im August*, 274.

for the Jews and opposed their inhumane treatment. The order did not want to bring more problems upon itself by accepting a Catholic Jew. Even though Father Rechmann maintained that Fritz Rosenbaum's calling was authentic and gave a positive reference, the aspirant was not accepted into the order in September 1938.

In the *Reichskristallnacht* (November 9–10, 1938) Fritz Rosenbaum was also attacked. When he told his attackers that he was Catholic, he was beaten even more severely. Covered with blood, Fritz sought refuge with Father Rechmann, who brought him—that same night—to the safety of his sisters' home in Düsseldorf (Germany). Once more, Rosenbaum asked the provincial to accept him into the Franciscan Order. Even though it was perilous to accept a Jew into an order that had already been outlawed, the provincial did not think he could refuse Rosenbaum any longer.

On March 1, 1939, a fellow brother brought Fritz Rosenbaum, who had a valid passport with the required "J" for Jews, to the formation house of the German Franciscans, Saint Ludwig's, which was located in Vlodrop in the Netherlands. This friary was on the German border, and it had been founded during the time of the *Kulturkampf*[6] as the formation house for the German Franciscans of the Province of Werl. Confronted with a growing number of refugees from Germany, the friary required Fritz to obtain official permission from the Department of Justice in The Hague to stay in the Netherlands. This permission arrived soon.[7]

---

[6] See n. 32 in chap. 2 (p. 76 above) about the *Kulturkampf*.
[7] See Kutzner in Moll, *Zeugen*, 765.

To avoid further complications, Rosenbaum's Jewish identity was for the time being hidden. He was presented to his fellow brothers in the community as Fritz Rensing. He received various tasks. Since he had worked in his father's textile business, he was assigned, among other places, to the friary sewing room. Later he worked in the laundry and many other places where assistance was needed.

During his work, Fritz came to know his future brothers better. His conversations were often about religious topics. His love and knowledge sometimes made these discussions into lively adult catecheses about religious themes. Many noticed especially his childlike devotion to Mary. In the heat of conversation he could appear somewhat nervous. He could also lash out rather fiercely about the situation in Germany under the authority of the Nazis, and he declared that after the Jews the Catholics would get their turn. In those days, not yet everyone recognized the intentions of the Nazis.[8]

On September 1, 1939, the Second World War began with the German invasion of Poland. That same month, Fritz began his retreat in preparation for his clothing. On the vigil of Saint Francis (October 3, 1939), he was received into the Third Order Regular of Saint Francis. He received the habit of the order as well as his religious name of Brother Wolfgang.

---

[8] About the Nazi future plans for Catholics and the Nazi judicial processes that had the intention of harming the Church, see H. Hockerts, *Die Sittlichkeitsprozesse gegen katholische Ordensangehörige und Priester (1936–1937)* (Mainz, 1971); H. Hürten, "'Endlösung' für den Katholizismus? Das nationalsozialistische Regime und seine Zukunftspläne gegenüber der Kirche", *Stimmen der Zeit* 203 (1985): 534–46; P. Hamans, "Na de joden de katholieken", *Katholiek Nieuwsblad* 22:34 (May 20, 2005): 10.

After the *Blitzkrieg* in the east, there was speculation about a German invasion in the Netherlands. It became too dangerous for Brother Wolfgang to be so close to the border. The friary in Vlodrop would, in fact, have to be vacated in 1941 at the command of the occupying forces. His local superior, therefore, sent the novice Brother Wolfgang to a house of the Dutch province of the Franciscans in Woerden on November 16, 1939.

On May 10, 1940, the Germans invaded the Netherlands. All Germans residing in the Netherlands had to report. Afterward, Brother Wolfgang was permitted to return to the friary. On the Solemnity of Saint Francis (October 4, 1940), Brother Wolfgang professed his vows as a member of the Third Order Regular of Saint Francis in the hands of the guardian (the superior) after High Mass in the chapel of the friary at Wilhelminastraat 13 in Woerden. After his profession, Brother Wolfgang was assigned to work in the friary's printing office.[9]

On August 2, Brother Wolfgang was picked up by the German police at 7:00 A.M. The community was at prayers at that hour. The police waited at the door of the chapel. Brother Wolfgang had to go outside and was not even given time to eat anything. He got into the car, and it drove away.[10] The car brought him first to The Hague. Then he was taken to Amersfoort, Westerbork, and finally to Auschwitz.[11]

[9] See Kutzner in Moll, *Zeugen*, 765–64.

[10] See Mohr and Prégardier, *Passion im August*, 276; Kutzner in Moll, *Zeugen*, 766.

[11] See NIOD, Archive 250 I, Westerbork camp, inventory no. 239, list A, no. 17; R. Kempner, *Twee uit honderdduizend, Anne Frank en Edith Stein: Onthullingen over de nazimisdaden in Nederland voor het gerecht in München* (Bilthoven, 1969), 109. On the list that was written up on August 4, 1942, in Amersfoort

In a letter, the guardian of Woerden informed his fellow German brothers of the sad news. He wrote, "You can understand how terrible this was for him and for us. I will never forget his last sad glance!" The house chronicle from the friary in Woerden also describes Brother Wolfgang's arrest: "Deported, first to The Hague, then to Amersfoort, then to the Westerbork camp in Drenthe. A few days later he was deported with a large Jewish transport to the east." [12]

His religious brothers lost a faithful member of the community. They recount that "he was very much appreciated and loved by all because of his piety, fraternity, and his willingness to help." Moreover, they tell us that "he was an example for the whole community. In the morning, he was always the first in choir, and then he served as many Holy Masses as possible.... Everyone who knew him is convinced that he was a very holy religious." [13]

He was never heard from again. It was not until February 15, 1952, that the Department of Justice's Commission for Missing Persons informed the Franciscans that Brother Wolfgang had been transported from Westerbork to Auschwitz on August 7, 1942. It is suspected that he died on September 30, 1942, as the result of exhaustion or gassing. [14] He was twenty-seven years old.

---

in preparation for the transport to Westerbork, we read under no. 62: "Rosenbaum, Fritz, J. 5–27–15, religious brother." Kempner, *Twee uit honderdduizend*, 108. His name also appears on the transport list that was prepared for Auschwitz in Westerbork on August 7, 1942.

[12] As quoted by Kutzner in Moll, *Zeugen*, 766.

[13] Ibid.

[14] The Dutch Red Cross: File EU 110.877.

For nine of those years he belonged to the Church. He was very happy in the Catholic faith. After Father Rechmann received the news of his death, he wrote, "That good Brother Wolfgang! It goes without saying that he is now with God. He always loved his Savior so deeply, after all. I will never forget how he knelt in ardent prayer every day in the church."[15]

In the parish of Saint Francis in Witten, this murdered Catholic Jew is depicted in a stained glass window together with Saint Teresa Benedicta of the Cross (Edith Stein). On the occasion of the thirtieth and fiftieth anniversary of his death, his home parish held services in his memory.[16]

---

[15] The Reverend Rechmann, as quoted by Kutzner in Moll, *Zeugen*, 766.

[16] See O. Mund, *Blumen auf den Trümmern: Blutzeugen der NS-Zeit: Wolfgang Rosenbaum u.a.* (Paderborn, 1989); O. Mund, "Bene qui vivit, bene latuit. Zum 50. Todestag von Edith Stein und Bruder Wolfgang Rosenbaum", *Franziskanische Studien Heft* 2/3 (Werl, 1992).

Chapter 14

SISTER JUDITH MENDES DA COSTA, O.P.

Judith Henriëtte Mendes da Costa was born on August
15, 1895, to Portuguese-Jewish parents living in Amsterdam. Her father, Emmanuel, and her mother, Esther Hen-
riques de Castro, were both of Portuguese-Jewish origin.

Sister Judith Mendes da Costa, O.P.
Photo: Congregation of the Dominican Sisters of
Saint Catherine of Siena in Voorschoten

There were seven children in the family, Judith being the youngest. Her parents were devout Jews. Her father was a stockbroker, and the family was well-to-do. Judith was twelve years old when her father died in 1907. After the father's death, the family had to leave their manor located at Herengracht 105 in Amsterdam and went to live in a smaller house in the same city.

A number of Catholics worked in the da Costa household. Judith's mother once said, "They are honest, polite, and cheerfully fulfill their duty." [1] For the first seven years of her life, Judith was entrusted to the care of a Catholic nanny. Even though this woman did not practice the faith, Judith noticed at an early age that the Catholic environment was different from that of her own family. When she was seven, Judith went to elementary school. Instead of playing in her room, she now spent more time in the living room, where the Jewish house liturgy, the daily prayers, the celebration of the Sabbath, and the Jewish feasts took place. A Jewish tutor came to the house to teach Judith about the ceremonies, the Jewish feasts, and the basics of the Hebrew language. He also told stories from what the Christians call the Old Testament. Already in her childhood, Judith noticed the strictness of the Jewish rules, the exactness with which they were to be kept, and the abyss that yawned between this exactitude and personal sins. She could not see how this fit with "the good God" she knew from the biblical stories. [2]

[1] Sister Judith Mendes da Costa, *Sister Judith Mendes da Costa, Dominican Sister of the Congregation of St. Catherine of Siena in Voorschoten, Amsterdam 1895–1944 Auschwitz: Autobiografie*, publication in possession of author (Voorschoten, 2006), 8.

[2] See Sister M. Emerentia Peters, in *Als een brandende toorts: Documentaire getuigenissen over Dr. Edith Stein (zuster Teresia Benedicta a Cruce) en medeslachtoffers* (Echt: Friends of Dr. Edith Stein, 1967), 193.

When Judith was fourteen years old, Jesus Christ came into her life. One evening she went with her mother and sister to a theater featuring a movie about the life of Jesus. Later she writes about her experience that evening, "I could not speak; it was all too much for me. It was as though my soul had been shocked."[3] Judith began her search for "Christ and his Truth" in liberal and orthodox Protestant circles.

In the meantime, she was attending high school. After finishing school, she went to work as an office clerk in the business of one of her distant cousins. She began to date and eventually became engaged to a young Catholic man, who, however, wholly neglected the duties of his faith. Still, it was her fiancé who pointed her to the Catholic faith. Judith began to visit Catholic churches and was impressed by the beauty of the liturgical celebrations.

Through an advertisement, she heard of conferences for non-Catholics that were held in the parish of Saint Dominic located on the Spuistraat in Amsterdam. Here she was introduced to the teachings and practices of the Catholic Church. She placed herself under the spiritual direction of Father Matthias Frehe, O.P. (who died in 1967). This same priest was later also Dr. Lisamaria Meirowsky's confessor. It would still be a long time, however, before she could wholly and freely surrender herself to the triune God.

Judith knew that a decision to join the Church would entail a break with her family. She had already seen this in the case of her oldest sister, who had also been on her way to the Church. Her sister had not dared to take the

---

[3] Sister Judith Mendes da Costa, O.P., as quoted by Peters in *Als een brandende toorts*, 194.

final step, however, had suffered a nervous breakdown, and was admitted to the psychiatric hospital Het Apeldoornse Bos. During the night of January 21–22, 1943, this sister was picked up from the hospital by the Nazis and was later gassed.[4] Another sister and brother were deported to Germany. They never returned.

Even though Judith had the discouraging example of her sister's nervous breakdown, she proceeded resolutely. She was twenty-eight years old when she was baptized in Saint Dominic's church in Amsterdam at 4:00 P.M. on October 10, 1923. On October 14, she received her First Holy Communion in the Rosary Church in the same city.[5] In the winter of the same year she was confirmed by the Most Reverend Augustinus J. Callier, Bishop of Haarlem (1903–1928). The Dominican priest who was her spiritual director advised her not (yet) to make known that she had become Catholic. A Protestant friend told one of Judith's brothers, however. The result was a big quarrel and the expected subsequent break with her family. Since the death of her father, Judith had always slept with her mother. They loved one another very much, and Judith had been the mother's favorite. Her mother had always honored her for her piety and her noble character. Now she damned her daughter. For days, Judith did not dare to come near her. She began to sleep in an attic room in her mother's house. After a number of days, she once again approached her mother, who was then calmer. Not another word was spoken about the incident. Her relationship with her brothers, however, remained more difficult.

---

[4] See Peters, in *Als een brandende toorts*, 194–95.
[5] See Sister Judith Mendes da Costa, *Autobiografie*, 28–29.

Every morning Judith left the house at 6:45 A.M. in order to attend Holy Mass. Afterward she went to work and did not return home until 11:30 P.M. In that way, she could avoid meeting her brothers. Judith lived this way, almost as a homeless person, for three years. She no longer felt at home with her own family. Judith describes the words that she would hear in her heart: "'You no longer belong here! Go away, go away!' The loyal home hearth seemed to call this out to me. That was painful, a piercing pain deep in my soul." [6]

She broke her engagement with her fiancé because she did not want to be married to a non-practicing Catholic. All of this cost her so much energy that she did not even report to the office for a few days. She would later be fired from her place of employment, where she had worked up to the position of deputy manager. Judith then became a nanny, but this did not work out. She was not suited for this task, nor had she ever been trained for it.

The Catholic Judith drew strength from her prayers and from the conviction that she carried her suffering for the salvation of the Jewish people. In Catholic circles she found new friends and acquaintances. She became a member of a sewing circle that made liturgical garments and accessories for the missions. She was also zealous for the recently founded Association of Prayer for Israel.

Judith was alone in the world. She was very happy in the faith, but she repeatedly had to endure heavy setbacks, her health suffering under the pressure of the various circumstances of her life. It was in this setting that

---

[6] Sister Judith Mendes da Costa, O.P., as quoted by Peters in *Als een brandende toorts*, 196.

she began to sense her vocation to the religious life. On September 1, 1928, she entered the Dominican Sisters of Saint Catherine of Siena in Voorschoten. On April 29, 1929, she received the religious habit. She made her temporary profession on April 30, 1930, and her final profession on April 30, 1933.

Sister Judith became a happy Dominican with an always radiant look. A fellow sister said the following about Sister Judith:

> Sister Judith's fourteen years of professed life were undoubtedly one loving encounter with God. Everything was a loving encounter with him, whether she was typing reports of the patients' illnesses at Berg en Bosch Sanatorium, or whether she was united with him in prayer. She found the happiness that came from this meeting just as much when she was given peace and consolation after Holy Communion as in the desolation and emptiness with which God tests his own. Her joy lay hidden in the daily struggle between the oversensitivity of her delicate heart and the disappointments and humiliations, the fierce blows of life, of which she had such a large share.
>
> Everything was a meeting of love with God for this happy child of God: the flowers in her office, which she tended with such care; the beauty of the woods surrounding the sanatorium; the simplicity of a child's words of gratitude; the smile of a sick person to whom she had been able to say a kind word; the service rendered to a fellow sister.
>
> Everyone around her noticed her reverence for the Most Holy Sacrament, "Oh, if you knew what it means to go to Communion, if you knew how long I had to search for faith." In her rich prayer life she was ever a

true Dominican, who valued, above all, the contemplation of God and things divine.

At the same time, the ardent convert, who was always conscious of the smaller duties of religious life, truly understood that it was her solemn Dominican duty to allow others to drink from the fruits of her own contemplation. And here lies perhaps the tragedy of her religious life. The profundity of her inborn desire for God was rivaled only by her desire to bring others the truth for which she herself had longed so long. And yet . . . she was never directly involved in the apostolic charitable works of the congregation. She was assigned a task at the typewriter. She knew, though, how to elevate her small duties in the beautiful light of her burning longing for souls. Every letter that she typed had an apostolic intention, as she once told a fellow sister. In the same way, she saw every occasion in her surroundings to do a service for someone. Most heartily she sympathized with everyone. With the words, "Who is doing it? He, he!" she could console a saddened or hurt person. Her finger then pointed upward, and in her eyes there was the mix of seriousness and roguishness that wholly unmanned others.

Day after day she was of service to her sisters. And she waved off every thanks for her quickly offered help with the cheerful, "Cohen Company, first quality, quick service!" The great desire to embrace suffering, struggles, and sacrifices was motivated by the thought that this could serve the salvation of her people.[7]

It would be a mistake to think that Sister Judith was safe in the convent and was simply living happily there.

[7] Ibid., 197–98.

In the 1920s she lost two of her brothers who had refused to reconcile themselves with her. She hoped in vain that her youngest brother would find his way to the Church. The Nazi Jewish persecution prevented his journey to the Church from being crowned with holy baptism.

On January 10, 1934, her mother died. When Sister Judith learned that her mother was dying, her prioress offered her the opportunity to go home, assist her mother, and say goodbye to her. "No, prioress [she said], there are rabbis at the death bed. They have the right to spit on me because I am a deserter. I do not want to cause my mother that grief." [8]

After the occupation, Sister Judith saw how Jews were picked up and deported to Germany. She was repeatedly offered help to go into hiding. Although she did not want to endanger her order or the sanatorium, she also said, "If I have to go, I shall offer my life for the salvation of Israel." [9]

On Sunday, August 2, 1942, Sister Judith was picked up from the convent and Berg en Bosch Sanatorium in Bilthoven. In her autobiography she recounts these events:

Before the Consecration I was suddenly inspired to pray most intensely for a moment. This had happened before, and I immediately obeyed the inner voice. Not two minutes had passed before I heard the doorbell at our guest quarters and thought, "It is probably a visitor for one of the sisters." Some time later, our prioress came to get me from the chapel, and as I was following her I thought—not suspecting anything bad— "Probably visitors for me!"

[8] Ibid., 198.
[9] Ibid.

At the entrance of the church the prioress said to me, "Do not be shocked. There are two policemen who have come for you because you are a Jew. . . . They are in the large parlor, and you must just act very normal." I took a deep breath (!), and entered full of courage. Then the questioning began.

"Are you a Jew?"

The prioress answered, "She is Catholic."

"You have four Jewish grandparents?"

"Yes", I said.

"Then we must arrest you."

"Can you just do that?" the prioress asked firmly.

"Here are the authorizations for the arrest", and they showed her the papers.

"She may certainly change first?" the prioress asked.

It was permitted, and I also received a list of things I was allowed to bring. I had fifteen minutes to get ready. They asked if I had possessions, to which the prioress replied that we have a cell with a table, bed, chair, and a closet with some clothes.

"We must seal that cell and closet", they said.

We went there, and I ran upstairs, not to change my clothes, because I was wearing my Sunday clothes (!), but in order to remove everything from my closet that could be a danger. I quickly put all that under my neighbor's bed.[10]

A large suitcase was packed with all the necessities: two woolen blankets, food for two days, a plate, mug, fork, and spoon. Sister Judith received the blessing of the chaplain, and as he gave her a firm handshake, he said, "Be strong! I will think of you every day during the Holy

---

[10] Sister Judith Mendes da Costa, *Autobiografie*, 81.

Mass." Sister Judith asked him, "Will you please pray to
the Holy Spirit, so that I will know what I must respond?"
The chaplain promised to do so. A large group of sisters
saw Sister Judith off. A military policeman carried her
suitcase. The prioress accompanied her to the car. As Sister Judith got in, the prioress said, "Be strong and trust
in God. He will not abandon you." Sister Judith once
more pressed her hand. She thanked her prioress for everything she had done for her and said, "Our dear Lord
goes with me, and everything will be fine. Do not worry
about me. Will you please ask the sisters to pray for me?"
Then the car drove away in the direction of the town of
Bilthoven.

Sister Judith writes of what happened next:

We went to the police station in Bilthoven, where I
had to get out. "You go inside, otherwise many will
look", the policeman who was carrying my suitcase
said. In the station there were a few men and ladies
wearing stars. I also wore one on my black coat. The
prioress had pinned it on at the last moment. I thought,
"Yes, now I am once again among Jews." But it turned
out to be different!

"I am glad", one lady told her husband, "that I could
still go to Holy Mass first and receive Holy Communion. Now I am at least strengthened!" It was a rev-
elation for me! "Catholic, too", I rejoiced deep inside.[11]

More and more Catholic Jews were gathered inside
and outside the police station. All were brought to
the Dutch Theater in Amsterdam by bus.

When the bus began to move, a firm man's voice
asked, "Are all here Catholic?" "Yes", it sounded as

though in one voice. A lady from Maartensdijk, dressed
in black, knelt next to me and asked, "Sister, may I
kiss your cross?" I held it up to her and signed the
cross on her forehead!

Then a small boy who was sitting next to his mother
came up to me. The mother was crying and constantly looked in my direction with a sad gaze full of
compassion. The little boy said, "Mother says that I
must ask you if I may kiss your cross."

"Are you Catholic?" I asked.

"No," he said, "but my mother is." I gave him the
cross and signed his forehead also with a cross. . . .[12]

Sister Judith mustered up new courage for herself. "Do
not worry now. Enjoy the moment." She also found consolation in a citation from Saint John of the Cross. "Do
not be disheartened in sad circumstances, because you
never know how through a secret disposition of God,
your suffering can change into joy and can serve your
eternal salvation." When the circumstances became more
critical, Sister Judith found strength in the sentence,
"When you have to face something difficult, then approach
it as though one were going to a wedding!"[13]

The arrestees were brought into the auditorium of the
Dutch Theater. About two hundred Catholic Jews were
gathered here, and Sister Judith was the only religious
among them. One man said to her, "Sister, we have no
priest. You now represent the Church to us!"[14]

Around 2:00 P.M., it was announced in the auditorium
that all who were in a mixed marriage (a Jew with a

[12] Ibid., 83.
[13] Ibid.
[14] Ibid., 84.

non-Jew) and their children could go home again. Someone mischievously said to Sister Judith, "Sister, you must
stay. You are married to a Jew!" [15] Thirty-six Catholic
Jews remained in the theater.

Father Reuzenaar from the Waterlooplein (a square in
Amsterdam) came to the theater. Sister Judith recounts:

> He shook my hand and asked me if I knew if there
> were people who would like to go to confession. I replied
> that I did not know and that I could scarcely ask.
>
> "It seems to me best if you do not keep talking to
> me but, instead, walk back and forth a bit through
> the auditorium. Those who want to speak to you will
> come to you." The priest thought that an excellent
> idea, and I went back to the people.
>
> "Sister, do you know that priest?" they asked.
>
> "No, but he asked if some of you would like to go
> to confession. I answered that I could scarcely inquire,
> but I suggested that he walk back and forth a bit. Those
> wanting to approach him would do so." Immediately
> a young woman stoop up and went to the priest, and
> they sat next to one another in the first row left.
>
> Her mother came to sit next to me and told me
> her daughter's life story. She had always been an exem-
> plary Catholic, had married a Jew two months ago,
> and had since neglected her faith. "You see, Sister,
> now she is telling the priest everything." I consoled
> her and spoke to her of God, who in his great good-
> ness had brought her daughter here precisely for this
> reason. She cried out of happiness and gratitude.
>
> Later the young woman came to me. "Oh, sister, I
> am so happy that you said that about confession. If I

[15] Ibid.

had not known that, I would have never dared approach him!" She went to her mother, and I left them alone. More people went to confession.[16]

There was a good, even jovial atmosphere in the theater. The prisoners mutually supported one another. Sister Judith distracted the people by telling them jokes and praying the rosary. The military police guarding the complex came in to look every once in a while. At 9:00 P.M., Sister Judith went to sleep.[17]

> In the morning around 4:45 A.M. (whether one considers it early or late, that is the time I always get up) I woke up. It was becoming light, and I thought, "Get up immediately before the others, so that you can freely go your way!" I did it immediately. Wearing my coat, I took my toiletries and clothing to the washing area, where I could peacefully dress myself. Afterward, I went downstairs to pray my morning prayer and the Little Hours. Meditation followed. In the break room we had breakfast, including coffee, in common.[18]

In the afternoon, Sister Judith even received permission to go to a convent (the Saint Hubertus Institute) across from the theater. There they had set the table for her; she could go to pray in the chapel; and she asked all the sisters and children for prayers. After half an hour she had to be back in the theater.[19]

On Monday, August 3, an old Redemptorist priest from Keizersgracht (a street in Amsterdam) also came toward

[16] Ibid., 85.
[17] See ibid.
[18] Ibid., 86.
[19] See ibid., 87–88.

evening. He did his best to obtain Sister Judith's release. Toward this end, she had to give him the names of her four Portuguese grandparents. This visit gave some other detainees the opportunity to go to confession. That evening, two hundred non-Catholic Jews arrived. They would be brought to Westerbork along with the Catholic Jews.[20] The Redemptorist priest had fifty chocolate bars sent to Sister Judith. Packages and suitcases that the prisoners were allowed to take on the approaching journey were brought into the theater.

On Tuesday, August 4, around 1:00 A.M., the group left the theater. Afraid to lose one another, the Catholic Jews held one another's hands. From the darkness a man's voice called, "Where is the sister! The sister must stay close to us!" Sister Judith called very calmly in response, "Here is the sister; I am with you." She realized anew how important her presence was for the Catholics. "God is so good, that he would give me, poor, weak nothing, strength to be of some consolation and comfort to those people in that terribly black night."

Together with the other Jews, the group of Catholics went by tram to the Central train station. Sister Judith describes the situation:

> I will never in my life forget the misery there. A miserable drizzle made the whole event even sadder. Flashlights mysteriously lit up the human wretchedness of those who had been picked up and were waiting in long rows for their turn to enter the station. We Catholics held one another again by the hand, or by the skirt, because we wanted to be together in the train,

---

[20] See ibid., 89.

too. "Curb", the one walking ahead would say and we would pass it on. In that way we arrived at the entrance of the station. The train was waiting at the platform, and we could already board.[21]

Sister Judith ended up in a compartment with the Westering family, which consisted of the father, mother, a daughter who was a Third Order member of Saint Francis, and a son who was in the Franciscan novitiate and had been picked up there.[22]

Very early on the morning of Tuesday, August 4, the train arrived in Hooghalen in Drenthe.[23] According to the liturgical calendar, it was the memorial of Saint Dominic. With her group, Sister Judith left the train station in Hooghalen for the Westerbork camp. The walk would last about an hour and fifteen minutes. Once again she suggested they pray the rosary out loud. She was afraid that one of the accompanying soldiers would silence her by hitting her face. She prepared herself for that and intended to offer the soldier the other cheek if she could.[24]

On the way, two wagons, pulled by horses, passed them. They were filled with people and luggage. Among those who sat on them, there were also about six religious. In the camp they became acquainted with these religious. They were two Trappistine sisters, two Trappist priests, and one brother, all from one family, and a Carmelite, doctor in philosophy, from Echt. This was Sister Teresa Benedicta.

---

[21] Ibid., 91.

[22] See ibid. This family is not listed on the transport list of August 7, 1942, from Westerbork to Auschwitz.

[23] See Sister Judith Mendes da Costa, *Autobiografie*, 92.

[24] See Peters in *Als een brandende toorts*, 160.

Life in the camp was tense, unpleasant, and deprived of every comfort, as Sister Judith recounts in the excerpts already cited in chapter 1.[25]

In Westerbork, an unfriendly German asked about the golden profession ring he saw on her finger.

"Are you married?"

"Yes," Sister Judith responded proudly, "to the Church."

"That does not count", the Nazi responded. She had to give up her cherished profession ring.[26]

All prisoners had their photograph taken, holding in front of them a small chalkboard on which a number had been written.[27] Since she had to wait an hour and a half here, Sister Judith wrote a letter to her superior general and her prioress.

After the picture had been taken, Sister Judith had to report immediately to the camp's deputy commander. His office was in a large building near the entrance of the camp. Sister Judith recounts:

A man opened the window and asked my name.

"Are you related to Professor Mendes da Costa?" he asked.

"Yes!" I responded.

"Is his first initial S., and does he live in Amsterdam, on P.C. Hoofdstraat?"

I confirmed everything.

"Then your departure to Germany has been postponed for the time being."

I thanked him and immediately left.[28]

---

[25] See chap. 1.

[26] Peters in *Als een brandende toorts*, 163–64, 199.

[27] See ibid., 164.

[28] Sister Judith Mendes da Costa, O.P., as quoted by Peters in *Als een brandende toorts*, 165.

In Westerbork camp Sister Judith lived full of confidence. She regularly prayed an ejaculatory prayer to the Blessed Mother. She described the effect of such an ejaculatory prayer: "The next moment I was wholly at peace. Mother was so near me, even though I did not see her. It was as though I felt her maternal protection." [29] On Thursday, August 6, the evening before the First Friday, Sister Judith united herself to the prayers of her community during their holy hour. "I counted upon the prayers of my beloved community. I prayed much, both alone and with the people. I did not ask God to be freed, because above all else his holy will had to be accomplished in me. I told our dear Lord, 'If I receive a respite, it is good. If I have to go to Silesia, it is also good. But if I may return to "Berg en Bosch," then I will be very grateful to you, even though I cannot ask you for it.'" [30]

Initially Sister Judith was told that she had to go along to the east, but it later turned out that this had been a mistake. When it became clear that she had not come to Westerbork by means of Amersfoort, a request that she not go to the east was drafted. The barrack leader informed Sister Judith that the report had been received and that she would not leave for the east Thursday night. She had to leave the barrack immediately, along with the others who had received a postponement. Sister Judith gave the apples, cheese, jam, and other treats she had received in the camp (probably from Sophie van Berckel) to others and gave her black coat to a lady. "Then I said goodbye to the others. 'Until we meet again,' I said, 'because I

[29] Ibid.
[30] Ibid., 166.

will surely follow you after some time. Be of good courage. I will think of you.' " [31]

The next night the others left to meet death in Auschwitz. Sister Judith was released on August 15, 1942, because
of her Portuguese Jewish origins. She broke out in tears.
It was difficult for her "to have to leave good friends in
misery and to be the only one to regain freedom".[32] She
received a respite of a year and a half. Between August
1942 and February 1944 she wrote the recollections from
which this biography is taken. She entitled it *Grasped by
God*. Sister Judith's spiritual disposition and readiness to
sacrifice become clear in the words with which she looks
back to her first deportation in August 1942. In her notes,
she called the fourteen days in Westerbork "my most beautiful time". One thought dominated her mind and prepared her to accept all suffering: "If I have to go to
Germany, I will go as to a wedding!" [33]

During the last decades of the sixteenth century,
Portuguese Jewish refugees had found hospitality in
Amsterdam. The Portuguese Jewish community in the
Netherlands in 1943 included twenty-two families—273
persons in all. Their deportation was initially postponed.[34] At the end of 1943, a rumor circulated that
the Portuguese Jews would be deported to Portugal. It
was the ruse by which the Nazis tried to prevent the
Jews from panicking. Later the Nazis decided that

[31] Ibid., 167.
[32] Ibid., 199.
[33] Ibid.
[34] The Archives of the Archdiocese of Utrecht, no. 76, include an extensive report about the Jews with a Portuguese background. See also R. Kempner, *Twee uit honderdduizend, Anne Frank en Edith Stein: Onthullingen over de
nazimisdaden in Nederland voor het gerecht in München* (Bilthoven, 1969), 133.

Portuguese Jews were also "inferior people" and did not consider it responsible to let them go to Portugal. They, too, had to be murdered.

Sister Judith wanted to take the sacrifice of the deportation upon herself. She even rejoiced in it. She said to a fellow sister:

> My life here [in Bilthoven] is not hard enough. I would like to do much more for him. I owe him so much gratitude. I would be glad once more to lead the life of a prisoner, also in order to be a support for my fellow prisoners. I always think back with great gratitude to what I was able to do in the few days [of imprisonment]. How happy I would be if God would once again give me that grace and if I would have it even harder this time.[35]

God accepted her readiness for sacrifice. On February 2, 1944, she was arrested in Bilthoven for the second time. Before she left, she asked the blessing of a Dominican priest who happened to be there. The angelus bells rang as the car drove off. The sisters prayed together, "Behold the Handmaid of the Lord." Sister Judith, together with the other Portuguese Jews, was brought to Westerbork. In two letters she informed the sisters that camp life in Westerbork had in the meantime become much stricter. She soon became ill there, but she did not mind that. It was much more difficult for her to live without the sacraments and without the consolation of others who shared her faith. She was the only Catholic among the Jews in the camp then. She remained in

[35] Sister Judith Mendes da Costa, O.P., as quoted by Peters in *Als een brandende toorts*, 200.

Westerbork until February 25, 1944, at which time she was brought to Theresienstadt. On May 16, 1944, she left there for Auschwitz, where her earthly existence ended. It is not wholly clear if her death was the consequence of exhaustion or if she was gassed. The date given for her death is July 7, 1944.[36]

---

[36] See Peters in ibid., 193.

APPENDIX

LIST OF MURDERED CATHOLIC JEWS

A list of the Catholic Jews who were murdered in response to the letter of the Dutch bishops of July 26, 1942, has never before been published. There is a good reason why this has not been done before: it is a complicated undertaking to compile such a list. There are many lists that must be compared with one another. Moreover, the exact meaning of these lists is not always clear.

The list that follows is therefore probably not complete. It is a first attempt, which will hopefully be completed and, where necessary, corrected in the future. This list also makes it possible to carry out a future study of the lives of those persons listed whose biographies are not yet known. In that way, one could provide faces for the names.

Most arrestees were gathered in the Amersfoort camp on August 2, 1942, were brought to Westerbork on August 4, were deported to Auschwitz on August 7, and were gassed there on August 9. The September 30, 1942, date of death is a juridical determination of the latest possible date the deported persons would have died. Events did not proceed according to this chronology for all the Catholic Jews.

The list of arrests from the district of Amsterdam has not yet been recovered. Those who were arrested there were brought from Amsterdam directly to Westerbork. For this reason, their names did not appear on the transport list that was prepared in Amersfoort. The Catholic Jews from the district of Amsterdam are therefore missing—with one exception—from the list that follows.

The criteria for being included in this list are that the person in question was arrested in response to the bishops' letter of July 26, 1942, and that he was afterward not released, even if the person in question was murdered earlier or later than August 9. The list includes eighty-three persons: thirty-one men and fifty-two women. Of the twelve religious on this list, there were four men: two priests and two brothers. There were six women religious and two third-order members. A total of seventeen lay families were deported (married couples with or without children, brothers, and sisters). Of the families, the Hamburger family was the largest, with a mother and five children. The children were ages nine to seventeen. From the Löb family, six members also died, and these were all adults. The youngest member on this list is Branca (or Bianca) Schupper, who was born on March 18, 1942, in The Hague. She was not even six months old when she was murdered. The oldest who was murdered was Marianne Hertz, who was born on January 14, 1882. At the time of her arrest, she was sixty years old.

The first name "Israel" or "Sara" is very common in the list. This is rarely a given first name. In order to emphasize the Jewish character, the Nazis added the first name "Israel" to every male Jew and "Sara" to every female Jew.

I here take the occasion to thank in a particular way Mr. V. Laurentius, staff member of the Dutch Red Cross in The Hague in the War Aftercare Department, for his cooperation in the realization of this list.

Arend,[1] Antoine Franciscus den
Born: February 5, 1905, in Rotterdam
Deportation from Westerbork: August 7, 1942
Died: September 30, 1942, in Auschwitz

Arend-Ossendrijver,[2] Femina den
Born: January 20, 1909, in Rotterdam
Deportation from Westerbork: August 7, 1942
Died: September 30, 1942, in Auschwitz

Arend,[3] Leendert den
Born: February 23, 1934, in Rotterdam
Child
Deportation from Westerbork: August 7, 1942
Died: August 9, 1942, in Auschwitz

Arend,[4] Marcus den
Born: July 27, 1940, in Rotterdam
Child
Deportation from Westerbork: August 7, 1942
Died: August 9, 1942, in Auschwitz

Bak-Meiler,[5] Sebilla
Born: August 18, 1886, in Bergschenhook
She lived at Schellinglaan 11 in Voorburg. She was on
    the list of arrests from The Hague.

[1] List Amersfoort-Westerbork (list A–W) (August 4, 1942); transport list
Westerbork-Auschwitz (transport list W–A) (August 7, 1942), A, no. 9.
[2] Ibid.
[3] Ibid.
[4] Ibid.
[5] List of 23 Catholic Jews in mixed marriages (list of 23); list A–W (August
15, 1942); transport list W–A (August 17, 1942), A, no. 5.

Deportation from Westerbork: August 17, 1942
Died: August 19, 1942, in Auschwitz

Behr,[6] Ilse Johanna

Born: August 12, 1901, in Krefeld (Germany)
Office clerk
At the time of her arrest on August 2, she lived at Leyenbroek 73 in Oosterhout.
Deportation from Westerbork: August 7, 1942
Died: September 30, 1942, in Auschwitz

Berliner-Rosenthal,[7] Berta Sara

Born: October 22, 1896, in Ibbenbüren (Germany)
No profession
Deportation from Westerbork: August 7, 1942
Died: September 30, 1942, in Auschwitz

Berliner,[8] Liselotte

Born: December 4, 1908, in Rheine (Germany)
No profession
Deportation from Westerbork: August 7, 1942
Died: September 30, 1942, in Auschwitz

Bing,[9] Dr. Fritz

Born: December 12, 1882, in Nürnberg (Germany)
Lawyer

---

[6] On the list of arrests from Breda, she is listed as no. 1; list A–W (August 4, 1942); Kempner, *Twee uit honderdduizend*, 107; transport list W–A (August 7, 1942), A, no. 10.

[7] List A–W (August 4, 1942); Kempner, *Twee uit honderdduizend*, 108; transport list W–A (August 7, 1942), A, no. 10.

[8] Ibid.

[9] On the list of arrests from Tilburg; list A–W (August 4, 1942); Kempner, *Twee uit honderdduizend*, 108; transport list W–A (August 7, 1942), A,

Baptized, together with his entire family, on March 19, 1932, in Mannheim (Germany). According to civil records, he left Mannheim on February 24, 1934, and moved to The Hague.
Deportation from Westerbork: August 7, 1942
Died: September 30, 1942, in Auschwitz

Bing-Hachenburg,[10] Grete
Born: May 10, 1890, in Mannheim (Germany)
Deportation from Westerbork: August 7, 1942
Died: August 9, 1942, in Auschwitz

Bing,[11] Heinz Wolfgang
Born: June 9, 1922, in Wurzburg (Germany), lived in Mannheim (Germany)
Deportation from Westerbork: August 7, 1942
Died: September 30, 1942, in Auschwitz

Bock,[12] Edith
Born: August 23 (or 29), 1907, in Vienna (Austria)
Teacher; stateless (had been Austrian)
She lived at Katendrechtselagedijk 231A, Rotterdam.
Deportation from Westerbork: August 7, 1942
Died: August 9, 1942, or September 30, 1942, in Auschwitz
See biography in the present work.

---

no. 13; http://www.bundesarchiv.de/gedenkbuch/index.html. Christopher Smider has written an article about the Bing family that will be published in the fifth edition of the German martyrology, *Zeugen für Christus*.
    [10] On the list of arrests from Tilburg; list A–W (August 4, 1942); transport list W–A (August 7, 1942), A, no. 13.
    [11] Ibid.
    [12] On the list from Rotterdam; list A–W (August 7, 1942); Kempner, *Twee uit honderdduizend*, 107; transport list W–A (August 7, 1942), A, no. 7.

Bock,[13] Helene (Leni) Luise Maria Theresia
Born: June 25, 1912, in Vienna (Austria)
Office clerk; stateless (had been Austrian)
She lived at Katendrechtselagedijk 231A, Rotterdam.
Deportation from Westerbork: August 7, 1942
Died: August 9, 1942, or September 30, 1942, in Auschwitz
See biography in the present work.

Bock,[14] Sister Charitas (Thérèse [Resi] Christina Clementina)
Born: June 13, 1909, in Vienna (Austria)
Final profession: August 15, 1931, in Moerdijk
Address: Moerdijkersteenweg 49 (Sacred Heart Convent [H. Hartklooster] added in pencil). Hooge en Lage Zwaluwe
Deportation from Westerbork: August 7, 1942
Died: August 9, 1942, or September 30, 1942, in Auschwitz
See biography in the present work.

Davidson,[15] Rachel
Born: September 11, 1888, in The Hague
Dutch nationality
Office clerk
She lived at Bilderdijklaan 16 in Voorburg.
Deportation from Westerbork: August 7, 1942
Died: August 9, 1942, in Auschwitz

[13] On the list from Rotterdam; list A–W (August 4, 1942); Kempner, *Twee uit honderdduizend*, 108; transport list W–A (August 7, 1942), A, no. 8.

[14] On the list from Breda, no. 3; list A–W (August 4, 1942); Kempner, *Twee uit honderdduizend*, 107; transport list W–A (August 7, 1942), A, no. 7.

[15] Amersfoort lists (August 4, 1942); Kempner, *Twee uit honderdduizend*, 108; transport list W–A (August 7, 1942), A, no. 6.

Dohm-Gütherz,[16] Susanna Felicitas

Born: April 1, 1903, in Dresden (Germany)

She lived at Beukenlaan 33B in Oosterbeek.

Deportation from Westerbork: August 17, 1942

Died: August 30, 1942, in Auschwitz

Feitsma,[17] Jacob

Born: April 13, 1895, in Amsterdam

Unmarried; translator

He lived at Biesboschstraat 65I in Amsterdam

He was brought to Westerbork on August 4, by way of the Dutch Theater in Amsterdam.

Deportation: August 7, 1942

Died: September 30, 1942, Auschwitz

He is the only one of the Catholic Jews deported by way of the Dutch Theater whose name is known.

Geus,[18] Louis de

Born: July 15, 1908, in Amsterdam

Artist

Deportation from Westerbork: August 7, 1942

Died: September 30, 1942, in Auschwitz

[16] List of arrests from the district of Arnhem (August 15, 1942); list of 23; list A–W (August 15, 1942); transport list W–A (August 17, 1942), A, no. 5.

[17] Jewish Council File in Archive Wartime Documentation of the Dutch Red Cross; list A–W; transport list W–A (August 7, 1942), A, no. 6; Institute for Wartime Graves; Sister Judith Mendes da Costa, *Sister Judith Mendes da Costa, Dominican Sister of the Congregation of Saint Catherine of Siena in Voorschoten, Amsterdam 1895–1944 Auschwitz: Autobiografie*, unpublished (Voorschoten, 2006).

[18] List A–W (August 4, 1942); Kempner, *Twee uit honderdduizend*, 108; transport list W–A (August 7, 1942), A, no.13.

Goldschmidt,[19] Annemarie Louise Sara

Born: January 31, 1922, in Munich (Germany)
Student
Deportation from Westerbork: August 7, 1942
Died: August 9 or September 30, 1942, in Auschwitz
See biography in the present work.

Goldschmidt,[20] Elfriede Karoline Ida Sara

Born: August 4, 1923, in Munich (Germany)
Student
Deportation from Westerbork: August 7, 1942
Died: August 9 or September 30, 1942, in Auschwitz
See biography in the present work.

Hamburger (de Man) -Kalker,[21] Eva Jeannette Maria

Born: April 10, 1905, in Rotterdam
Married to Salomon Herman Hamburger (de Man) on
    March 19, 1924
Housewife
Deportation from Westerbork: August 7, 1942
Died: August 9, 1942, in Auschwitz
See biography in the present work.

Hamburger (de Man),[22] Johannes (Jan) Willem

Born: February 3, 1925, in Utrecht

[19] List A–W (August 4, 1942); Kempner, *Twee uit honderdduizend*, 109; transport list W–A (August 7, 1942), A, no. 6.

[20] Ibid.

[21] List A–W (August 4, 1942); Kempner, *Twee uit honderdduizend*, 108; transport list W–A (August 7, 1942), A, no. 13.

[22] List A–W (August 4, 1942); Kempner, *Twee uit honderdduizend*, 108; transport list W–A (August 7, 1942), A, no. 17; Kempner, *Twee uit honderdduizend*, 109.

Student

Deportation from Westerbork: August 7, 1942

Died: Official date given is September 30, 1942, in Auschwitz (but possibly in 1944 in France)

See biography in the present work.

Hamburger (de Man),[23] Anna (Anneke) Maria Henriëtte

Born: November 8, 1928, in Woerden

Child

Deportation from Westerbork: August 7, 1942

Died: August 9, 1942, in Auschwitz

Hamburger (de Man),[24] Joachim (Jochie) Albertus Maria

Born: September 3, 1930, in Berlicum

Child

Deportation from Westerbork: August 7, 1942

Died: August 9, 1942, in Auschwitz

Hamburger (de Man),[25] Magdalena (Magdaleentje) Johanna Maria

Born: February 5, 1932, in Berlicum

Child

Deportation from Westerbork: August 7, 1942

Died: August 9, 1942, in Auschwitz

[23] List A–W (August 4, 1942); Kempner, *Twee uit honderdduizend*, 108; transport list W–A (August 7, 1942), A, no. 13.

[24] Ibid.

[25] Ibid.

Hamburger (de Man),[26] Petrus (Pieterje) Christianus Maria

Born: May 19, 1933, in Berlicum
Child
Deportation from Westerbork: August 7, 1942
Died: August 9, 1942, in Auschwitz

Hertz,[27] Marianne

Born: January 14, 1882, in Holzminden (Germany)
Deportation from Westerbork: August 7, 1942
Died: August 9 or September 30, 1942, in Auschwitz

Hertz,[28] Siegfried

Born: January 30, 1915, in Sittard
Tailor/factory worker; Dutch nationality
He lived at Putstraat 90 in Sittard.
Deportation from Westerbork: August 7, 1942
Died: August 18, 1942, in Auschwitz

Ikkersheim,[29] Margareta

Born: December 8, 1919, in Bandung (Indonesia)
Maid
Deportation from Westerbork: August 7, 1942
Died: August 9 or September 30, 1942, in Auschwitz

[26] Ibid.
[27] List A–W (August 4, 1942); transport list W–A (August 7, 1942), A, no. 7.
[28] On the list of arrests from the district of Maastricht; list A–W (August 4, 1942); Kempner, *Twee uit honderdduizend*, 108; transport list W–A (August 7, 1942), A, no. 15.
[29] List A–W (August 4, 1942); Kempner, *Twee uit honderdduizend*, 108; transport list W–A (August 7, 1942), A, no. 14.

Jacobs-Hollander,[30] Pauline
Born: July 8, 1883, in Antwerp (Belgium)
She lived at Oranjestraat 5 in Tilburg.
Deportation from Westerbork: August 17, 1942
Died: August 19, 1942, in Auschwitz

Kantorowicz,[31] Dr. Ruth Renate Frederike
Economist
Born: January 7, 1901, in Hamburg (Germany)
Deportation from Westerbork: August 7, 1942
Died: August 9 or September 30, 1942, in Auschwitz
See biography in the present work.

Klint,[32] Elisabeth (Betje)
Born: March 14, 1890, in Amsterdam
She lived at Elandstraat 122 in The Hague.
Deportation from Westerbork: August 7, 1942
Died: August 9, 1942, in Auschwitz

Köstenmann,[33] Arthur Israel Erwin
Born: May 20, 1884, in Vienna (Austria)
He lived in Udenhout and was on the list of arrests from
    's-Hertogenbosch
Deportation from Westerbork: August 17, 1942
Died: August 30, 1942, in Auschwitz

---

[30] List of 23; list A–W (August 15, 1942); transport list W–A (August 17, 1942), A, no. 5.

[31] List A–W (August 4, 1942); Kempner, *Twee uit honderdduizend*, 109; transport list W–A (August 7, 1942), A, no. 15.

[32] List A–W (August 4, 1942); Kempner, *Twee uit honderdduizend*, 107; transport list W–A (August 7, 1942), A, no. 16.

[33] List of 23; list A–W (August 15, 1942); transport list W–A (August 17, 1942), A, no. 5.

Langer-Winnekowa,[34] Chawa Siskowna

Born: May 23, 1906, in Orel (former U.S.S.R.)
Housewife
Deportation from Westerbork: August 7, 1942
Died: August 9, 1942, in Auschwitz

Langer,[35] Sinaida Leopoldovna

Born: January 1, 1932, in Pavschino (Ukraine)
No profession
Deportation from Westerbork: August 7, 1942
Died: August 9, 1942, in Auschwitz

Leeuw–van Weezel,[36] Rosalie Elisabeth de

Born: May 30, 1903, in Amsterdam
Housewife
Deportation from Westerbork: August 7, 1942
Died: August 9, 1942, in Auschwitz
She is probably the daughter of Gerrit van Weezel.

Leeuw,[37] Alexander de

Born: May 9, 1935, in The Hague
Child
Deportation from Westerbork: August 7, 1942
Died: August 9, 1942, in Auschwitz

[34] List A–W (August 4, 1942); Kempner, *Twee uit honderdduizend*, 108; transport list W–A (August 7, 1942), A, no. 10.

[35] Ibid.

[36] List A–W (August 4, 1942); Kempner, *Twee uit honderdduizend*, 108; transport list W–A (August 7, 1942), A, no. 17; Kempner, *Twee uit honderdduizend*, 109.

[37] Ibid.

Leeuw,[38] Richard Gerrit de
Born: February 13, 1937, in Amsterdam
Child
Deportation from Westerbork: August 7, 1942
Died: August 9, 1942, in Auschwitz

Löb,[39] Sister Hedwigis, O.C.S.O. (Lien or Lina)
Born: March 3, 1908, in Rijswijk
Final profession: May 4, 1933
Deportation from Westerbork: August 7, 1942
Died: September 30, 1942, in Auschwitz
See biography in the present work.

Löb,[40] Father Ignatius, O.C.S.O. (George or Joris)
Born: September 25, 1909, in Hoensbroek
Priestly ordination: June 6, 1936
Deportation from Westerbork: August 7, 1942
Died: August 19, 1942, in Auschwitz
See biography in the present work.

Löb,[41] Brother Linus, O.C.S.O. (Robert)
Born: October 15, 1910, in The Hague
Final profession: March 19, 1937
Deportation from Westerbork: August 7, 1942
Died: September 30, 1942, in Auschwitz
See biography in the present work.

[38] Ibid.
[39] Peter Steffen and Hans Evers. *Scheuren in het Kleed: Het joos-Katholleke gezin Löb 1881–1945* (Nijmegen: Volkhof Pers, 2009).
[40] Ibid.
[41] Ibid.

Löb,[42] Sister Maria-Theresia, O.C.S.O. (Dorothea or Theodora)

Born: October 22, 1911, in Sawah Loento (Indonesia)
Final profession: May 13, 1934
Deportation from Westerbork: August 7, 1942
Died: September 30, 1942, in Auschwitz
See biography in the present work.

Löb,[43] Father Nivardus, O.C.S.O. (Ernst)

Born: October 29, 1913, in Sawah Loento (Indonesia)
Priestly ordination: June 3, 1939
Deportation from Westerbork: August 7, 1942
Died: August 19, 1942, in Auschwitz
See biography in the present work.

Löb,[44] Hans Jozef

Born: October 11, 1916, in Sawah Loento (Indonesia)
Arrested: August 28, 1942
Left from Westerbork for Auschwitz on August 31, 1942
Died: February 20, 1945, in the Buchenwald concentration camp
See biography in the present work.

Löwenfels,[45] Sister Maria Aloysia, P.H.J.C. (Luise) (Dernbacher Sisters)

Born: July 5, 1915, Trabelsdorf (Germany)

[42] Ibid.

[43] Ibid.

[44] Archive of the Cistercian Abbey of Our Lady of Koningshoeven, Berkel-Enschot; Kempner, *Twee uit honderdduizend*, 130–31; also Steffen and Evers, *Scheuren in het kleed*, 387.

[45] List of arrests from the district of Maastricht (August 2, 1942); list A–W (August 4, 1942); Kempner, *Twee uit honderdduizend*, 108; transport list W–A (August 7, 1942), A, no. 15.

First profession: September 12, 1940
Deportation from Westerbork: August 7, 1942
Died: August 9 or September 30, 1942, in Auschwitz
See biography in the present work.

Luik or Kuik-Koperberg,[46] Sophie van

Born: December 11, 1896
Deportation from Westerbork: August 7, 1942
Died: September 30, 1942, in Auschwitz

Meirowsky,[47] Dr. Lisamaria

Born: September 7, 1904, in Grudziądz/Vistula (Poland)
Physician; member of the Third Order of Saint Dominic
Deportation from Westerbork: August 7, 1942
Died: August 9 or September 30, 1942, in Auschwitz
See biography in the present work.

Menkel,[48] Hans

Born: November 14, 1907, in Eitorf (Germany)
Wallpaper-hanger
Unmarried and lived in Nijmegen after 1936.[49]
Deportation from Westerbork: August 7, 1942
Died: September 30, 1942, in Auschwitz

---

[46] List A–W (August 4, 1942); transport list W–A (August 7, 1942), A, no. 9.

[47] List of arrests from Tilburg (August 2, 1942); list A–W (August 4, 1942); Kempner, *Twee uit honderdduizend*, 108; transport list W–A (August 7, 1942), A, no. 17; Kempner, *Twee uit honderdduizend*, 109.

[48] List of arrests from the district of Nijmegen; list A–W (August 4, 1942); Kempner, *Twee uit honderdduizend*, 108; transport list W–A (August 7, 1942), A, no. 4.

[49] See the biography by Helmut Moll, which will be published in the fifth edition of the German martyrology, *Zeugen für Christus*.

Merkelbach-Van Enkhuizen-Grünbaum,[50] Hermine, divorced from Bock

Born: September 29, 1886, in Leobersdorf (Austria-Hungary)

Mother of the three Bock sisters

She lived at Katendrechtselagedijk 231A in Rotterdam.

Deportation from Westerbork: August 17, 1942

Died: August 19, 1942, in Auschwitz

See biography in the present work.

Mesritz,[51] Elias

Born: March 7, 1908, in Duisburg-Laar (Germany)

Butcher; Dutch nationality

He lived at Flakkeeschestraat 95B in Rotterdam.

Deportation from Westerbork: August 17, 1942

Died: September 30, 1942, in Auschwitz

Michaelis,[52] Sister Mirjam, C.S.J. (Trier) (Elisabeth)

Congregation of the Sisters of Saint Joseph in Trier

Born: March 31, 1889, in Berlin (Germany)

Final profession: 1935

The list of arrests from Maastricht of August 2, 1942, notes that she lived in Convent Mariënwaard no. 23. For profession, it says "religious sister"; for nationality, it says German.

Deportation from Westerbork: August 7, 1942

---

[50] List of arrests from the district of Rotterdam (August 15, 1942); list of 23; list A–W (August 15, 1942); transport list W–A (August 17, 1942), A, no. 5.

[51] Ibid.

[52] List of arrests from Maastricht; list A–W (August 4, 1942); Kempner, *Twee uit honderdduizend*, 108; transport list W–A (August 7, 1942), A, no. 13.

Died: August 9, 1942, in Auschwitz
See biography in the present work.

Ossendrijver,[53] Leendert
Born: July 25, 1886, in Rotterdam
Fruit exporter; Dutch nationality
He lived at Rosestraat 164B in Rotterdam.
Deportation from Westerbork: August 7, 1942
Died: September 30, 1942, in Auschwitz

Ossendrijver-Oss,[54] Gerdina
Born: November 22, 1894, in Den Bosch
Housewife; Dutch nationality
She lived at Rosestraat 164B in Rotterdam.
Deportation from Westerbork: August 7, 1942
Died: September 30, 1942, in Auschwitz

Praag,[55] Bertha Amelia van
Born: January 2, 1914, in Amsterdam
She lived at Langnekstraat 46 in The Hague.
Deportation from Westerbork: August 7, 1942
Died: September 30, 1942, in Auschwitz

Praag,[56] Selma van
Born: January 24, 1918 in Amsterdam
She lived at Langnekstraat 46 in The Hague.

---

[53] List of arrests from Rotterdam; list A–W (August 4, 1942); Kempner, *Twee uit honderdduizend*, 107; transport list W–A (August 7, 1942), A, no. 13.
[54] Ibid.
[55] List of arrests from The Hague; list A–W (August 4, 1942); transport list W–A (August 7, 1942), A, no. 7.
[56] Ibid.

Deportation from Westerbork: August 7, 1942
Died: September 30, 1942, in Auschwitz

Reis,[57] Alice Maria
Born: September 17, 1903, in Berlin (Germany)
Nurse
Deportation from Westerbork: August 7, 1942
Died: August 9 or September 30, 1942, in Auschwitz
See biography in the present work.

Rosenbaum,[58] Brother Wolfgang, O.F.M. (Fritz)
Born: May 27, 1915, in Witten/Ruhr (Germany)
Profession: October 4, 1940
Deportation from Westerbork: August 7, 1942
Died: August 9 or September 30, 1942, in Auschwitz
See biography in the present work.

Sanders-Platz,[59] Elvira (Elviere)
Born: September 15, 1891, in Cologne (Germany)
Housewife and widow
Deportation from Westerbork: August 7, 1942
Died: August 9 or September 30, 1942, in Auschwitz
See biography in the present work.

---

[57] List of arrests from Enschede; list A–W (August 4, 1942); Kempner, *Twee uit honderdduizend*, 108; transport list W–A (August 7, 1942), A, no. 2; Kempner, *Twee uit honderdduizend*, 110.

[58] List A–W (August 4, 1942); Kempner, *Twee uit honderdduizend*, 108; transport list W–A (August 7, 1942), A, no. 17; Kempner, *Twee uit honderdduizend*, 110.

[59] List A–W (August 4, 1942); transport list W–A (August 7, 1942), A, no. 7.

Schupper,[60] Wolf

Born: November 6, 1903, in Dubiecko (Poland)
Deportation from Westerbork: August 31, 1942
Died: July 31, 1943 in Fürstengrube subcamp
The whole Schupper family left the Netherlands and was
brought to Auschwitz on August 31, 1942.

Schupper-Hirsch,[61] Piroska

Born: March 3, 1911, in Mukachevo (Ukraine)
The Schupper Family lived at Spaarnedwarsstraat 7 in
The Hague. They were brought to the Westerbork Jew-
ish Transit Camp (*Juden Durchgangslager Westerbork*) on
August 4, 1942.
Deportation from Westerbork: August 31, 1942
Died: September 3, 1942, in Auschwitz

Schupper,[62] Tonia Rachel

Born: April 5, 1938, in The Hague
Child
Deportation from Westerbork: August 31, 1942
Died: September 3, 1942, in Auschwitz

Schupper,[63] Hela

Born: February 15, 1941, in The Hague
Child

[60] List A–W (August 4, 1942); transport list W–A (August 31, 1942), A,
no. 11.
[61] Jewish Council File in Archive Wartime Documentation of the Dutch
Red Cross; list A–W (August 4, 1942); transport list W–A (August 31, 1942),
A, no. 11; *Staatscourant* 27 (July 1950).
[62] List A–W (August 4, 1942); transport list W–A (August 31, 1942), A,
no. 11.
[63] Ibid.

Deportation from Westerbork: August 31, 1942
Died: September 3, 1942, in Auschwitz

Schupper,[64] Branca or Bianca
Born: March 18, 1942, in The Hague
Deportation from Westerbork: August 31, 1942
Died: September 3, 1942, in Auschwitz
She was not yet six months old and was the youngest of
    the murdered Catholic Jews in this group.

Soester,[65] Hendrika Rosalie (divorced from Walg)
Born: January 31, 1912, in Rotterdam
Deportation from Westerbork: August 7, 1942
Died: September 30, 1942, in Auschwitz

Spanjaard,[66] Martin
Born: July 30, 1892, in Borne
On list of August 4 no profession is listed.
Music conductor, composer, and teacher
Deportation from Westerbork: August 7, 1942
Died: September 30, 1942, in Auschwitz

Spanjaard-Okladek,[67] Eleonora Maria Hedwig
Born: March 10, 1901, in Vienna (Austria)
Housewife

[64] Ibid.

[65] List A–W (August 4, 1942); transport list W–A (August 7, 1942), A, no. 2; Kempner, *Twee uit honderdduizend*, 110.

[66] List A–W (August 4, 1942); Kempner, *Twee uit honderdduizend*, 108; transport list W–A (August 7, 1942), A, no. 10.; list A–W (August 4, 1942); Kempner, *Twee uit honderdduizend*, 108; transport list W–A (August 7 1942), A, no. 10.

[67] List A–W (August 4, 1942); Kempner, *Twee uit honderdduizend*, 108; transport list W–A (August 7, 1942), A, no. 10.

Deportation from Westerbork: August 7, 1942
Died: September 30, 1942, in Auschwitz

Speijer-Bendin,[68] Emmy

Born: January 9, 1888, in Dorstfeld, near Dortmund (Germany)[69]

On the transport list of August 7, 1942, three persons who went voluntarily to Auschwitz are listed. These are people who did not want to leave their beloved ones alone. Among the volunteers is also Jacob Speijer, born on May 14, 1892. He could have been Emmy's husband.[70]

Deportation from Westerbork: August 7, 1942
Died: August 9, 1942, in Auschwitz

Stein,[71] Rosa Maria Agnes Adelheid

Born: December 13, 1883, in Lublinitz (Germany)
Member of the Third Order of Carmel in Echt since June 25, 1941
Deportation from Westerbork: August 7, 1942
Died: August 9, 1942, in Auschwitz
See biography in the present work.

Stein,[72] Saint Teresa Benedicta of the Cross, O.C.D. (Dr. Edith Teresa Hedwig)

Born: October 12, 1891, in Breslau (Germany)
Final profession: April 21, 1938, in Cologne (Germany)

[68] List A–W (August 4, 1942); transport list W–A (August 7, 1942), A, no. 11.

[69] See http://www.bundesarchiv.de/gedenbuch/index.html (Dec. 2009).

[70] Transport list W–A (August 7, 1942), A, no. 28.

[71] List A–W (August 4, 1942); Kempner, *Twee uit honderdduizend*, 109. Transport list W–A (August 7, 1942), A, no. 2; Kempner, *Twee uit honderdduizend*, 110.

[72] Ibid.

Deportation from Westerbork: August 7, 1942
Died: August 9, 1942, in Auschwitz
See biography in the present work.

Tichelhoven-de Oliveira,[73] Esther

Born: May 22, 1896, in Rotterdam
She was divorced and had four children from her first
    marriage. They were ages 25, 23, 22, and 21. At the
    time of her arrest she lived at Zutfensestraat 27 in The
    Hague.
Deportation from Westerbork: August 7, 1942
Died: September 30, 1942, in Auschwitz

Velleman,[74] Jacob

Born: August 10, 1911, in Leeuwarden
Deportation from Westerbork: August 7, 1942
Died: September 30, 1942, in Auschwitz

Vogel-Löwenstein or Loewenstein,[75] Gertrud

Born: August 7, 1904, in Hagen (Germany)
Lived in Mönchengladbach (Germany) before coming to
    the Netherlands.[76]
Housewife
Deportation from Westerbork: August 7, 1942
Died: September 30, 1942, in Auschwitz

[73] List of arrests from The Hague; list A–W (August 4, 1942); transport list W–A (August 7, 1942), A, no. 15.

[74] List A–W (August 4, 1942). On the transport list W–A (August 7, 1942), A, no. 13, Jacob Velleman is listed with the birthdate of September 10, 1911.

[75] Amersfoort lists (August 1942). On the list from Amersfoort to Westerbork of August 4, she is listed under her husband's name, Vogel; Kempner, *Twee uit honderdduizend*, 107; transport list W–A (August 7, 1942), A, no. 15.

[76] See http://www.bundesarchiv.de/gedenkbuch/index.html (Dec. 2009).

Vries,[77] Samuel de
Born: April 22, 1884, in Amsterdam
Scholar
Deportation from Westerbork: August 7, 1942
Died: September 30, 1942, in Auschwitz

Weelen-Lopes Cardozo,[78] Sara
Born: April 22, 1887, in Amsterdam
Deportation from Westerbork: August 17, 1942
Died: August 19, 1942, in Auschwitz

Weezel,[79] Gerrit van
Born: March 7, 1882, in Amsterdam
Musician
He was probably the father of the above-mentioned Rosa-
    lie de Leeuw–van Weezel.
Deportation from Westerbork: August 7, 1942
Died: September 30, 1942, in Auschwitz

Weiss,[80] Arpad
Born: April 16, 1896, in Solt (Hungary)
Soccer coach; Hungarian nationality
He lived at Betlehemstraat 10A in Dordrecht.
Deportation from Westerbork: October 2, 1942
Died: January 31, 1944, in Auschwitz

[77] List of arrests; list A–W (August 4, 1942); Kempner, *Twee uit honderd-duizend*, 108; transport list W–A (August 7, 1942), A, no. 11.

[78] List of 23; list A–W (August 15, 1942); transport list W–A (August 17, 1942), A, no. 5.

[79] List A–W (August 4, 1942); Kempner, *Twee uit honderdduizend*, 108; transport list W–A (August 7, 1942), A, no. 17; Kempner, *Twee uit honderddui-zend*, 109.

[80] List of arrests; list A–W (August 4, 1942); Kempner, *Twee uit honderd-duizend*, 108; transport list W–A (October 2, 1942), A, no. 23.

Weiss-Rechnitzer,[81] Ilona
Born: October 7, 1908, in Szombathely (Hungary)
Housewife; Hungarian nationality
She lived at Betlehemstraat 10A in Dordrecht.
Deportation from Westerbork: October 2, 1942
Died: October 5, 1942, in Auschwitz

Weiss,[82] Robert
Born: July 12, 1930, in Milan (Italy)
Child with Hungarian nationality
He lived at Betlehemstraat 10A in Dordrecht.
Deportation from Westerbork: October 2, 1942
Died: October 5, 1942, in Auschwitz

Weiss,[83] Klara
Born: October 2, 1934, in Milan (Italy)
Child with Hungarian nationality
She lived at Betlehemstraat 10A in Dordrecht.
Deportation from Westerbork: October 2, 1942
Died: October 5, 1942, in Auschwitz

Welling-Spier,[84] Froukje
Born: November 29, 1883 (or January 29, 1884), in Haarlem
She lived at Douwes Dekkerstraat 37 in The Hague.
On the list of arrests from The Hague
Deported on October 2, 1942
Died: October 5, 1942, in Auschwitz

[81] Ibid.
[82] Ibid.
[83] Ibid.
[84] List of 23; list A–W (August 15, 1942); transport list W–A (October 2, 1942), A, no. 23.

Wil(l)heim-Wiesenberg,[85] Johanna H.
Born: September 25, 1888, in Vienna (Austria)
Deportation from Westerbork: August 7, 1942
Died: August 9, 1942, in Auschwitz

Wil(l)heim,[86] Kurt Joseph
Born: March 19, 1909, in Vienna (Austria)
Deportation from Westerbork: August 7, 1942
Died: September 30, 1942, in Auschwitz

[85] List A–W (August 4, 1942); transport list W–A (August 7, 1942), A, no. 10.
[86] Ibid.

BIBLIOGRAPHY

Archives of Utrecht, the Netherlands (*Het Utrechts Archief*). Archives, Archdiocese of Utrecht, inventory numbers 76–77.

Cisterican Abbey of Our Lady of Koningshoeven (*Cisterciënzer-abdij O.L. Vrouw van Koningshoeven*). Archives. Berkel-Enschot, the Netherlands.

Cistercian Abbey of Our Lady of Koningsoord (*Cisterciënzerinnen-abdij O.L. Vrouw van Koningsoord*). Obituary list. Berkel-Enschot, the Netherlands.

Congregation of the Holy Ghost (*Congregatie van de H. Geest*). Archives. Gemert, the Netherlands.

Dutch Institute for War Documentation (*Nederlands Instituut voor Oorlogsdocumentatie*, NIOD), Amsterdam.

Archive 250 F, Amersfoort camp, inventory number 14:

Lists of arrests from the various districts (August 2, 1942).

Transport list from Amersfoort to Westerbork (August 4, 1942).

Transport list from Amersfoort to Westerbork (August 15, 1942).

BDC H 213, pages 1586/1688.

Archive 250 I, Westerbork camp, inventory number 239:

Transport list from Westerbork to Auschwitz (August 7, 1942), a total of 29 pages.

Dutch Red Cross, The Hague. War Archives (*Het Nederlandse Rode Kruis Den Haag, Oorlogsarchief*):

Jewish Council File.

Documents EU (European) 2.883, 61.891, 100.605, 101.453 up to and including 457, 108.796, 108.797, 110.877, 141.026 up to and including 141.031, 184.554, 197.197, 197.200, 197.201, 197.202.

Notes concerning the number of Catholic Jews brought into
the Amersfoort camp:

Inventory no. 52 (Westerbork), request no. 370:

Transport list Westerbork-Auschwitz (August 7, 1942).

Transport list Westerbork-Auschwitz (August 17, 1942).

Transport list Westerbork-Auschwitz (August 31, 1942).

Inventory no. 52 (Westerbork), request no. 371:

Transport list Westerbork-Auschwitz (October 2, 1942).

Inventory no. 84 (Amersfoort), box VI:

List of 23 Catholic Jews in mixed marriages.

Transport list Amersfoort-Westerbork (August 4, 1942).

Institute for Wartime Graves (*Oorlogsgraven Stichting*).

Stein, Edith. Letter to Pope Pius XI of April 1933. *Der Pilger: Bistumblatt der Diosese Speyer* 8 (February 23, 2003): http://www.zenit.org/german/visualizza.phtml?sid=31603.

Literature

Abbink, G. "In memoriam mgr. dr. J.A. Geerdinck 1902–1977". *Analecta voor het aartsbisdom Utrecht* 50 (1977): 247–66.

Akkermans, G. In *Bedevaarten in Nederland*. Volume 3: Province Limburg, edited by P. Margry and C. Caspers et al., 188–97. Hilversum, 2000.

Als een brandende toorts: Documentaire getuigenissen over Dr. Edith Stein (zuster Teresia Benedicta a Cruce) en medeslachtoffers. Echt: Friends of Dr. Edith Stein, 1967.

Arborelius, A. *Edith Stein. Biografie*. Gent, 1987.

Aukes, H. *Het leven van Titus Brandsma*. Utrecht, 1985.

———. *Kardinaal de Jong*. Utrecht, 1956.

Batzdorff, S. *Edith Stein—meine Tante: Das jüdische Erbe einer katholischen Heiligen*. Würzburg, 2000. Translated as *Aunt Edith: The Jewish Heritage of a Catholic Saint* (Springfield: Templegate Publishers, 1998).

———. *Edith Stein: Selected Writings*. Springfield: Templegate Publishers, 1990.

Bergen, W.v. "Bij een grafsteen". *Heemkundevereniging Geleen* 3 (1985): 140–56.

Bergh, S. van den. *Deportaties. Westerbork, Theresienstadt, Auschwitz, Gleiwitz, Bussum.*

Bromberg, R. "Trappisten met davidster". *De Bazuin* 38 (January 15, 1955): 8; (January 22, 1955): 8; (January 29, 1955): 8.

Buitkamp, J. *Moerdijk van bezetting tot bevrijding.* Moerdijk, 1979.

Cammaert, A. *Het verborgen front: Geschiedenis van de georganiseerde illegaliteit in de provincie Limburg tijdens de Tweede Wereldoorlog.* Volumes 1–2. Leeuwarden, 1994.

Cistercian Abbey of Our Lady of Koningshoeven (*Abdij O.L.Vrouw van Koningshoeven*). Website, 2006: www.koningshoeven. nl/.

Clara, Sister. "Edith Stein, zuster Benedicta". *Samen* 15 (1978): 8–9.

Coenen, J. *Hertog Jan en de Zummerse mens: Een overzicht van de geschiedenis van Someren en Lierop.* Someren, 2001.

Dam, C.v. "Jodenvervolging in de stad Utrecht". In *De Joodsche gemeenschap in de stad Utrecht (1930–1950).* Zutphen, 1985.

Dam, H. *De NSB en de kerken: De opstelling van de Nationaal-Socialistische Beweging in Nederland ten opzichte van het christendom en met name de Gereformeerde Kerken 1931–1940.* Kampen, 1986.

Die sieben christlichen Makkabäer (Geschwister Löb). Dahlem (Eifel): Trappisten-Abtei Maria Frieden, 1988. Leutesdorf am Rhein: Johannes-Verlag, 1964.

Elders, L., editor. *Edith Stein: Studies over haar leven, spiritualiteit, filosofische werk.* Brugge, 1991.

Frequin, L., and A. Terstegge. *Titus Brandsma/Die Geschwister Löb: Vervolgter Glaube—Vernichtetes Leben.* Munich, 1982.

Friedländer, S. *Pius XII en het Derde Rijk. Documenten.* Amsterdam, 1965.

Frijtag Drabbe Künzel, G. von. *Kamp Amersfoort.* Amsterdam, 2003.

Joosen, W., and M. Kooistra-Kruyf, editors. *Geschiedenis van Someren in de Tweede Wereldoorlog.* Someren, 1984.

Graef, H. *Edith Stein een vrouw van onze tijd.* Bilthoven, 1955.

Guth, K. *Jüdische Landgemeinden in Oberfranken (1800–1942)*. Bamberg, 1988. 301–8.

Haas, A. de. In *Zeugen für Christus: Das deutsche Martyrologium des 20. Jahrhunderts*, edited by H. Moll, 882–85. Paderborn, 2001.

———. *Luise Löwenfels: Een "vergeten" martelares*. Geleen, 1998.

Hamans, P. "De Nederlandse bisschoppen waarschuwden in 1934 al voor het fascisme". *Katholiek Nieuwsblad* 12, no. 36 (1995): 22–23.

———. "Getuigen van het geloof tot in de dood". *Emmaüs* 36 (2005): 31–40.

———, editor. *Getuigen voor Christus: Rooms-Katholieke bloedgetuigen uit Nederland in de twintigste eeuw*. Published by the Liturgical Commission of the Dutch Bishops' Conference, commissioned by the Bishops of the Province of Utrecht, 2008. 's-Hertogenbosch, 2008.

———. "Martelaar voor de sacramenten van de kerk. Pastoor Otto Neururer". *Eucharistie en Geestelijk Leven*, 23 (2000): 193–202.

———. "Na de joden de katholieken". *Katholiek Nieuwsblad* 22, no. 34 (2005): 10.

———. "Opdat wij onze vrijheid waard blijven". *Katholiek Nieuwsblad* 11, no. 59 (1994): 16–18.

———. "Pius XII en de Jodenvervolging". *Emmaüs* 25 (1994): 67–80.

———. "Rooms-Katholieke Kerk en fascisme in Nederland". *Communio Internationaal Katholiek Tijdschrift* 13 (1988): 374–84.

———. "Waarom zweeg Pius XII". *Katholiek Nieuwsblad* 11, no. 47 (1994): 15–20.

Heemskerk, W. *De heilige Edith Stein en haar tijd*. Sittard, 2005.

———. "Rosa Stein, de grote onbekende naast haar zus Edith". *De Sleutel: Informatieblad Bisdom Roermond* 22, no. 5 (1994): 9–11.

Heggen, Sister Ancilla, O.C.D. "Recollections of Edith Stein by Her Sisters". *Carmelite Digest* 3, no. 1 (Winter 1988): 21–29.

Hockerts, H. *Die Sittlichkeitsprozesse gegen katholische Ordensangehörige und Priester (1936–1937)*. Mainz, 1971.

Hoogbergen, Dr. T. G. A. Interview of September 9, 2006.

Hürten, H. "'Endlösung' für den Katholizismus? Das nationalsozialistische Regime und seine Zukunftspläne gegenüber der Kirche". In *Katholiken, Kirche und Staat als Problem der Historie: ausgewählte Aufsätze 1963–1992*, edited by H. Hürten, 174–89. Paderborn: Schöningh, 1994.

Jong, L. de. *Het Koninkrijk der Nederlanden in de Tweede Wereldoorlog*. Volume 5. The Hague, 1974; Volume 6/1. The Hague, 1975.

Jonge, A. *Het Nationaal-Socialisme in Nederland: Voorgeschiedenis, ontstaan en ontwikkeling*. The Hague, 1968.

Joosten, L. *Katholieken en fascisme in Nederland 1920–1940*. Hilversum, 1964.

Jungels, C. "Rosa Stein". In *Zeugen für Christus: Das deutsche Martyrologium des 20. Jahrhunderts*, edited by H. Moll, 335–38. Paderborn, 2001.

Kempner, R. *Twee uit honderdduizend, Anne Frank en Edith Stein: Onthullingen over de nazimisdaden in Nederland voor het gerecht in München*. Bilthoven, 1969.

Kutzner, E. In *Zeugen für Christus: Das deutsche Martyrologium des 20. Jahrhunderts*, edited by H. Moll, 763–67. Paderborn, 2001.

Lapide, P. *De laatste drie pausen en de joden*. Hilversum, 1967.

Leeuw, A. van der. *Die Deportation der römisch-katholischen Juden aus den Niederlanden im Monat August 1942*. Written in 1966. NIOD, archive 785, Notes for historical work, inventory number 136. Amsterdam, 1966.

Levy, U. *De onvoorstelbare jaren 1939 tot 1947*. Eersel, 1995.

Linssen, M. "Edith Stein, Zuster Theresia Benedicta A Cruce O.C.D." *Een-Twee-Een* 15 (1987): 304–52.

———. *Edith Stein: Kiezen voor de waarheid*. Gent, 1998.

Manning, A. "De Nederlandse katholieken in de eerste jaren van de Duitse bezetting". *Archief voor de geschiedenis van de Katholieke Kerk in Nederland* 21 (1979): 105–29. Also in Jaarboek Katheliek Documentatie Centrum (1978).

Mendes da Costa, Sister Judith. *Sister Judith Mendes da Costa, Dominican Sister of the Congregation of St. Catherine of Siena in Voorschoten, Amsterdam 1895–1944 Auschwitz: Autobiografie*. Unpublished. Voorschoten, 2006.

Mesters, G. "Rosa Maria Agnes Adelheid Stein". In *Getuigen voor Christus. Rooms-Katholieke bloedgetuigen uit Nederland in de twintigste eeuw*, edited by Dr. P.W.F.M. Hamans, 562–67. Published by the Liturgical Commission of the Dutch Bishops Conference, commissioned by the Bishops of the Province of Utrecht, 2008. 's-Hertogenbosch, 2008.

Meyer, R., editor. *Concentratiekampen, systeem en de praktijk in Nederland*. Bussum, 1970.

Mohr, A., and E. Prégardier, editors. *Passion im August (2.–9. August 1942): Edith Stein und Gefährtinnen: Weg in Tod und Auferstehung*. Zeugen der Zeitgeschichte, 5. Annweiler: Plöger, 1995.

Moll, H., editor. *Zeugen für Christus. Das deutsche Martyrologium des 20. Jahrhunderts*. 2 vols. Paderborn, 2001. Fourth edition, 2008.

———. In *Zeugen für Christus: Das deutsche Martyrologium des 20. Jahrhunderts*, edited by H. Moll, 885–88. Paderborn, 2001.

Mund, O. "Bene qui vivit, bene latuit. Zum 50. Todestag von Edith Stein und Bruder Wolfgang Rosenbaum". *Franziskanische Studien Heft* 2/3. Werl, 1992.

———. *Blumen auf den Trümmern: Blutzeugen der NS-Zeit: Wolfgang Rosenbaum u.a.* Paderborn, 1989.

Munsters, Sister Maria Teresita. In *Als een brandende toorts: Documentaire getuigenissen over Dr. Edith Stein (zuster Teresia Benedicta a Cruce) en medeslachtoffers*, 210–35. *Echt:* Friends of Dr. Edith Stein, 1967.

Neyer, M. Amata, O.C.D. *Edith Stein aus meinem Leben*. Freiburg, 1987.

———. *Edith Stein: Her Life in Photos and Documents*. Translated by Waltraut Stein, Ph.D. Washington, D.C.: ICS Publications, 1999.

———. *Edith Stein: Wie ich in den Kölner Karmel kam*. Würzburg, 1994.

———. "Heilige Schwester Teresia Benedicta a Cruce". In *Zeugen für Christus: Das deutsche Martyrologium des 20. Jahrhunderts*, edited by H. Moll, 892–97. Paderborn, 2001.

Oosten-Neuwahl, Dr. N.M.E., van, granddaughter of Elvira Sanders-Platz. Interview. Leiden.

Ossanna, F. "Sie wurde getötet im Lager Auschwitz am 9. August 1942; genauso wie ihre Schwester Edith gab Rosa ihr Leben aus Liebe für Christus". *Osservatore Romano* (May 22, 1992). Translated by H. Kretzers into Dutch in *Een-Twee-Een* 20 (1992): 553–56.

Peters, Sister M. Emerentia. In *Als een brandende toorts: Documentaire getuigenissen over Dr. Edith Stein (zuster Teresia Benedicta a Cruce) en medeslachtoffers*, 159–67, 193–201. Echt: Friends of Dr. Edith Stein, 1967.

Poorthuis, M., and T. Salemink. *Een donkere spiegel: Nederlandse katholieken over joden: Tussen antisemitisme en erkenning 1870–2005*. Nijmegen, 2006.

Posselt, Sister Teresia Renata de Spiritu Sancto. *Edith Stein: Jodin, geleerde, Carmelites*. Bilthoven, 1952.

———. *Edith Stein: The Life of a Philosopher and Carmelite*. Edited by Susanne Batzdorff, Josephine Koeppel, and John Sullivan. Washington, D.C.: ICS Publications, 2005.

Prégardier, E. In *Zeugen für Christus: Das deutsche Martyrologium des 20. Jahrhunderts*, edited by H. Moll, 139–42, 260–63, 309–12, 326–28, 397–401. Paderborn, 2001.

Presser, J. *Ondergang: Vervolging en verdelging van het Nederlandse Jodendom (1940–1945)*. 2 vols. The Hague, 1965.

Recollections of daughter Anna Sanders of her mother Elvira Sanders-Platz, written for her oldest daughter, Nitha, part 7 (1997).

Salemink, T., and J. de Maeyer, editors. "Katholicisme en antisemitisme". *Trajecta* 15 (2006).

Sander, Xaverius. Information on the website: http://www.janvanhout.nl/pluche2/pers/plup_sander_1204.htm.

Schaller, A. "Die lieben Kinder von Koningsbosch sind bei uns: Zwei Mädchen aus München starben mit Edith Stein". *Münchener Kirchenzeitung*, October 10, 1999: 9.

Schilz, L. *Schwester Mirjam Michaelis: Opfer von Auschwitz*. Trier, 1993.

Schippers, H. *Zwart en Nationaal Front*. Amsterdam, 1986.

Schray, D. "Holocaust: Annemarie und Elfriede Goldschmidt". *Heliandkorrespondenz* 4 (1992).

Snoek, J. *De Nederlandse kerken en de joden 1940–1945: De protesten bij Seyss-Inquart, hulp aan joodse onderduikers, de motieven voor hulpverlening*. Kampen, 1990.

Steffen, Peter, and Hans Evers. *Scheuren in het Kleed: Het Joods-Katholleke gezin Löb 1881–1945*. Nijmegen: Volkhof Pers, 2009.

Stein, Edith. *Aus dem Leben einer jüdischen Familie: Das Leben Edith Stein, Kindheit und Jugend*. Edith Stein Werke, vol. 7. Freiburg: Herder, 1965. Translated into Dutch by P. Romaeus Leuven, O.C.D., as *Mijn jeugd: Uit het leven van een joodse familie* (Brugge-Utrecht, 1967). Translated into English by Josephine Koeppel, O.C.D., as *Life in a Jewish Family*. Edited by L. Gelber and Romaeus Leuven, O.C.D. The Collected Works of Edith Stein, vol. 1 (Washington, D.C.: ICS Publications, 1986).

————. *Briefauslese (1917–1942). Mit einem Dokumentenanhang zu ihrem Tode*. Edited by the Kloster der Karmelitinnen Maria vom Frieden, Köln. Freiburg: Herder, 1967.

————. *Self-Portrait in Letters*. Translated by Josephine Koeppel, O.C.D. Edited by L. Gelber and Romaeus Leuven, O.C.D. The Collected Works of Edith Stein, vol. 5. Washington, D.C.: ICS Publications, 1993.

————. *Kreuzeswissenschaft: Studie über Joannes a Cruce*. Edith Steins Werke, vol. 1. Freiburg: Herder, 1942. Second edition, 1983. Translated into English by Josephine Koeppel, O.C.D., as *The Science of the Cross: A Study of St. John of the Cross*. Collected Works of Edith Stein, vol. 6 (Washington, D.C.: ICS Publications, 2002).

Stephanie, Sister. "Herinneringen aan zuster Benedicta". *De Sleutel* 15 (1987): 5–7.

Stokman, S. *Het verzet van de Nederlandsche bisschoppen tegen nationaal-socialisme en Duitsche tirannie*. Utrecht, 1945.

Stratmann, F. In *Als een brandende toorts: Documentaire getuigenissen over Dr. Edith Stein (zuster Teresia Benedicta a Cruce) en medeslachtoffers*, 207–9. Echt: Friends of Dr. Edith Stein, 1967.

————. *In der Verbannung: Tagebuchblätter 1940–1947*, 194–97, 250–54. Frankfurt, 1962.

Vaartjes, G. *Herman de Man: Een biografie.* Soesterberg, 1999.

Vermeiren, K., and G. van der Donck. *Het gegeven leven van de broeders en zusters Löb.* Cisterciënzer getuigen van onze tijd. Vitorchiano, 2006.

Westerholz, S. "Das Schicksal der jüdischen Nonne Luise Loewenfels aus Trabelsdorf". In *Mesusa: Lebensbeschreibungen und Schicksale: Spuren jüdischer Vergangenheit an Aisch, Aurach, Ebrach und Seebach*, edited by J. Fleischmann, vol. 4, 269–309. Mühlhausen, 2004.

————. "Luise Löwenfels und ihre Familie". *Sammelblatt des Historischen Vereins Ingolstadt* 111 (2002): 189–270.

INDEX